D1502098

❖ **Some Other World to Find** ❖

T his world clean fails me: still I yearn.
  Me then it surely does concern
Some other world to find. But where?
In creed? I do not find it there.
That said, and is the emprise o'er?
Negation, is there nothing more?
This side the dark and hollow bound
Lies there no unexplored rich ground?
Some other world: well, there's the *New*—
Ah, joyless and ironic too!

                                    —*Clarel*

Some Other World to Find

❖❖❖❖❖❖❖❖❖❖❖❖❖❖❖❖❖❖❖❖❖❖❖❖❖❖❖❖❖❖❖❖❖

Quest and Negation in the Works of
Herman Melville

BRUCE L. GRENBERG

University of Illinois Press
Urbana and Chicago

"On the Death of Friends in Childhood"
Copyright © 1981 by Donald Justice.
Reprinted from *The Summer Anniversaries*
by permission of Wesleyan University Press

This book is printed on acid-free paper.

Library of Congress Cataloging-in-Publication Data

Grenberg, Bruce L. (Bruce Leonard), 1935–
    Some other world to find : quest and negation in the works of
Herman Melville / Bruce L. Grenberg.
        p.   cm.
    ISBN 0-252-01625-4 (alk. paper)
    1. Melville, Herman, 1819–1891—Criticism and interpretation.
2. Quests in literature.   3. Negation (Logic) in literature.
I. Title.
PS2388.Q5G7   1989
813'.3—dc19   88-39406
                                                                    CIP

Contents

For
Charlie Henbest and Tony Ingrassia

We shall not ever meet them bearded in heaven,
Nor sunning themselves among the bald of hell;
If anywhere, in the deserted schoolyard at twilight,
Forming a ring, perhaps, or joining hands
In games whose very names we have forgotten.
Come, memory, let us seek them there in the shadows.

—Donald Justice

Acknowledgments

A large number of people have had a hand in bringing this book to fruition, and I would like to express my gratitude to them for their assistance. First, I would like to thank the Canada Council, which many years ago granted me a leave fellowship to pursue a year of reading unencumbered by the usual responsibilities of teaching. That reading, they might be surprised to learn, did finally yield a product. Second, my very special thanks go to my friend and colleague, Bickford Sylvester and to another, long-distance colleague and friend, Milton Stern, both of whom displayed uncommon generosity of spirit in reading what proved to be a very rough draft of the book. The process of refining my thoughts on Melville continued through a fairly lengthy dialogue by correspondence with Bernard Rosenthal and Joseph Flibbert, who consistently maintained that fine critical balance of pointing out weaknesses of argument and expression while encouraging the main effort. The book, of course, is much the better for the contributions of these readers; that it isn't better than it is rests with me.

In addition, I would like to thank the editorial staff of the University of Illinois Press for their assistance, particularly Ann Lowry Weir, who was invariably helpful and patient; and Mary Giles, who copyedited the manuscript. Very special thanks go to my daughter, Vaile, whom I adore anyway, but who displayed more than love in deciphering an unreadable script and putting it into an uncooperative word processor. Last, but not least, my gratitude, my sympathy, and my love go to my wife, Maida, who learned what it was like to live with a monomaniac on a fiery quest.

Introduction

If thou judgest thyself, I know thou wilt judge candidly; and
then I shall not be harmed or offended, whatever be thy
censure. For though it be certain that there is nothing in this
treatise of the truth whereof I am not fully persuaded, yet I
consider myself as liable to mistakes as I can think thee; and
know that this book must stand or fall with thee, not by any
opinion I have of it, but thy own. If thou findest little in it
new or instructive to thee, thou art not to blame me for it.
It was not meant for those that had already mastered this
subject, and made thorough acquaintance with their own
understandings, but for my own information, and the satisfaction
of a few friends, who acknowledged themselves not to
have sufficiently considered it.

—Locke, *An Essay Concerning Human Understanding*

There are probably easier tasks in life than that of trying to collect
and articulate one's chameleon thoughts on the complex chameleon works of Herman Melville. It is dramatic testimony to the living
and lasting power of Melville's art that so many people have expended
so much energy in attempting that task for themselves. Of course, one's
own questionings of Melville are complicated by a broad and deep critical literature, and in writing this book, nearly one hundred years after
Melville's death, I have found my task both eased and burdened by
those critics who have gone before. There are countless critics of Melville's art who hold my rather substantial I.O.U.s—F. O. Matthiessen,
Willard Thorp, Lawrance Thompson, Milton R. Stern, Charles Feidelson,
Jr., Merrell Davis, Howard P. Vincent, Charles R. Anderson, John D. Seelye,

C. Hugh Holman, Paul Brodtkorb, Jr., to name but a few—debts no less great simply because they never will and never can be called in.

For all their help, however, the great readers of Melville have charted no single or simple course, and in the past twenty years Melville scholarship and criticism have become more and more specialized—focussing upon single works, particular elements or themes in works, or restricted periods in Melville's career. Although much of this criticism is extremely valuable in itself and has been useful to me in formulating my own ideas, there is a danger that we are ceasing to see, or even look for, the "whole" Melville. There is an additional, related, danger that by emphasizing certain works at the expense of others we are quietly polemicizing the Melville canon and perpetuating a partial and distorted view of Melville's total accomplishment as a writer.

In this book I attempt to redress what I consider to be this imbalance, my central purpose being to provide an articulated and coherent statement of the formative ideas operating in Melville's art from *Typee* to *Billy Budd*. Although Melville was not a systematic philosopher, he possessed a singularly critical intelligence, and at the heart of all his writing is the centering focus of humanity's persistent attempts to leap from demonstrable, manifold experience to the persuasive, comprehensive meaning of that experience. Because Melville is first and foremost a writer of fiction, I concentrate upon his fictional canon; however, in establishing what I see as a continuity of thought, theme, and character in this fiction I suggest some ways in which it is consistent with *Clarel*, Melville's longest and most ambitious poem.

Contrary to most studies of Melville, in this book I make virtually no effort to define Melville's "personal" beliefs, attitudes, and convictions, and devote little space to the oft-rehearsed external events of Melville's life and times.[1] Although some critics find it irresistible to identify Melville the man with the artist-Melville, I am persuaded by the simple, persuasive truth of Charles Feidelson's assertion that "'Herman Melville (1819–91)' remains largely unknown, so that all attempts to identify the omnipresent voice of the novels with Melville as he lived and breathed have been self-defeating."[2] The "Melville" that I refer to in the following pages, therefore, is Feidelson's "literary personality, a created figure who inhabits a created world,"[3] and when I write of "Melville's" attitudes or changing perspectives I am referring ultimately to the artist-Melville, who is defined, and can only be defined, by the works themselves.

I should not like to be mistaken for a proponent of a simplistic "New Criticism," however. I do not see each work as an entity unto itself, outside space and time, but, on the contrary, attempt to show how reading Melville's works as a whole establishes an expanding context of values that aids us in understanding each work—not at the expense of the others, but as an individual expression integral to the whole. Although this entire book is devoted to defining these complex forces at work in Melville's mind and art, it is useful at the outset to outline them in broad, synoptic terms.

Although many critics have commented in a general way on the dialectical nature of Melville's fiction,[4] there is no definable synthesis of thesis and antithesis in his works, and, thus, it is probably more accurate to speak of Melville's fiction in terms of a dynamic, in which essentially contrary forces of mind and imagination operate to produce the contrary, irreducibly vital energies of art. To the degree that these forces are persistent we shall find a sort of familiarity in all Melville's works; to the extent that Melville never ceased taking new postures toward them, this familiarity becomes a difficult one for readers to define.[5] My method has been simplified as much as possible to counteract this inherent complexity. I shall discuss each work individually (as far as that is ever possible) and chronologically (for the most part), my intention being to illuminate on the one hand the intrinsic values of each work and on the other the development of Melville's art.

Beginning with *Typee*, Melville records humanity's attempts to comprehend its complex experience or its complex world: the two formulations are in every sense one.[6] What characterizes Melville's life-long struggle in this regard is his absolute determination to leave no questions unasked and his brute honesty in depicting the answers to those questions—be they ever so unexpected or confounding.[7] Melville's first six novels, *Typee, Omoo, Mardi, Redburn, White-Jacket,* and *Moby-Dick,* are all built around quests, and although the immediate objects of those quests vary from book to book, they are intimately related in that taken all together they represent the goals of Enlightenment man and Romantic man. Tommo, Omoo, Taji, Redburn, White-Jacket, Ahab, and Ishmael, each in his own way seeks completion: the idea of an ordered plenary universe, or of a universe that *can* be ordered and mastered by mind and will, is an assumption shared by the protagonists of all six novels. Yet, clearly, each of these quests fails. Indeed, the power of these first six novels springs from Melville's ability to present convincingly the persistent quest for totality and, equally convincingly, to show how futile that quest is. Thus the first six novels stand as studies in philosophical chiaroscuro—the light of aspirations constantly playing against the darkness of defeat.

In *Typee*, the claims made upon Tommo by civilization and by primitivism are mutually demanding and mutually exclusive. Happy neither as sailor nor as native, Tommo does not reject the Typee valley, nor "return" to civilization so much as he sets out to find "some other world." But the other world Tommo finds in *Omoo* is time-ridden and dominated by the force of history, and it does not satisfy Tommo-Omoo's desire to transcend his prior experience so much as it defines his inability to do so.

Mardi is Melville's unrestrained effort to capture the totality of human experience, and its "failure" lies in the problem Melville set for himself. In *Mardi*, the quest for unified experience and mind is thwarted by the limitations of time and space, but more important, Melville's narrative stresses the mutability of the physical world and the essential unreliability of the mind's perception of it. In its putatively comprehensive exploration of the "pre-modern" assumptions of the predictability and reliability of humanity, God, and Nature, *Mardi*'s failure to provide a justification of a "Newtonian," ordered universe almost becomes a dead end.

The assumption of an ordered universe is, as Melville expresses it in *Mardi*, a belief most difficult to relinquish, and in *Redburn, White-Jacket,* and *Moby-Dick* we witness Melville's determination to leave no question unasked in his efforts to explore the foundations of that belief in the face of more and more evidence that it cannot be verified. In *Redburn* and *White-Jacket* Melville comes perilously close to a final, self-confounding answer to the problems that he had set for himself in *Mardi*, yet he does not hold himself back much in those two novels. Returning, as it were, to earlier experiences, he explores the two elemental themes of death and free will, which constitute the ultimate determinants of the human quest.

The limitations of time—the absolute form of which is death, the limitations of space, the indeterminability of free will, the mutability of nature, and the unreliability of perception and the mind in general are all brought together in *Moby-Dick*. *Moby-Dick* is a tri-focal novel, "centering" upon Ahab, Ishmael, and Moby Dick separately, alternately, and simultaneously. And the disintegration of the novel's ending dramatizes the tragedy of the human desire to find some certain significance in all things. The self acting (Ahab), the self thinking (Ishmael), and the object of the self's actions and thoughts (Moby Dick), are infinitely discrete. Far from being able to comprehend the universe, the composite self of Ahab-Ishmael cannot even comprehend itself, and with this conclusion Melville signals the tragic end of the "Rationalist-Romantic" quest.

Neither Melville's art nor his mind ends with *Moby-Dick*, however. Rather, the tragic conclusion of *Moby-Dick* serves as prolegomena to the fiction of total disillusionment that follows. Clearly there is a darkness in Melville's early novels: Tommo is doomed to wander perpetually among dissatisfying worlds, Taji does not find Yillah, Redburn is an Ishmael if not a Cain afloat, White-Jacket is trapped between the two worlds of unattainable felicity and inescapable horror, and both Ahab and Ishmael fail magnificently to grasp the elusive phantoms of their dreams and nightmares. Yet each has had his dream and pursued it relentlessly, if not successfully, to the utmost. Each has been the vessel of a great and heroic struggle between high aspiration and tragically incomplete experience. But the darkness that sets in with *Pierre* is thrice black, for in *Pierre* aspiration itself is self-defeating, and in the works that follow *Pierre*, aspiration, hope, and dream, if they exist at all, exist only as faint recollections of long-dead beliefs of times long past.

Beginning with *Pierre* and concluding with *Billy Budd*, Melville charts an uncompassed world in which dreams exist only as illusions or, even worse, delusions, in which motivations are without value and acts are without significance, a blindman's buff sort of world in which innocence and guilt, honesty and falsehood are mere "perspectives" and Truth is but a ragged-edged sham. This dark world of *Pierre, The Piazza Tales, The Confidence-Man, Israel Potter, Clarel*, and *Billy Budd* eludes the definitive modern concepts of existentialism, absurdism, or even, finally, nihilism. Rather, its peculiar darkness derives from Melville's complex nineteenth-century sensibilities in which his passionate speculations upon heroic aspiration and youthful ideals do not blind him to the bleak truths of this world, and his tragic awareness of those truths leads not to a black despair but to a courage that can gaze upon dreams and disillusionment with an equal eye. If for no other reason, that "courage to be" makes Melville's voice a profound one in our time as well as in his own.

1

Typee and *Omoo:*
Green Thoughts in a Green Shade

> It is no light undertaking to separate what is original from
> what is artificial in the present nature of man, and to know
> correctly a state which no longer exists, which perhaps never
> existed, which probably never will exist, and about which it is
> nevertheless necessary to have precise notions in order to
> judge our present state correctly.
>
> —Rousseau, "Preface" to *The Discourse on Equality*[1]

Typee and *Omoo* are apprentice works; however, neither *Typee* nor *Omoo* can accurately be termed "simple" in the sense of creating a unified, uncomplicated effect. What one does find in *Typee* and *Omoo* is a radical, relatively unmodulated mode of expression that serves as vehicle for the oppositional forces of Melville's mind. And although the disproportion between vehicle and burden frequently gives to these two books the appearance of inexperience and irresolution, the precise nature of the conflicts present suggests the complex motivation of all Melville's art.

Typee

In light of the sharply divided religious and cultural commitments of the reading public in the 1840s, we are not surprised by its mixed reaction to *Typee*. The religious and moral watchdogs of both England and America could scarce do anything but castigate "An apotheosis of barbarism"[2] and scorn Melville's "habits of gross and shameless familiarity not to say unblushing licentiousness, with a tribe of debased and filthy savages of Marquesas . . . ."[3] On the other hand, more Romantic spirits could rejoice at finding "Mr. Melville's book . . . full of things strange and queer to the ears of Broadway and Chestnut Street,"[4] and rise occasionally to outright hyperbole: "Enviable Herman! A happier dog it is impossible to imagine than Herman in the Typee valley."[5] Even more predictable, from our vantage point, were the countless statements to the general effect that Mr. Melville ought to "learn the worth of the morality taught by the Christian missionary, before he ventures to criticize his motives, or to disparage his work."[6]

For those interested in understanding *Typee* as a work of art, the most significant result of this contemporary criticism of the novel is that both factions, however opposed in judgment, were in agreement that *Typee* was a simple, polarized narrative that lauded the simple native life and attacked the values of Christian civilization. Although in our relatively sophisticated age we tend to react against evangelism and zeal and find Melville's licentiousness rather tame, we persist in seeing *Typee* as a book of polarized and polarizing values.[7] We in our own form of high morality speak of Melville's "social consciousness" and alternately speak of his romanticism, primitivism, or self-liberation.[8] But this prevailing view of the novel, whether expressed in nineteenth- or twentieth-century terms, is simplistic, and expresses more our reductive critical mentality than Melville's creative mentality.

To cast significant doubt upon this neatly categorized critical vision of *Typee* is easy enough. Although one thrust of the book presents the Typee natives as pure, innocent children of nature facing destruction by the corrupt power of frigate-Christianity, a counterthrust of approximately equal force asserts the natural corruption of flesh-eating, idol-worshipping, whimsically violent and ignorant savages whose only possible redemption lies in the saving force of culture and benign Christianity. One can also point to a first-person, controlling narrator who simultaneously lauds the native life and plots an escape from it every waking moment, a narrator who "goes native," but with all the nicety of a proper Christian gentleman. Or, to cap Melville's apparent "confusion," one might examine the whole *Typee-Omoo* sequence of Tommo's adventures, wherein he deserts one ship because of its uncivilized conditions, finds "paradise" with a blue-eyed Marquesan, flees this haven for another unknown ship, mutinies, etc., etc.

By looking at *Typee* in this fashion it is true that we have replaced simple bivalence with ambiguity. But for all the book's complexity it would be wrong to conclude that Melville was merely confused. Although Melville's experiences in the Marquesas and the Sandwich Islands, on the *Acushnet* and the *United States,* were traumatically, startlingly inconsistent with his intellectual and emotional expectations, in *Typee* and *Omoo* Melville attempts to assimilate and comprehend that disjunctive experience, to square his experience with his cultural, familial, and personal mold, in short, to order and unify the disparate elements of his highly varied life.

In a real sense we have asked the wrong questions of *Typee.* The true issue is not which culture will prevail—the answer to that is self-evident. Nor should we ask of the novel which culture Melville "favors"—for there is, properly speaking, no answer to that question at all. Christian, Western culture and heathen, Polynesian naturism do form the poles of Melville's experience and mentality in *Typee,* but rather than play one against the other, Melville sets himself the task of wedding the two and putting them to rest in harmonious felicity.[9]

That *Typee* is, in fact, a "problem" novel is indicated by Melville's total disregard for convincing motivation. Tommo jumps ship largely because of bad food and little prospect of a good voyage: Melville doesn't even tell us why Toby leaves. This same sense of irrational, totally arbitrary action pervades the sailors' descent into the Typee valley, the primary, critical action that determines the whole course of the narrative. As the narrative progresses, not only are we at a loss to explain the narrator's contradictory impulses to remain and to flee, but we are also unable to determine the motives of the Typees in treating Tommo alternately as a recovered child and as an untrustworthy prisoner.

Neither in the beginning, through the middle, nor at the end does Melville provide clear or even adequate motivation for what is going on. One might casually attribute this failure to first-book inexperience, and undoubtedly this plays a part in the whole truth. But this *ex nihilo* quality in the tale also suggests the character of unresolved essential conflict, and by examining the book in this light, one finds a number of otherwise obdurate difficulties at least partially explained. *Typee* is romance, not literal dream, but the terms of its conflicts are elemental to Melville's developing mind and yield something like a paradigm of Melville's artistic concerns in the novels that follow in such rapid succession.

One finds abundant evidence in *Typee* pointing toward an "easy" interpretation. Almost everyone reading the book for the first time would unhesitatingly agree that the primary thrust of the tale is toward a romantic praise of the free, uncomplicated life of the savage in nature—a praise expressed largely in contrast to a pervading criticism of restrictive, unintegrated civilized life. The evidence for such generalization is so rife that it scarcely bears repetition, let alone refutation. One thinks immediately of the portrait of the "patriarch-sovereign of Timor" and the "polished, splendid Frenchman," Du Petit Thouars (*T,* 27:201).[10] Or one recalls perhaps the most glaring example of Melville's cultural comparisons—his disquisition on the contract-free, coinless society of Typee in contrast to the "thousand sources of irritation that the ingenuity of civilized man has created to mar his own felicity," the hydra-heads of the monster Money (*T,* 17:126). Evidence of this movement in the book can be found, in fact, on almost every page.

However strong this evidence appears in itself, there are qualifying and opposing ideas in the book which are represented with equal force. Not merely incongruities of narrative and thought, but radical antinomies of mind insinuate the book and shape its meaning and form. Even granting that Melville probably included the anecdote of Kory-Kory's laborious fire-making (Chapter 14) as comic interlude or even "filler," the sketch sounds a discordant note in the purportedly unrelieved felicity of savage life. And there are other, more significant, values at odds with the overall pattern of development. One suspects a double edge to Tommo's seeming praise, that "the minds of these simple savages, unoccupied by matters of graver moment, were capable of deriving the utmost delight from circumstances which would have passed unnoticed in more intelligent communities" (*T,* 19:144), for within that verdant recess Tommo frequently falls prey to a "deep dejection . . . , which neither the friendly remonstrance of my companion, the devoted attentions of Kory-Kory, nor all the soothing influences of Fayaway could remove" (*T,* 14:104). Not unqualified ecstasy, but an inconclusive alternation of delight and woe is the result of Tommo's being "cut off . . . from all intercourse with the civilized world" (*T,* 14:104).

Ultimately, Tommo's disorienting experience forces him to rethink the suppositions of Western culture. His radical isolation from his informing culture, however eagerly sought, creates in him an ambivalent attitude, a sense of "eager uncertainty," toward all the factors of his experience. As a result, the events, characters, and ideas of his narrative are fraught with radically opposing values and implications. The simplicity of the Typees is also seen as narrowness: "The little space in which some of these clans pass away their days would seem almost incredible" (*T,* 4:27). Unanimity of brotherly feeling among the tribe, whereby "there hardly appeared to be any difference of opinion upon any subject whatever," and due to which "they all thought and acted alike" (*T,* 27:203), can and does become oppressive to the man who not many years earlier had dearly loved an argument for its own sake. And the most piercing anomaly in terms of our response to plot and theme is Tommo's categorical assertion that "the continual happiness, which . . . appeared to prevail in the valley, sprung principally from that all-pervading sensation

which Rousseau has told us he at one time experienced, the mere buoy-
ant sense of a healthful physical existence" (*T,* 17:127)—a most strange
apology by the Tommo who remains semi-invalid throughout his residence in nature and recovers only upon his return to civilization and a
"quack" physician.

But these numerous and important contradictions do not constitute
the deepest conflict in the book. Beneath the contradictions lurk yet
deeper oppositions that defy resolution. These are seen most clearly in
Melville's attitude toward the Marquesans (especially Fayaway—the first
of Melville's markedly synecdochal characters) and in his attitude toward
religion, both the Marquesan and Christian.

Melville's description of the noble Marquesans emphasizes, above
all, "the European cast of their features" (*T,* 25:184), and, indeed, the
people Melville chooses to typify the ideal state of nature are, in reality,
"European natives." The fairest of all these autogenous hybrids is Fayaway—whose Polynesian hair "flowed in natural ringlets over her shoulders," whose "strange blue eyes" seemed "most placid yet unfathomable," whose "soft and delicate hands" can only be compared to those of
a "countess," and whose feet "were as diminuitive and fairly shaped as
those which peep from beneath the skirts of a Lima lady's dress" (*T,*
11:86). At this level of ambiguous expression, the erstwhile contrasts
between native and civilized characteristics are transformed into comparisons and analogues. And at this point we begin to suspect that Tommo's allegiance lies with neither native nor with civilized culture, but
with some ideal realm not yet seen by land or sea.

If we examine in its totality Tommo's attitudes toward religion in *Typee,* we find a similar, persistent inability to fasten upon any realistic op-
tion and a concomitant yearning for some ideal fusion of possibilities.
Tommo in the most overt fashion attacks the Christianity of the missions
which forces itself upon alien cultures and spells the long, painful death
of those cultures (*T,* 26:195–96). Thus, Tommo argues on the one hand
that the Marquesans (and all Polynesians) would be better off left to
themselves, where a natural democracy (*T,* 25:185–86) might operate,
and where "common sense law" might prevail, impelled by an "indwell-
ing . . . universally diffused perception of what is *just* and *noble* . . ." (*T,*
27:201). On the other hand, he can, and does, assert: "let the savages be
civilized, but civilize them with benefits, and not with evils; and let hea-
thenism be destroyed, but not by destroying the heathen" (*T,* 26:195).
However attractive this statement of benevolent conversion might be to
Tommo, and to us, it is precisely such an ideal accommodation of the
two cultures that Melville in *Typee* and *Omoo* depicts as impossible. And

yet it is equally clear in these books that this is the *only* solution that Tommo would find acceptable.

If Christianity falters in *Typee,* the primitive religion of the Typees, the only stated alternative, never enters the race. However strongly Tommo is drawn to the Typees, he is immediately and irrevocably appalled by the heart of their culture—the religion of Taboo. Tommo's journey into the "solemn twilight" and "cathedral-like gloom" of the Taboo groves is redolent of Goodman Brown's penetration into the Satanic forest.

And Melville repeatedly links the Typees' highest religious expression directly with their most inhuman, revolting practice—cannibalism. His description of the Taboo groves is immediately followed by "Midnight Misgivings," and although at the time these misgivings are groundless, they point ahead to the "Mysterious Feast" of Chapter 32, which, structurally, precipitates Tommo's flight from the valley. His horror at the Typees' desire to tattoo him is heightened by his discovery that "the whole system of tattooing was ... connected with their religion ... " (*T,* 30:220). What Tommo instinctively fears in the Typees' religion, and indeed in their whole culture, is revealed in his spontaneous revulsion at the idea of being tattooed: "I now felt convinced that in some luckless hour I should be disfigured in such a manner as never more to have the *face* to return to my countrymen, even should an opportunity offer" (*T,* 30:219). He fears, in short, for his identity, both self-defined and as it is defined by the opinion of his civilized culture.

Although Tommo's sympathies, perspectives, and ideas seem intractably tangled in careless contradiction, certain basic lines of force control the book in its totality. Out of the inconsistency, contradiction, and paradox operating in plot, character, and theme, there is clearly discernible a powerful impetus toward an accommodating comprehensiveness. If Matthew Arnold's "Stanzas from the Grande Chartreuse" offers a gloss upon Melville's specifically religious quandary, a more complete analogue to the totality of *Typee* (and *Omoo*) is found in Marvell's "The Garden." Like the speaker in Marvell's poem, Melville's protagonist retreats, at least momentarily, to a pseudo-Paradise, wherein he too can exclaim:

> What wond'rous Life is this I lead!
> Ripe Apples drop about my head;
> The Luscious Clusters of the Vine
> Upon my Mouth do crush their Wine;
> The Nectaren, and curious Peach,
> Into my hands themselves do reach;
> Stumbling on Melons, as I pass,
> Insnar'd with Flow'rs, I fall on grass.

But for Melville, as for Marvell, mere sensuous delight is not enough; the mind and soul must enter and, through apprehension, transcend mere experience:

> Mean while the Mind, from pleasure less,
> Withdraws into its happiness:
> The Mind, that Ocean where each kind
> Does streight its own resemblance find;
> Yet it creates, transcending these,
> Far other Worlds and other Seas,
> Annihilating all that's made
> To a green Thought in a green Shade.[11]

This "creative annihilation" of manifold sensuous experience into a green unity of the soul and all its apprehensions is the ultimate goal of Tommo in *Typee*, But whereas for Marvell the statement becomes attainment, for Tommo the statement merely serves as a bitter reflection upon the recalcitrant terms of his own dilemma. The radically discordant elements of his experience refuse to be annihilated into a unity.

The basic ambiguities and ambivalences in *Typee* constitute, as it were, the prolegomena to the ambiguities and ambivalences in the next five novels. On the one hand, all experience, no matter how various or contradictory, has prima facie value as actuality. And Melville depicts the human response to this reality as immediate, playing over the texture of reality as a Typee might fondle a string of beads, a paddle, his own tattoos, a cocoa-nut, or his woman. Compelled toward freshness, contrast, even contradiction, this force, as Melville depicts it, is essentially expansive and "multilinear," projecting the self into each object of experience, thrusting it toward an infinity that is accretionary in process, an infinity to be attained only in the exhaustion of all possible experience. The other force operating in the self is essentially restrictive and "curvilinear."[12] Assimilative of completed experience, it is synthetic in process and impels one toward a unity deriving from necessary experience.[13] Beginning with *Typee*, Melville depicts the self's determined, even desperate, efforts to square this multiplicity with this drive to unity.

Neither force, as Melville defines it, is intrinsically self-defeating or even debilitating. Even together, although opposed radically, they do, in fact, provide the motive power to Melville's art through *Moby-Dick*. Yet there is in their conjunction an inherent instability that causes Melville problem after problem and that, ultimately, leads to the collapse of his grand intention in *Moby-Dick* and *Pierre*. In the early works we see Melville working out to a clearer and clearer definition, the tragic terms of a high and noble mind that has set for itself an impossible task.

One scarcely is tempted to call *Typee* a tragedy, yet in its quality as a "problem" narrative we see the incipient forms of *Mardi* and *Moby-Dick*, which certainly are tragedies. Tommo, like Faust, is trapped by his own inability to say "Enough!" Each experience is sought, yet none is satisfying. The individual elements of his experience remain disappointingly discrete—native and civilized, heathen and Christian—so that not even compromise is possible.[14] Melville offers no possibility for a positive interaction of the two cultures, nor does he suggest any kind of "suburbanite" civilized primitivism: there is no Walden Pond in Polynesia. Nukuheva and Tahiti, as border environments where one might have civilized trappings yet commune with nature, are, in fact, the targets of Melville's most scornful attack. Tommo demands the best of possible worlds; he requires an ideal, composite reality that will include all the good and exclude all the bad features of his real experience. The closest Tommo ever gets to his "green thought in a green shade" is in Chapter 7, when he treats us to a fairly conventional description of the unspoiled beauty of Polynesia, viewed as "the gardens of Paradise" (*T,* 7:49). There is, however, another prospect that Tommo finds even more impressive. In Chapter 6, Melville provides the first of several Pisgah visions in his fiction when Tommo stands atop "what seemed to be the highest land on the island" and looks down upon "the lonely bay of Nukuheva, dotted here and there with the black hulls of the vessels composing the French squadron" (*T,* 6:40). Tommo exclaims that it was "altogether the loveliest view I ever beheld, and were I to live a hundred years, I should never forget the feeling of admiration which I then experienced" (*T,* 6:40).

Significantly, both descriptions are of distant perspectives.[15] Tommo's eye is able to comprehend the whole without concern for distracting detail. Yet even to Tommo, the scene first cited is fragile to the point of appearing hallucinatory (he has just talked about his fever), and he fears that the harsh reality of a spoken word might shatter it. The second passage cited gives the sense of an "objective," real scene, although of ideal composition. Even the heretofore hated French frigates have aesthetic value here, and the significance of the scene lies in its evocation of the desired ideal composition of the two cultures: for at least this one fleeting instance civilization and nature are integrated in Tommo's experience. Tommo's experience of this harmony once in the book is critical in defining all that he would like to achieve, yet there is a pervasive dramatic irony here, for ultimately this momentary concord is set against his persistent failure to achieve a lasting reconciliation of his conflicting impulses.

Typee remains, then, an open-ended, unresolved "problem" narrative, and it does little more than broach the problems that are to persist in

Melville's fiction for the next four years. In view of Melville's central conception of the human dilemma in *Typee,* it is little wonder that he should be persistently torn between the urge to push narrative to a conclusion and the compulsion to dwell upon any and all interesting, however unassimilable, factors. What is clear in *Typee,* becomes clearer in *Mardi,* and is almost miraculously hidden in *Moby-Dick,* is Melville's inability or unwillingness to give dominant control to plot, to place any fetters upon the impetus to express direct intuitions without regard for form or overall effect.[16] The friction in his early novels between narrative plot and thematic structure but reflects Melville's desire to capture humanity's conflicting, even self-negating, desires to find some intrinsic unity in experience and, at the same time, to explore what appears as endless possibility.

Typee is a particularly good place to begin an examination of this difficult problem, because in this first book the lines of conflict are drawn clearly. The plot of Tommo's adventures is simple. Dissatisfied with life aboard ship, he strikes out on a straight line at the earliest possible opportunity—that is, when the ship touches land.[17] This rectilinear movement is soon deflected by the actualities of terrain and disorientation, but does, in fact, finally lead to the paradise of the Typee valley and Fayaway. Viewed in terms of its own implications, Tommo's flight should end here. He "should" settle in the valley of beauty and abundance beyond belief with the fairest maiden of the land and, if compelled to write for some inexplicable reason, should send his MS out to be found in a bottle, if at all. Strangely enough, not only did Melville not remain in his Typee valley, but he does not even allow his fictional self to remain. Instead, he writes surely one of the strangest endings to a novel in all nineteenth-century literature.

The ending of the novel has provoked considerable commentary but relatively little controversy. The prevailing critical view is that Tommo's striking of Mow-Mow represents a violent rejection of primitivism in favor of civilization. But Tommo takes leave of the Typees with a blow *and an embrace.* When Tommo embraces Fayaway, gives gifts to Kory-Kory and Marheyo, and almost simultaneously strikes out at Mow-Mow, he aptly symbolizes his almost perfect ambivalence. Weeping fondly over an impossible present and past, he sets out in desperate search of "some other world." The emphatic ambiguity of *Typee*'s ending emphasizes and derives from Melville's difficulty in containing the book's complex thought structure and resolving its conflicts through the agency of narrative. Faced with the series of contrary alternatives that arise out of his views on civilized and primitive life, Christianity and Taboo, enthusiasm and restraint, the physical and the mental life, Tommo is unable to arrive at any clear-cut choice. Strictly speaking, he finds it equally unsatisfactory either to leave or to remain in the Typee valley. And, in fact, the relationship between *Typee*'s plot and its thematic structure might be described as an uneasy suspension. Tommo's headlong descent into the valley and his precipitate rush to the beach are direct lines of movement, but during the whole central portion of the book, from the tenth to the last chapter, plot movement is suspended by Melville's explorations into the realm of meanings and values.

Such persistent inquiry into meaning and value does not lead inevitably to plot suspension; in such sprawling, thoughtful books as *Middlemarch* or *The Brothers Karamazov,* plot moves not only in spite of, but also through, complex thought structures. But as Melville conceives humanity the compulsion to synthesize and the like compulsion to extend to new experience lead necessarily to a radical impasse of thought. Working essentially disjunctive forms of thought (either/or), Melville inverts the Ramean dialectic and arrives not at answers—but questions. Because Tommo's highly varied experience refuses to be contained by any single available dogma or principle, all dogmas and principles are found wanting, and he is left in a state of unsatisfied yearning for wholeness.

Hence, however dissatisfying Tommo's reluctant escape from the Typees might appear on the surface, in one sense it does adequately reflect Melville's correct intuition that the questions raised by *Typee* have not been answered and that continued exploration is necessary. Whatever practical reasons prompted Melville to write *Omoo* and *Mardi,* there is little question that in essence they are continuations of the themes, ideas, and questions first brought to light in *Typee.*

Omoo

On the most superficial level *Omoo* is a mere extension of *Typee.* We have the same narrator-protagonist, and his adventures pick up in *Omoo* where they left off in the first book. Further, the themes of civilization-primitivism and Christianity-paganism carry over into the second book. Discovery through experience forms *Omoo*'s plot, comprehension through thought forms its total structure, and, throughout the novel, the impasse between the narrator's insistence upon unity and the recalcitrant multiplicity of his experience persists unabated. More important than these similarities in the two books, however, are the fairly subtle but profound changes at work in Melville's defining expression of these root conflicts and questions. Tommo's flight from the Typees represents his failure to resolve the dilemma of conflicting impulses and values, and this dilemma, in turn, becomes the object of scrutiny in *Omoo,* forcing Melville into a clearer definition of its implications.

In the writing of *Omoo* Melville reveals, although somewhat obliquely, the roots of mind that will support the growth of his emergent genius. Mutability, evil, and death appear as controlling themes in this book and assume their primacy as categorical realities with which one must come to terms. Further, it is in *Omoo* that we have the first example of Melville's continuing preoccupation with the relationship between human action (viewed variously as the product of free will, fate, and necessity) and human understanding (in terms of its dependence upon perception, conception, and imagination), with the correlative problem of distinguishing between appearance and reality, truth and falsehood.

The abstract generality of Melville's inquiry in *Typee* prevented a full depiction of Tommo's failure to resolve his contradictory impulses. And the book's suspended movement (in plot, character, and thought) is the result. In *Omoo,* however, Melville is forced to begin with this impasse and construct his narrative upon it. It is in this light that the dilatory description of life aboard the *Julia* with which *Omoo* opens has meaning. The aimless drifting of the *Julia* best reveals Tommo's state of mind at the end of *Typee* and clearly shows, on the one hand, Melville's determination to go beyond the dilemma of that book and, on the other, his deep awareness of the difficulty in doing so.[18] The extent of Melville's dilemma is perhaps best indicated by the very length of the *Julia* episode: it constitutes more than a third of the book.

Following the *Julia* section, Melville enters upon a fairly lengthy discussion of the state of affairs in Tahiti, and this too appears at first glance to be redundant—a repetition of similar remarks made in *Typee.* But in order to pass beyond the concluding irresolution of *Typee,* Melville alters significantly the terms of his concern with the question of how civilized and primitive cultures interact. Whereas in *Typee* Melville strives to hypothesize in Tommo's experience an ideal realm incorporating the best attributes of primitive and civilized existence, in *Omoo* his art turns directly to the actuality of intercourse between the two in a specific time and place—mid-nineteenth-century Tahiti. In shifting from an ideal to a more critical mode of apprehension and expression, Melville frequently gives the impression that in the actuality of Tahiti one finds the worst of both worlds preserved at the expense of all ideal expectation and hope. In contrast to Tommo's hope when he jumped ship at Nukuheva, the confluent cultures in Tahiti show the savage to be not truly civilized but, rather, perverted, and civilized men and women to be not liberated by nature, but, rather, bitterly reminded of their own incapacities as natural beings. The dreamy ideal of *Typee,* the discourse that becomes a novel, becomes the nightmare reality of *Omoo,* the novel that becomes a satire.

Melville's conception of the Polynesian as essentially nature's child continues from *Typee* to *Omoo.* That Melville should consider these people "godless" and at the same time created and maintained by providence in a state of nature is not exactly inconsistent, for he depicts the Polynesian as existing in the Edenic realm of pre-conscious impulse (cf. *O,* 45:174).[19] The irony in *Omoo* is that the role of the Serpent in this Eden is played by Christianity itself. Melville's attack upon Christianity as a destructive, self-interested power is virtually absolute in its implications, for he is saying quite clearly that the most natural of God's children are those least suited to the Christianity that Europe professes (cf. *O,* 45:175).

This essential incompatibility of the two cultures manifests itself in all their interactions. Melville lays the blame for the Tahitians' depravity directly at the door of the church. Deprived of their natural amusements by the moral rigor of Christianity, the Tahitians "have sunk into a listlessness, or indulge in sensualities, a hundred times more pernicious, than all the games ever celebrated in the Temple of Tanee" (*O,* 47:183). And reflexively, the depravity that was "in a measure unknown before . . . intercourse with the whites" (*O,* 48:188), drives the missionaries into self-righteous seclusion, rendering their mere presence a sham, their "conversions" a despicable hypocrisy (*O,* 48:187–88).[20]

But Melville is not content in *Omoo* merely to rehash the accusations of *Typee.* He no longer conceives of primitivism and Christianized civilization as mere alternate modes of being. Rather, they are depicted as simultaneous, if incompatible and incongruous, manifestations of total being. Hence, the cultural interaction at Tahiti provides Melville a synecdoche of the human capacity to give full vent to total potentiality. And hence, the threatened destruction of Polynesia by civilization forebodes, for Melville, the reduction of the self's potentiality by a destructive force within the self. In *Omoo,* Melville voices his fears that, through civilization and Christianity, the complex self is becoming disintegrated.

The implications of this disintegration take shape in the bewildered predicament of Tom. Far behind is the ideal aspiration of "civilized nature" in the Typee valley. At Tahiti it is impossible for Tom to be a savage, and he finds it equally impossible to identify totally with the civilization that brings disease, corruption, and death to nature and nature's children. To delineate the terms of Tom's disintegration, which ultimately consists of a partial orientation to each culture yet a definitive separation from both, Melville employs two techniques, both of which are to become habitual in his art. First, he splits his protagonist into two figures—in this book, Tom and Dr. Long Ghost. Basically incompatible as personalities, they are immediately and irrevocably bound throughout the book as companions. Somewhat schizoid in effect, this dualistic personification of irresistibly intimate but conflicting orientations allows Melville to present dramatically a complex experience of single actions and, hence, to present with immediacy the multiplicity of human attitudes and responses. Thus, Long Ghost throughout his adventures embodies the vestigial force of primitivism. Although somewhat educated, his perception is always unsophisticated and immediate, his needs (particularly the sexual) are primary and demanding, and his conscience (except for his compulsive attachment to Tom) is practically nonexistent. Tom, although consistently less forceful than Long Ghost, is the directional force in their wanderings and controls the outcome of the book. Although he cannot stop Long Ghost (a name suggestive of both phallicism and repression) in his headlong impulses, he can at least attempt to direct him in a mutually satisfying course of action.

To indicate his composite protagonist's isolation within the two cultures (each of which can satisfy only partially), Melville makes "him" a rover—an "Omoo"—"a person wandering from one island to another, like some of the natives, known among their countrymen as 'Taboo kannakers'" (*O,* "Preface":xiv). Not simply a deserter (as in *Typee*), Tom/Long Ghost in *Omoo* becomes the prototypic, wandering Ishmael. That Melville should conceive of wandering specifically as island-hopping is understandable enough since his own experience consisted of jumps from the Marquesas to Tahiti to the Sandwich to the Galapagos islands. But in *Omoo,* Melville's imagination is teased with the idea of islands as separate and discrete entities that nevertheless participate in the generic identity of the archipelago, and although it is not until *Mardi* that Melville hits upon the archipelago as the image of unified disparateness, in *Omoo* he depicts in rudimentary terms the human quest to reconcile the many and the one. The Omoo travels outside the bounds of all restricting culture (reminding one of Marnoo in *Typee*), paradoxically with the intention of synthesizing all cultural values and becoming the taboo ("holy") person.

Tom and Long Ghost's exploration of this island consists of two basic movements, one rectilinear as they penetrate to the heart of the island at Tamai, the other curvilinear as they circle the island to Taloo, Partoowye, and a new ship. The rectilinear movement is unilateral and overtly sexual (with Long Ghost assuming the dominant role), and its outcome is reflexive, sending the two wanderers back to their starting point at Martair to begin their circling of the island. The very intensity of the dance of the

Tamai maidens carries its own completion and leads no further, which might suggest man's ambivalent satisfaction amid dissatisfaction with sexual experience and expression.[21] The circular motion around the island, dominated by Tom, is motivated by a desire to "see things," and in contrast to the physical-sexual experience of Tamai, this desire seems comprehensive in intent but infinitely expansive in implication. When Tom takes ship in Partoowye, Long Ghost departs (never to be seen or heard from again), and "By noon, the island had gone down in the horizon; and all before us was the wide Pacific" (*O,* 82:316). Melville discovers in *Omoo* the basic elements of plot as movement and countermovement, and he also awakens to the possibility of the journey seen as quest, wandering expressed as wondering, and, by implication, rest conceived as attainment and completion.

In *Omoo,* Melville's concern with the cultural conflicts of "Polynesia civilizing" expands into a concern with humanity generically conceived. Ultimately, Melville's attitude is philosophic, its unstated aspiration being that of all philosophy, to attain an integrated vision of the self amid an infinitely complex environment. Because Melville was not a systematic philosopher, however, the labelling of his concerns as "metaphysical" or "ontological" gives him at once too much and too little credit. Melville's questions are those asked by all thinking individuals, and in his art he attempts to explore and express fully the complex human realm of action and thought, time and eternity, mutability and permanence, life and death.

This "philosophic" dimension in *Omoo* exists largely as a rough outline of things to come, but if there is one central idea that impels Melville in the direction of *Mardi, White-Jacket,* and *Moby-Dick,* it is his conception of time. Although Melville's experience in the Pacific was primarily spatial, the irregular inroads of civilization in the various island groups projected an artificial but nevertheless meaningful spectrum of temporal process. In the Marquesas Melville could still find primitive culture relatively unmodified by civilization; in Tahiti he witnessed the first stages of nature and natives being violated by European, Christian society; and in Hawaii he was the shocked witness of the future awaiting those primitives who might survive (at least nominally) the onslaught of culture.[22]

In *Typee,* Melville could compare and contrast the two conflicting cultures in rather direct terms, but when he places the sequel, *Omoo,* in Tahiti, he opens his artistic vision to the mind's persistent questioning of time. There is simply no way for him to avoid examining Tahiti in comparative terms, as one stage further along than the primitive world he had portrayed in *Typee.* And for Melville, this primary questioning of time thrusts upon him a host of related questions. The idea of sequential action, intention and implication, cause and effect, and ultimately mutability and death all force themselves upon Melville and demand consideration.

Time, first and last, signified to Melville change, alteration, and mutability. It is the sea of flux upon which one floats for a moment, only to sink and vanish for eternity. Infinite in itself, it provides the individual with but a meager portion of its possibilities. This flux of time can be treated comically in *Omoo,* as when Melville traces in caricature the fallen state of Tahiti's rulers, by telling us of "Pomaree Vahinee I., the granddaughter of the proud Otoo," who has had to go into "the laundry business" (*O,* 80:306). More frequently, Melville perceives time as the careless destroyer. After describing the singular beauty of the Tahitian cathedral of nature, Omoo evokes powerfully his sense of mutability: "But the chapel of the Polynesian Solomon has long since been deserted. Its thousand rafters of habiscus have decayed, and fallen to the ground; and now, the stream murmurs over them in its bed" (*O,* 44:169). Temples are raised and temples decay, but time flows ceaselessly and carelessly through both. Only change is permanent: only flux remains.

The significance of this concept of time is inestimable. The endless alteration of human experience and the world through time places an insurmountable obstacle in the way of Melville's desire for a unified comprehension. If Marquesans can "become" Tahitians, and Tahitians Hawaiians, what is the real nature of the individual? Is there anything permanent even in European culture or beliefs? Although these questions remain undeveloped in *Omoo* and their full implications are only realized fully in *Moby-Dick, Pierre,* and the later works, Melville's conception of the self's positive thrust toward a unified vision takes initial shape in *Omoo,* and the seeds of annihilative vision are planted in the same soil.

If time, as Melville considers it in *Omoo,* suggests the impermanent and mutable face of reality, the end of humanity, insofar as we are slaves of time, is seen to be death. And Melville makes the connection between time, change, and death explicit in the crucial Chapter 49, where he concludes the subject of "Tahiti As It Is." In this chapter, Omoo declares the Tahitian prospects as "hopeless": "like other uncivilized beings, brought into contact with Europeans, they must remain stationary until utterly extinct" (*O,* 49:192). Melville sees the process of time as inexorable, history's judgment upon the outmoded as absolute. He ends Chapter 49 with the prediction of Teearmoar: "The palm-tree shall grow,/The coral shall spread,/But man shall cease" (*O,* 49:192).

Melville's attitude toward death throughout *Omoo* is notably different from his treatment of it in *Typee.* In the first book, death exists as a threat

for Tommo, is seen sacramentally in Chapter 24 in the "Effigy of a Dead
Warrior," and is viewed as a necessary consequence to the enmity between the various tribes. In no instance does Melville present death as
having significant "meaning" per se; it is merely fact. In *Omoo*, although
death remains factual, it almost always carries a particular burden of
meaning: it signifies the end of the individual. More explicitly, it signifies
a curtailment of possibility. It is the end, first of all, to the deceased's
potential for action and thought and, thus, diminishes the self's potentiality absolutely. Moreover, death puts an end to the individual's potential
as an object of another's action and thought and diminishes all individuals to just that extent.

The self is thus virtually defined by its tenuous existence in a mutable
world. The passage through life is seen to be a continuous leaving behind
of possibility—with the final haven, death. Melville's description of the
sea burial in Chapter 12 of *Omoo* explicitly defines this end to individual
existence amid the continuance of existence per se. The drunken mate
tips the plank bearing the dead seaman, and the ship glides on "while the
corpse, perhaps, was still sinking" (*O*, 12:45). Furthermore, Melville's
conceptions of time and death are integral to his early view of evil. Not
until *Mardi* does Melville explore fully the nature and implications of
evil, but in *Omoo* we have some evidence that Melville views evil (like
time and death) primarily as a restrictive force.

With time and death, evil forms a triad of limitation upon man's will to
infinity and perfection. Most significant for Melville's later development
is his assertion in *Omoo* that evil arises as a result of misdirected will,
misread possibilities, and unfortunate circumstances. For example, he
can in good conscience berate the missions for forbidding all that is
meaningful to the Tahitians and then conclude by saying, "Doubtless, in
thus denationalizing the Tahitians, as it were, the missionaries were
prompted by a sincere desire for good; but the effect has been lamentable" (*O*, 47:183). He can thus consider evil, and must have in such
instances, as a disjunction between intention and result based upon ignorance of the real situation. What distinguishes Melville's definition of
evil in *Omoo* from that of the later books, like *Moby-Dick, Pierre,* and
The Confidence-Man, is that in *Omoo* Melville still depicts evil as a con-
tingency—accidental, not integral to the world as it is. Most significantly,
it is only by creating a protagonist who entertains this illusion that Melville can allow Tommo to attempt the ideal construct of *Typee* and to
wander relatively unscathed though the ambiguous world of *Omoo*.

Are these values and terms of reference so clear and well defined in
Omoo? The answer is yes and no. These values do operate within the
narrative as told by Tom, and they are clearly defined so long as we ac-

cept at face value Tom's claim to objective reporting. We can mitigate the ambiguity in Tom's attitudes toward his experience and the ambivalence intrinsic to his conceptions of time, death, and evil by merely referring to the "truth" in the book as being Tom's truth. And yet such subjective relativism is clearly not Melville's intent in Tom's assertion that he is motivated by "an earnest desire for truth and good" (*O*, "Preface":xv), and that he merely desires "to set forth things as they actually exist" (*O*, 48:184), for in these statements, Melville's narrator makes an unequivocal claim to the truth of his observations.

Although the narrator seems confident enough on most occasions in *Omoo*, there are occasional hints of uncertainty. Thus, in discussing the "moral and religious condition of the island at large" in Chapter 48, he modestly affirms, "Upon a subject like this . . . it would be altogether too assuming for a single individual to decide; and so, in place of my own random observations . . . I will here present those of several known authors, made under various circumstances, at different periods, and down to a comparative late date" (*O*, 48:186). Thus unobtrusively, Melville introduces into his art the theme of epistemology—the self's access to knowledge and potential for attaining truth and certainty. In one sentence Tom modifies his own self-assured "objectivity" by an appeal to authority ("known authors") and to comprehensive perspective, both modal ("made under various circumstances") and temporal ("at different periods, and down to a comparative late date").

This appeal is much more than a modification of Tom's narrative. Under its influence his claimed objectivity and authority are rendered merely dimensional, and to this extent the values and terms of his narrative are not so clearly defined as I have been arguing. Melville establishes a hiatus between the teller and the tale, but although this hiatus might be an attempt on Melville's part to assert the "facts" of the narrative regardless of what the narrator makes of them, the implications of such technique point him in a far different direction. The independence of tale and teller not only undercuts the asserted authority of the teller, but it also creates a radical division between act and thought. Thus, when Melville bifurcates his protagonist in *Omoo*, he is commenting indirectly upon the variability of "fact" and the elusiveness of "truth." Reality and truth are too complex for the single vision and must be encompassed by alternative visions if they are to be apprehended. In the most significant sense, attempts to achieve this encompassment through concerted social effort are exactly what Melville depicts in *Mardi* and *Moby-Dick.*

This discussion of the simple *Omoo* has become quite complex. And yet it is not finished. For Melville's tentative probings at the nature of human limitations (time, death, incomplete vision) have ethical significance as well. In fact, Melville's art is dominated by ethical concerns, and the quest for the true and the beautiful is simultaneously a quest for the good.

It is probably easiest to see the implications of *Omoo* by looking back upon it from the vantage point of the later novels, but even without this reflective advantage it is clear that Melville creates in his first two novels some difficult problems for himself. Melville defines in *Omoo* the external and internal limitations of individual human potential, while at the same time he defines humanity's insistence on the possibility of an ideal synthesis. By so doing, he delineates our apprehension of the world as a realm of absolute values that we have no certain means of attaining. In terms of Melville's inherited religious assumptions, he depicts a nineteenth-century universe in which the idea of a theocentric universe is retained, but without the necessary belief in the ordering concept of Christ the Mediator and Redeemer. Consequently, the self is turned inward upon its own changeable nature and is horribly flawed in its attempt to ascertain true morality. Although this formulation of humanity's plight becomes the foundation of Melville's tragic vision, in *Omoo* it functions more restrictively as a pained awareness of the uncertainty of truth and, hence, of virtue.

Melville's attempts to account for the evil situation in Polynesia and to discount the necessity of such evil fail to rectify the ethical paradox that evil is frequently wrought out of good intentions. This ethical dilemma is most forcefully expressed in Chapter 48 of *Omoo,* where "the earlier laborers [missionaries] in the work" are described as "strictly conscientious," but as "a class, ignorant, and in many cases, deplorably bigoted," a description that adds little credibility to the conclusion that more recent missionaries "have, nevertheless, in their own way at least, labored hard to make a Christian people of their charge" (*O,* 48:185). Here Melville virtually equates zeal, disinterest, and conscience with bigotry, ignorance, and (by the implicit results of mission work) evil.

By so questioning the correspondence of intention and effect, appearance, and reality, he foreshadows the ethical dilemma of his following books, in which the effort to distinguish and apprehend the good serves as a synecdoche for humanity's total effort to unify manifold experience, and thus serve equally the demands of experience and "truth." Just as important for our understanding of Melville's searching mind, this passage contains in rough form the ultimate ethical conundrum which, once clearly formulated by Melville, provides a definitive confutation of the self's insistent quest for certainty: if one is incapable of determining the reality behind appearance, then good and evil ultimately are indistinguishable to judgment. When Melville grasps the full force of that proposition, he will write *Pierre.*

In *Typee* and *Omoo,* the die of Melville's mind is cast, and the basic materials of his art are mined. From *Mardi* to *Moby-Dick,* his style, technique, and evaluations may and do alter, but he relentlessly, almost compulsively, pursues the root questions of his first "light romances" and changes course only when these questions are finally answered. From *Mardi* to *Moby-Dick,* Melville explores serially, cumulatively, and exhaustively all the variations on the essential human quest for certain and complete values. Even as he anatomizes this questing human spirit, he delineates the causes and implications of that questing spirit's failure. Rather than being ironic in tone, the four novels that follow *Typee* and *Omoo* are dialectical, in which the claims of aspirations and the counterclaims of experience meet on level terms.

2

Mardi:
Melville in the Banian Grove

Now, in a certain inclosure toward the head of the valley,
there stood an immense wild banian tree; all over moss,
and many centuries old, and forming quite a wood in itself;
its thousand boughs striking into the earth, and fixing there
as many gigantic trunks. With Tammaro, it had long been a
question, which of those many trunks was the original and
true one; a matter that had puzzled the wisest heads among
his subjects; and in vain had a reward been offered for the
solution of the perplexity. But the tree was so vast, and its
fabric so complex; and its rooted branches so similar in appearance; and so numerous, from the circumstance that every
year had added to them, that it was quite impossible to
determine the point.

—*Mardi*, 115:356[1]

Mardi might well be regarded as Melville's first consciously created work of art. Whatever values one attaches to the narratives of *Typee* and *Omoo*, the works appear products of Melville's immediate and unreflective response to his experience in the South Seas. This quality does not render the books "shallow," but it does give to their expression a quality of unreflective declaration. By contrast, *Mardi* is the work of Melville's critical and reflective mind, and its alternating passages of poetry and bombast, its notoriously convolute style and intricate structure testify equally to Melville's explosive mental development and his determined effort to contain and conserve the energy of that explosion in formal expression. In a very real sense, *Mardi* is best viewed as a continuation and discursive commentary on the art, thoughts, and implications of *Typee* and *Omoo*, for although one might detect in *Typee* and *Omoo* the roots of *Mardi*'s concern with the riddling questions of death, time, space, sexuality, and self, it is with *Mardi* that Melville holds nothing back in his attempt to push these questions to their ultimate implications and to find workable answers to them.

Perhaps the most striking feature of *Mardi* is its seeming uncertainty of direction. The first forty-one chapters, more or less believable as narrative, at least within the tradition of sailors' "yarns," seem to do little to prepare readers for the allegorical chapters that follow, and arising as it does, almost inadvertently, the allegorical quest for Yillah seems to proceed without clear direction or definitive conclusion. Not wishing to quarrel with this almost universal response to the book, I would like to suggest another, and rather different basis for our dissatisfaction in reading *Mardi*. Admitting many of the artistic imperfections that have been charged against Melville in *Mardi*, I believe that thematically and philosophically *Mardi* is not an "interesting failure," but a very successful book. Its very waverings and indecisions are reflections not so much of Melville's undeveloped art as of the way his mind was developing. And perhaps many of the dissatisfactions with *Mardi* spring from an unwillingness to accept the darker implications of Melville's journey into the mind.

Surely it is foolish to think that the shift from adventure-narrative to allegorical quest slipped into *Mardi* undetected by Melville. And Melville would have been something of a fool had he knowingly left his third, most ambitious book a botch from the beginning—with forty-one chapters leading nowhere and one hundred fifty-three springing from God knows where. In spite of the prevailing criticism of the book, it seems manifest that Melville saw a unity in the book that has eluded most readers, a unity that comprises more than a simple consistency of narrative point of view.[2] It is that unity and its implications for Melville's developing mind and art that I am trying to get at.

The opening chapters of the novel present us with a narrator who, not surprisingly, reminds us a great deal of Tommo-Omoo. He is young, romantic, naive, idealistic, and, most of all, bored with the minor role Fate has asked him to play in life. Literally and metaphorically, he is a young man "at sea" in a calm. Envisioning the universality of experience whereby "all things form but one whole; the universe a Judea, and God Jehovah its head" (*M*, 3:12), the narrator is oppressed by his confinement to the *Arcturion*, just as Tommo found the Typee valley and Tahiti confining to his more oceanic aspirations.

The narrator's characterization of the *Arcturion* at the beginning of Chapter 7 as a "maternal craft" (p. 24) reveals just how elemental are his bonds and his desire to escape them. The old *mother*ship with her "heart of oak" (p. 24), however loved and honored, is "exceedingly dull" (*M*, 1:5) to the young spirit that would be free to discover itself. Surely this is the significance of the jejune vision the narrator has at the end of Chapter 1, in which "Vistas seemed leading to worlds beyond" (*M*, 1:7–8).

Accordingly, the narrator plots his escape from this confining reality—in mid-ocean! This is Melville's romancing mind at work; having his protagonist jump ship in mid-Pacific doesn't suspend his reader's disbelief so much as prompt it.[3] Melville asks us to leave behind the more or less factual world of the *Arcturion* for the thrilling—and frightening—"endless sea" (*M*, 12:38). We are asked to join a narrator who, like Tommo and Omoo before and Redburn and Ishmael after, flees a known and secure reality in search of self, tries simultaneously to penetrate and transcend the facts of the world in an effort to grasp the comprehensive meaning of those facts. We are asked to enter the world of the mind.

The narrator's declaration of independence is fraught with immediate self-doubt and fear; once at sea in his "frail boat" (*M*, 9:29), with the security of social order and custom behind him, the narrator finds himself frighteningly close to the dense reality he would transcend. No painted ships upon painted oceans for Melville: "I commend the student of Ichthyology to an open boat, and the ocean moors of the Pacific" (*M*, 13:39). For Melville, the search for self through mind was not an abstract university exercise, but his rejection of authorized learning is not the same as, or even at all like, Jarl's unreflective rejection of all thought. The narrator, in contrast, thrives on the newly discovered wonders of the deep and concludes his rhapsody on the open Pacific thus: "Be Sir Thomas Browne our ensample: who, while exploding 'Vulgar Errors,' heartily hugged all the mysteries in the Pentateuch" (*M*, 13:39). With a Romantic or Transcendental arrogance, Melville is asking us to join his narrator in exploring the world as it truly is, not as it seems to be through habit and common perception.

In no other book does Melville so clearly reveal himself as a contemporary of Emerson, Thoreau, and Thomas Carlyle.[4] The open Pacific is not Walden Pond, however, and an open boat is nothing like a salon, be it in Concord or Cheyne Walk. "Devil Fish"—not loons; sharks and swordfish—not the divine soul of man, are the objects of Melville's unflinching gaze. To be sure, there is something "parlor-ish" about literature altogether, but Melville takes pains to show that mind proper must grow out of experiences and facts, all of which appear frightening and overwhelming.

The obdurate density of the world our narrator sets out to conquer is admirably reflected in his companion and alter-ego, Jarl. The narrator, for all his ruminations on the "Cathays of the deep" (*M*, 13:39), is forced to squat cheek and jowl with Jarl in his practical if somewhat hysterical probings of the water cask. This is no fairy voyage, but one in which exposure, dehydration, hunger, and the "ghastly White Shark" (*M*, 13:41) loom as threats to existence.

The mind can work upon, but not control, the reality that exerts itself suddenly and without warning: "ON THE EIGHTH DAY there was a calm" (*M*, 16:48). Thus simply the external world puts an end to the narrator's westering vision and its seven-day creation of "airy arches, domes, and minarets." And most emphatically this irresistible external power virtually annihilates the characteristic buoyancy of the narrator. This impenetrable density of fact and "event" will plague the narrator throughout his voyage and in his search for Yillah. It is the fatal encumbrance placed upon humanity's effort to understand the world. The density might most simply be defined as the carelessness of fact. Calms do not announce themselves as polite visitors: one awakes to them unprepared. And they leave with similar lack of ceremony (cf. *Mardi*, 16:50). Indeed, it is this quality of nature's unpredictability, with its implicit unconcern for human concerns, that most thwarts the narrator's efforts to control his own existence.

Emblematic of the unpredictable world of *Mardi* are the *Parki* episode and the Aleema sequence, which together prefigure the problems faced in the allegorical search for Yillah in the last two-thirds of the book. Both the *Parki* and Aleema's strange craft appear unannounced on the horizon, and both crafts are eminently mysterious in appearance. However strange they might seem to us at first appearance, and however odd they might appear to Jarl and the narrator, in retrospect they can be viewed as definitive of the main themes and purposes of *Mardi*. The *Parki*, with its violent history and ill-fated future—Samoa's self-mutilation and Annatoo's accidental, meaningless death—points to the violent discon-cert of all human endeavors and the failure of the social order. Aleema's craft, wrung from nature and appearing in a flock of birds (cf. *Mardi*, 39:126), yields its secret cargo [Yillah] only to violence, and then only partially, thus pointing to the impenetrable mystery of nature and its central meaning. Together, the two encounters define the arena of Taji's future quest, his aspirations, and his ultimate failure.

The *Parki*'s appearance is announced blankly, if not without signifi-cance for the reader, at the end of Chapter 18: "an event occurred" (*M*, 18:55). The next twenty chapters deal partly with Samoa's history and life aboard the *Parki*, partly with seeming digressions on ship's names, surgery, and swordfish. But from the clutter of narration and exposition, both presented in the tall-tale tradition of sailors' yarns, there emerges a fairly clear definition of nature and life in nature. Samoa's tale of the mutiny and of his savage killing of the helpless, if heretofore treacherous, mutineers is a clear enough introduction to the cruelty inherent in survival. And the harshness of survival itself is stated in a lightheartedly macabre description of Annatoo's amputation of Samoa's injured arm. This whole chapter, "Dedicated to the College of Physicians and Surgeons," exemplifies Melville's attempt to "read lessons to Buffon," that is, to derive truth from the heart of elemental experience. As the chapter concludes, the "vulgar errors" both of the "sensible man" with his "warm fireside and muffins" (M, 24:79) and of Edmund Burke, who mourned the departure of the epic age (M, 24:79) are thoroughly exposed by Melville's ironic image of "a heroic bivouac, in a wild beechen wood, of a raw gusty morning in Normandy; every knight blowing his steel-gloved fingers, and vainly striving to cook his cold coffee in his helmet" (M, 24:79). Whatever truth our narrator is to wring from nature and from himself will not be based on "common sense" or on the high seriousness of academic inquiry, but on the hard terms of an intractable reality.

Within the context of depicted life on the *Parki*, the narrator's self-posturing must be viewed as the worst kind of self-delusion. Far from being "the Grand Turk and his Vizier Mustapha sitting down before Vienna" (M, 20:64), the narrator and Jarl are hard put to keep the *Parki* floating, let alone sailing in the right direction. Samoa and Annatoo are the ones who have best adjusted to the world of the *Parki*. How arrogant, futile, and irrelevant seem the narrator's manipulations of Annatoo and Samoa and his secret self-promotion to "owner, as well as commander of the craft I sailed" (M, 29:97). He cannot forestall the calm, nor can he resist, or even prepare for, the storm that succeeds the calm (cf. M, 36:116–17)—the storm that kills Annatoo, sinks the *Parki*, and dashes the narrator's stout heart (cf. M, 37:120). The narrator, self-conceived in heroic-romantic terms, comes to know all too well the fragility of his powers and the terrors of the overwhelming world he had set out to conquer.

Melville marks the crucial significance of the *Parki* episode for us in Chapter 38, "The Sea on Fire." The chapter links the *Parki* disaster with the appearance of Aleema and Yillah in Chapters 39 through 43, and it is, thus, perhaps the most important chapter in the early part of the book. On the surface, the chapter is a digression on marine phosphorescence, comparable to the digressions on the swordfish and ships' names, but in rhetorical effectiveness the chapter prefigures some of the depths to be found in the later "Whiteness of the Whale" and "Cetology" chapters of

Moby-Dick. The phosphorescence, like all of the significant events in this portion of the novel, appears abruptly to Jarl and the narrator, who, awakened, behold "the ocean of a pallid white color, corruscating all over with tiny golden sparkles" (*M*, 38:121). Looking "like ghosts" to each other, they behold the crossing and recrossing trails of sharks and the schools of "Medusa" fish. Then "suddenly [again], as we gazed, there shot high into the air a bushy jet of flashes, accompanied by the unmistakable deep breathing sound of a sperm whale" (*M*, 38:121). Even this early in the book, and within the only partially developed metaphors of the literalized voyage of the *Chamois*, the sea has come to signify the infinite possibilities of the world, for earlier, on the book's opening page, Melville has defined the Cachalot as the whale "whose brain enlightens the world" (*M*, 1:3). But what a world and what an enlightenment—only the wondrous Cachalots seem able "to sport in these phosphorescent billows" (*M*, 38:121).

This occurrence immediately reminds the narrator of two previous occasions off the coast of Peru when he "beheld the sea white as a shroud" (*M*, 38:123), and he uses this recollection to "explain" the phenomenon. The chapter, indeed, falls rather neatly into two halves, the first offering a more or less objective description of the phenomenon, the second presenting a multiplex explication of its causes and significance. Thus this chapter, which structurally links the narrative-adventure of the *Chamois* and the *Parki* with the romantic quest for Yillah, stands as a microcosm of the complex relationship between phenomenon and explanation—fact and mind—which defines the structure and dominating theme of the novel. As Melville leads us deeper into his explorations of the mind's world, we will see just how thoughtful and appropriate is this original conceit—"The Sea on Fire."

The narrator's gloss upon the fiery sea has multiplicity as its most salient feature. There is no simple or single explanation for the phenomenon as perceived. Because "sailors love marvels, and love to repeat them" (*M*, 38:123), the narrator tells us first of Jarl's superstitious belief that the phosphorescence is caused by a "commotion among the mermaids" (*M*, 38:123). But dismissing this explanation even as he produces it, he proceeds to the more reliable theories of Faraday, who "might, perhaps, impute the phenomenon to a peculiarly electrical condition of the atmosphere" (*M*, 38:123). But even this hesitant supposition is no sooner stated than contradicted—"by many intelligent seamen, who, in part, impute it to the presence of large quantities of putrescent animal matter" (*M*, 38:123). And this contradiction is itself countered by the narrator's own observations that "there are many living fish, phosphorescent" (*M*, 38:123). The narrator's conclusion that these alternative and contradictory explanations "are only surmises; likely, but uncertain" (*M*, 38:123) seems not only uncertain in itself, but also muddle-headed.

As logical explanation, scientific or otherwise, the narrator's argument and conclusion are muddle-headed. As poetic statements of Melville's larger purposes, however, they are pure revelation. The wondrous nature of the world, giving substance to experience and serving as the object of mind, is marvellously ambiguous. It emanates light from life *and* death, the one (although which is not certain) serving as medium to the spectacular splendors of the other. The final end is—no doubt—certain: "alas, thrice alas, for the poor little fire-fish of the sea, whose radiance but reveals them to their foes, and lights the way to their destruction" (*M*, 38:124). But the call to that brilliant world of jewelled experience is irresistible. The mermaids ask us to linger in the chambers of the sea; Hero awaits "the approach of her Leander, who comes buffeting with his wings the aroma of the flowers" (*M*, 38:124).

Thus, precisely and poetically, Melville prepares us for Yillah and all that she signifies. She is the blonde sea-maid held secret captive in the heart of nature. She is irresistible and she is fateful. To seize her, or even attempt to, the narrator must plunge into an unknown, frightening world. And once he has plunged to those depths, he can never rise again. She is nature's secret prize, always sought, sometimes glimpsed or touched, but never held. In her very conception Melville shows his kinship with his Romantic contemporaries—Goethe, Byron, Shelley, Carlyle, Poe, Hawthorne, and Emerson. In her development, that is, her disappearance, Melville names himself forefather to our age—of Hemingway, Faulkner, Fitzgerald, of Sartre, Camus, Beckett, Nabokov, and the myriad faceless names of modern art.

As the vessel bearing the prized Yillah, Aleema's craft clearly symbolizes nature. It appears on the horizon "dancing into view . . . like one of many birds" (*M*, 39:126). The air and sea are joined to the earthly image of the canoe's yard—"a crooked bough, . . . to which the green bark was still clinging" (*M*, 39:128), and the fire of violence and death soon complete the picture of elemental nature. Aleema himself is a fitting captain for nature's vessel—an "old priest, like a scroll of old parchment, covered all over with hieroglyphical devices" (*M*, 40:130). Looking as "old as the elderly hills" (*M*, 40:130), he is an Aaron to his sons and the keeper of the "Eleusinian mysteries" (*M*, 41:131). He is, finally, the keeper and guardian of Yillah.

The antagonism between Aleema and the narrator is immediate and complete. Depository of all time, convention, and social restraint, Aleema is symbolized as the Nemesis to the narrator's search for independent action and awareness. Silent and invisible within Aleema's tent, Yillah is nature's prized secret, which the narrator is determined to possess at whatever risk or cost. Unmotivated in any narrative or dramatic sense, the narrator's determination to rescue her from Aleema forms an emphatic parallel with his reckless determination to abandon the *Arcturion* in mid-Pacific in search of the golden isles of the west.

The narrator's commitment to rescuing the captive is absolute, and he sees it is "best to set heedfully about it" (*M*, 41:131) just as he saw it best to plan carefully the flight from the *Arcturion*. But here, as there, events outrun plans, and the nice concern for the shedding of blood is forgotten in the murderous fight for life. As the climactic action of the *Chamois* adventure-narrative, "A Fray" clearly defines Melville's uneasy awareness of the separation between thought and act, mind and world. "Depart and you live; stay and you die" (*M*, 41:132) is Aleema's decree. Then: "No time to think. All passed quicker than it can be said. . . . A thrust and a threat! Ere I knew it, my cutlass made a quick lunge. A curse from the priest's mouth; red blood from his side; he tottered, stared about him, and fell over like a brown hemlock into the sea" (*M*, 41: 132–33). Yillah is "won."

The next ten chapters define Yillah's character and, by extension, the central theme of the novel. Commentators on *Mardi*, in an effort to view Melville as "modern" and therefore ironic in his treatment of quests and questers for the absolute, often ignore the simple fact that the narrator does actually possess Yillah for some considerable time before her disappearance.[5] And it is of considerable value to understand her presence if we are at all to understand her absence.

We initially identify Yillah with the inner secrets of nature, and it is irresistible to identify her further with the golden-tressed mermaids of the previous chapter and with the torch-bearing Hero who awaits her Leander [the narrator] described at the end of that same chapter. "More than mortal" (*M*, 43:137), "lovely enough to be really divine" (*M*, 43:139), as a self-conceived maiden of fairy tale, she tells an "unearthly" story of her home in Oroolia, "the Island of Delights" (*M*, 43:137). To possess her finally, the narrator does not discredit her dream world; he enters it by claiming for himself a divine origin in Oroolia and a dream past in which he was her lover (cf. *M*, 45:143)

This untoward behavior has profound implications for our proper understanding of Melville's purposes in *Mardi*. In the "romantic interlude" Melville defines and attempts to dramatize the romantic dream of a perfectly conceived universe perfectly experienced. It is the world of Israfel, of kingdoms by the sea, of Thoreau's Walden in spring and Emerson's moonstruck common, of Keats's faery landscape: "Was not Yillah my shore and my grove? my meadow, my mead, my soft shady vine, and my arbor?" (*M*, 46:145). In sum, this "romantic interlude" defines the timeless, unconfined world of unfettered mind and imagination.

Clearly, Melville might have ended his narrative with this rather conventional definition of the romantic imagination running free, or adrift, rather, in a harsh, recalcitrant world. In tone, the final sentence of Chapter 46 seems remarkably like a conclusion to the novel. Melville doesn't conclude his romantic tale there, however, and the conclusion of the novel is markedly altered from these vague ecstasies of Chapter 46. Melville could conceive of and even dramatize the same romantic ecstasies that inspired the British and American Romantics of the nineteenth century, but he could not, like Coleridge, Shelley, Keats, and Poe, relegate these ecstasies to some displaced world—of religion, mind, imagination, or art. In conception, and perhaps in aspiration, Melville was much more akin to Emerson and Thoreau; if these elevated moments were to be accepted as anything more than hallucination or willing self-deception, they had to be integral to one's persistent experience of the world. Thus, although for the idyllic moment the narrator harbors "some shadowy purpose of merely hovering about for a while," it is clearly only until he feels "more landwardly inclined" (*M*, 46:145)—that is, until he feels compelled to return to the world of unvarnished reality.

The idyll of "life and love ... united" (*M*, 51:159) continues for five days, but the dream begins to fade, "and Yillah pining for the shore, we turned our prow due west, and next morning came in sight of land" (*M*, 52:160). On the literal level of the narrative, this easy discovery of land would appear to be a remarkable bit of blind navigation, but the very contrivance of the incident points clearly to its true significance. However desirable as a sea-dream maiden, Yillah must be brought to the reality of the shore. Her destiny, as foretold by Aleema in a dream, is to descend into a whirlpool to "depths unknown"—at last "to well up in an inland fountain of Oroolia" (*M*, 43:138), and this Arethusian myth is, I think, a very apt image for Melville's purposes in the novel. Yillah does descend to depths unknown shortly after her arrival in Mardi, and Taji's quest for her throughout the remainder of the book is a Melvillean "diving" for truth in the world, a search for a unifying vision to encompass the multiplicity of human experience.[6]

It is in Mardi, on the island of Odo, that our narrator is first named: Taji, demigod, sailor from the sun. Polynesian myth aside, Taji is well defined within the Judeo-Christian tradition; he is half corporeal, half spiritual in nature. He requires his yams for sustenance but burns with a thirst for the higher meaning of life. Even as he and Yillah approach Mardi, the difficulty of their making an easy home there is strongly underscored. Yillah's "merry suggestion" to plant a mast on the highest hill and fly away to Oroolia (*M*, 52:161) is met by the narrator's chilling question: "alas! how weigh the isle's coral anchor, leagues down in the fathomless sea?" (*M*, 52:161).

Indeed, Yillah's fantasy and the narrator's response haunt the rest of the novel. Even in Odo, to preserve the purity of Yillah's dream vision Taji must retire from the main island "to a little green tuft of an islet" (*M*, 62:188). Ashore he is haunted by his guilt ("Am I a murderer, stars?" [*M*, 58:179]) and by the vague threat of Hautia (Chapter 61), who from the first brings disharmony into the idyll. Taji is, for the moment, rapt with joy in this "fairy bower in the fair lagoon, scene of sylvan ease and heart's repose" (*M*, 64:193), but just as suddenly as she appeared, Yillah departs. Fled is that vision and all that it entails. Edenic innocence, Romantic imagination, transcendental idealism all prove too delicate to survive even proximity to the real world of Mardi—"no land of pleasure unalloyed, and plenty without a pause" (*M*, 63:191). And a man—even though a demigod—by his Mardian nature cannot live for long retired from the world.

Melville's Mardian world and Taji's ensuing search for Yillah throughout that world are irredeemably humanistic, and the ensuing search for Yillah, or, more precisely, the attempt to realize humanity's highest dreams, takes place in a context almost totally devoid of religious and transcendental implications—at least until the searchers reach Serenia at the conclusion of the novel. The satire directed at religion in Chapters 105–117 is as self-limiting as it is self-evident. Whatever realm of values lies beyond this world of experience is for precisely that reason inconsequential.

The questions weighed and the possibilities raised by Taji's search spring first and finally from the self's worldly nature. Taji and his companions in the quest, Media, Yoomy, Babbalanja, and Mohi, constitute not only the multifaceted individual personality, as Lawrance Thompson, among others, has noted,[7] but also the multifaceted structure of civilized society. In a work so clearly concerned with philosophical questions, it is natural to stress the characters' identities as functions of the mind: Babbalanja (logic, reason, intuition, and even mystical perception), Yoomy (creative imagination), Mohi (memory), Media (volition), and Taji (the totality of all these who, nevertheless, exceeds the sum of their parts). But it is also noteworthy that Melville draws an analogy between the individual and his society. Thus, the considerable amount of political and social satire in *Mardi* is integral to Melville's conception of the individual, for without the integrity of individual understanding and behavior, social integrity and order are virtually impossible.

The early portion of the novel dealing with the *Chamois* adventures prepares us for the psychological and social partitioning of Taji in the satire-travelogue portion of the book. The narrator-Jarl dualism in the early chapters presents a rather simplistic dramatization of the mind-body relationship, and the narrator-Yillah dualism suggests a perfect, if fleeting, union of sense, mind, and imagination. The bonds joining Taji, Yoomy, Mohi, and Media in a single composite identity are much more elastic than those binding the narrator to Jarl and Yillah; indeed, this elastic relationship among the questers—threatening to break altogether periodically throughout the quest—reveals the disintegration of Taji's personality in a world without Yillah. In like manner, the disintegrated world of Juam, Willamilla, Ohonoo, and Vivenza is presented as a product of the disintegrated personalities of its rulers.

Thus, the quest for Yillah is both internal and external, the search for unity by the unintegrated self in a disintegrated world. The search takes place among the various islands of the Mardian archipelago—the central unifying metaphor of the book. Truly this is an apt metaphor for Melville's purposes, for the individual islands clearly signify the isolated and fragmented nature of individuals and states who through ignorance, weakness, stubbornness, or pride have cut themselves off from the world. But these same islands viewed together as an archipelago represent, or at least imply, the unified and integrated reality sought by Taji and his companions. Because all islands in Mardi belong to the same archipelago, it makes little difference what order is followed in examining them. In terms of Taji's quest, however, it is necessary that he visit them all.

Melville cannot, strictly speaking, be faulted in his concept of narrative strategy. Gower, Langland, Dante, Spenser, and Pierre Bayle would no doubt have understood, and even applauded, his intention to provide a cumulative-exhaustive panorama of the known world with running commentary on its meaning. Practically speaking, however, Melville either misjudged the sensibilities of his age (and ours), or he obstinately wrote the book as it seemed to him that it had to be written. In any case, the chronic problem for the critic of any fiction is, in the case of reading *Mardi*, very acute. The plenary concept of *Mardi* modifies severely the critical license we all employ in extracting crucial scenes, events, and passages to explain the "total" significance of a work. In a very meaningful sense, all critics of *Mardi* are doomed to fail just as Taji is doomed to fail in his search for Yillah. And we and he fail for the same reasons: We do not see all that is there to be seen, we cannot comprehend all that we see, and we cannot clearly state all that we have seen or comprehended.

The central themes and problems of *Mardi* are those of focus: how does one see the world? Taji and his companions look through the world in hopes of finding (seeing) the ultimate in Yillah. And the beliefs and behavior of all those they meet are presented as direct products of the ways they look at their world. This question of "vision" persists throughout the narrative, and the conclusion of the novel is, to use a rather homely figure, bifocal. But it is in the very beginning of the quest that Melville defines the complex nature of "seeing" and "knowing," particularly as they relate to "doing." At the very beginning of the search for Yillah, Melville clearly dramatizes in King Peepi and King Donjalolo the inherent limits to our ability to view the world steadily and whole, thus prefiguring the reasons why the quest must ultimately fail.

King Peepi strikes one initially as a cliché buffoon-king, wielding absolute power with an insouciant carelessness more frightening than a purposive tyranny. But Melville carefully defines his boy-king's perversity as a product of excessive, not deficient thought. The inheritor of "the valiant spirits of some twenty heroes, sages, simpletons, and demi-gods, previously lodged in his sire" (*M*, 67:202), Peepi becomes, "by reason of these revolving souls in him, . . . one of the most unreliable of beings" (*M*, 67:203). Melville here is not concerned merely with the unreliability of kingship or the dangers of absolute authority. Rather, he emphasizes the unreliability of human temperament per se. Personifying the various moods in Peepi as alternating "inherited souls," Melville dramatizes the concept that there are many "personalities" within each individual. And he is quick to see the radical implications of such whimsical variability of thought and behavior. One brief paragraph intervenes between the observation that in King Peepi's realm there is "nothing permanent but the island itself" and the far-reaching conclusion that insofar as he was "subject to contrary impulses, over which he had not the faintest control, Peepi was plainly denuded of all moral obligation to virtue" (*M*, 67:203). Arrived at so simply and stated so matter-of-factly, this proposition conceals for a moment its deadly dart. In fact, however, the whimsical farce of Chapter 67 effectively destroys two thousand years of Western ethical thought. Amid all its theological and ritualistic complexities, Judeo-Christian belief is founded ultimately on practical morality—which is to say "good behavior"—originating in "right reason" and true perception. And in denying the reliability of the origins of ethical judgment Melville denies the reliability of all consequent actions, not because there is no ultimate reality, but because that reality is ultimately unknowable.

The concept of unreliability and inconsistency in mind and personality is so commonplace in our psychiatric age that is is difficult for us to imagine the enormity of such a concept for the nineteenth-century mind. But the "pre-modern" world-picture assumed the reliability and consistency of perceiver, perceived, and perception; Newton and Locke shared the assumption that properly recognized causes yielded predictable effects. Hume horrified himself as much as his readers by the suggestion that cause-effect relationships were conventional rather than necessary, and Kant's synthetic vision can be viewed as a monumental attempt to salvage free will, God, and immortality—that is, Christianity and practical morality—by defining the predictable reliability of the mind—categorically as it were. All of the eighteenth-century thinkers were, in fact, obsessed with the relationship between cause and effect, for they recognized its centrality to all their thought. Melville annihilates the question altogether, and in doing so finds himself forced to voyage "chartless" through *Mardi*.

Unknown causes are bound to yield surprising and startling effects. And it is tempting for an admirer of Melville to justify the reckless progression of incident in *Mardi* as organically consistent with Melville's central theme. Leaving that boundless speculation to the side, it is certain that Melville sensed the implications of Chapter 67, for he pursues them directly in the sequence of events immediately following the visit to King Peepi of Valapee. In the visit to King Donjalolo of Willamilla, Taji confronts the stunning, crippling effects of the self's inability to see the world steadily and grasp it firmly. In the contrast between Taji's free-wandering, aspiring spirit and Donjalolo's sodden, degraded existence Melville depicts emphatically—if somewhat in caricature—the tragic difference between our self-conceived nobility and a sadly diminished reign in an enigmatic world.

Chapters 69 and 70 link the tales of Valapee and Juam. Much of the two chapters consists of a chatty introduction of Taji's fellow travellers, but amid the Polynesian pleasantries there lurks a sinister thread reminding us of the threats to Taji's quest. The bantering exchanges between Yoomy and Babbalanja in fact produce in the latter a skeptical, summary denial of any possibility of success in the search for Yillah: "All vanity, vanity, Yoomy, to seek in nature for positive warranty to these aspirations of ours" (*M*, 69:210).

Babbalanja thus defines both the dream and its impossibility. As we progress through the narrative we discover we must discount in varying degrees the statements made by various individual characters, but here, at the beginning of the quest, Babbalanja's measured pessimism carries great force for the reader. And certainly there is no question of perspectivism, or discounted value in the third appearance of Hautia's heralds. They come upon Taji and his companions just as they complete their "Paddle Chant"—a fitting paean to the questing spirit. Although the heralds are "hooded" and "enigmatical" (*M*, 70:215), Taji's response is one of spontaneous and deep perplexity and alarm (*M*, 70:215). Viewed merely as conditioned responses to an unexpected event, Taji's surprise and confusion appear natural, if somewhat excessive. But viewed within the context of the newly initiated quest for Yillah, these heralds of Hautia and these emotions of Taji's are ominous. Surprise, puzzlement, alarm, and confusion are antithetical to the security, certainty, peace, and contentment sought in Yillah. The "thrice waved oleanders," which Yoomy glosses "Beware—beware—beware" (*M*, 70:215), warn both Taji and reader of difficulties and uncertainties ahead.

The first stop of the searchers at Valapee had been a bad enough portent, for the King Peepi episode clearly illustrated the mind's inherent instability and briefly dramatized the futility of that mind's efforts to seize upon a stable reality. But the full import of the heralds' warning to Taji becomes apparent only after the questers' visit to Juam and Willamilla, the hereditary home of King Donjalolo. Melville takes great care in presenting Donjalolo as an alter-ego to Taji and in presenting Willamilla as a microcosm of the Mardian world. In Donjalolo's fretful confinement we see the heavy penalty exacted by recalcitrant nature on any aspirations to supreme dominion. In the bounty of Willamilla, which does not satisfy but merely gluts, in the beauty of its maidens, who do not sate but merely tire, Melville depicts his anti-Eden, a paradise that fails because human beings lack knowledge of good and evil. It is a daring concept, running directly against the grain of conventional Christian dogma, but Melville is unwavering: perfect innocence and salvation require perfect awareness, but our awareness is anything but perfect.

The secluded vale of Willamilla is so much like Taji's isolated "green tuft of an islet" off Odo that we half expect to find Yillah "immured in this strange retreat" (*M*, 71:217). We don't, of course, but we do find in Donjalolo a gloss upon Taji's character as a quester, and in the king's sweet imprisonment we find yet another forecast of Taji's failure. Donjalolo, like three of his forebears, and like Taji, is a "rover" (*M*, 72:221), but on the very day he had planned to set out to explore Mardi, his father committed suicide, thus entailing Donjalolo to remain in the valley forever. This absolute ban upon all travel by the reigning monarch of Juam is an inheritance from the past, the price Marjora and "the uttermost scion of his race" (*M*, 72:220) must pay for Marjora's murder of his brother Teei. The taint of murder itself links Donjalolo with Taji, but even more strikingly, Donjalolo, like Taji, is "the victim of unaccountable vagaries; haunted by specters, and beckoned to by the ghosts of his sires" (*M*, 73:223).

Both Marjora and Taji have committed murders to usurp power and supremacy; both have suffered an unforeseen guilt that in itself curbs the power they would exert. In these terms Melville retells the Christian myth of the fall—that much is obvious. Not so obvious, perhaps, is Melville's unorthodoxy in assigning values to the myth. Although he doesn't ignore Taji's crime, neither does he question the prize, and the inestimable worth of Yillah goes far beyond any Miltonic concept of "felix culpa." Rather, Melville seems to present the Faustian argument: to attain the beatitude of perfect knowledge (i.e., union with Yillah), any act, any crime is justifiable. He might even be making the Mephistophelian argument: to attain the beatitude of perfect knowledge, an act of crime and disorder is necessary. In any event, Melville's conclusion is inescapable: the act sufficient to seize perfection is also sufficient to destroy it.

Melville thus places his characters, his readers, and himself in a quandary: perfect awareness, which is infinitely desirable, is also infinitely unattainable. And Donjalolo is the epitome of humanity's unhappy fate in such a world; he is the figure of the mind forever incapable of grasping the world in itself. Melville constructs a fairly complex figure of concentric analogies to illustrate his point. That is, Donjalolo's mind is to his body as his person is to Willamilla, as Willamilla is to Juam, as Juam is to Mardi, as Mardi is . . . ad infinitum. At the center is finite mind, at the circumference infinite being, and however much we may desire to bridge center and circumference it is beyond our mortal power to do so. Yet, *Mardi* makes clear, it is also beyond our mortal power to stop trying. Not only is Mardi "forever shut out" once Donjalolo becomes king, but there is also a "law of his isle, interdicting abdication to its kings" (*M*, 73:223).

Trapped by his own inescapable limitations, frantic in his futile search for outlets, Donjalolo "in many a riotous scene, wasted the powers which might have compassed the noblest designs" (*M*, 73:223). Like King Peepi, Donjalolo gives way to a tangle of contradictory moods, motives, and acts. Like King Peepi, Donjalolo vacillates "between virtue and vice; to neither constant, and upbraided by both; his mind, like his person in the glen, . . . continually passing and repassing between opposite extremes" (*M*, 73:224). His is the madness of the hungry mind left nothing to feed upon except itself.

Melville thus gives us an all-too-clear picture of the causes behind instability of mind and action. Incapable of seeing the whole of anything, both Peepi and Donjalolo (and by implication Taji) can judge neither whole nor part and must act out the absurdity of a sovereignty based on ignorance. But in the Donjalolo episode Melville pushes his inquiry yet further, for he questions the power of the community as well as that of the individual. Although the possibility immediately suggests itself that a community of individuals acting in concert might well overcome the individual shortcomings of its members, Melville is quick to point out that truth is no more accessible to many than to one. When Donjalolo sends his emissaries to explore the neighboring isles (Chapter 82) he is dismayed to discover that his two wisest agents, "honest of heart, keen of eye, and shrewd of understanding" (*M*, 82:248), cannot agree on the simplest of facts—the color of a coral reef. Donjalolo's conclusion is immediate and far-reaching. His first observation is almost a truism—"how hard is truth to be come at by proxy!" (*M*, 82:249). But his next remarks probe deeper into the heart of *Mardi*, and of Melville's work as a whole: "How is it? Are the lenses in their eyes diverse-hued, that objects seem different to both; for *undeniable is it, that the things they thus clashingly speak of are to be known for the same*; though represented with unlike colors and qualities. *But dumb things can not lie nor err*" (*M*, 82:249, my emphasis).

Donjalolo's perception and statement of the problem do not lead to a happy relativism, although he does go on to say that "Truth dwells in her fountains; where every one must drink for himself" (*M*, 82:250). Donjalolo's skepticism leads rather to a dark pessimism: "For me, vain all hope of ever knowing Mardi! Away! Better know nothing, than be deceived" (*M*, 82:250). Because Melville presents nature, or "reality," as permanent and objective—"dumb things" that "can not lie nor err"—it is merely the unhappy fate of humanity, singly and collectively, that we cannot grasp this reality wholly. Babbalanja's summary comment is all too fitting: "My lord, I have seen this same reef at Rafona. In various places, it is of various hues. As for Zuma and Varnopi, both are wrong, and both are right" (*M*, 82:250).

The full import of Babbalanja's observation here is revealed in the "nursery tale" he tells later on the isle of Maramma about "nine blind men, with uncommonly long noses" who "set out on their travels to see the great island on which they were born" (*M*, 115:355). In their travels they come upon "an immense wild banian tree; all over moss, and many centuries old, and forming quite a wood in itself; its thousand boughs striking into the earth, and fixing there as many gigantic trunks" (*M*, 115:356). The problem posed by the tree is a familiar one: to determine "which of those many trunks was the original and true one" (*M*, 115:356). The fable of the nine blind men in the banian grove forms a clear analogy with the Donjalolo reef fable, and even more important, it constitutes a paradigm of the central quest motif in the novel and thus warrants close attention.

The banian tree as described reinforces the central metaphor of the book—the archipelago—in that it admirably suggests the confusing multiplicity of presumably unified nature. And the nine blind "wise men" (*M*, 115:356) may be viewed alternately as the various conflicting points of

view within the individual personality and as the various conflicting individual perspectives within society. In both cases, Melville poses his
problem in the form of an equation with no known quantities. Each of
the searchers is blind, and all of the trunks are rooted. Each searcher calls
upon his own experience to support his claim upon truth, and with no
court of appeal higher than the evidence of their own experience, the
searchers aggressively defend their respective claims to truth by "beating
each other with their staves, and charging upon each other with their
noses" (*M*, 115:356). In "Benito Cereno," *The Confidence-Man*, and
Billy Budd, Melville depicts the violence that springs from the unverifi-
able, and therefore isolating, nature of human experience. In *Mardi*,
Melville defines bluntly the inescapable absurdity of human aspirations
and pretensions to truth. None of the searchers individually, nor all of
them together, nor King Tammaro and his subjects looking on, can determine which, if any, of the blind men has seized the original trunk of
the banian.

This fable, like that of the reef, seems to invite some sort of philosophical relativism, but Melville does not respond to the invitation as we of
this century do. At this central point in his tale and in this, his most lucid
metaphor for its central theme, Melville remains consistent in his belief
that truth is permanent and abiding—whether or not the self has access
to it. There is a reef at Rafona, and there is one original trunk to the
banian tree, all other seeming trunks but branches. Indeed, this assumption of a "Newtonian," ordered universe, inherited from both the Judeo-
Christian and the pre-modern scientific traditions, is the cardinal belief
Taji finds most difficult to abandon in his journey through Mardi; his
continuing quest for Yillah dramatizes his persistent belief in a central,
ordering principle to life, even in the face of more and more evidence
that it can never be verified.

The episodes of King Peepi and King Donjalolo serve as a fitting introduction to Taji's quest. Yillah, the fairy maiden, embodies for Taji, his
companions, and for us, all the virtues that give the quality of certainty
to one's experience; yet Melville makes it clear at the outset that there
are inherent and formidable obstacles to our finding Yillah and the
certainty she promises. These contrary motivations are not accidental.
Nor do they lead merely to "meaningful ironies" in any puerile sense,
whereby all the rough-textured contrariety of human experience is reduced to the comforting forms of figurative language and academic definition. Nor is it meaningful to debate whether Melville is to be found in
the romantic-idealist Taji or in the skeptical Babbalanja, whether he is a
foolish transcendentalist or a flinty pessimist; the meaning of *Mardi* lies
in Taji, Babbalanja, Media, Mohi, Yoomy, and all the other characters we

encounter. Pessimism and optimism, idealism and materialism, hope and skepticism all lay claim to our sympathy and belief as we read.

The question begins to loom large: Where does all this contradiction of mind and inconclusiveness of experience ultimately lead? That is an appropriate query for the reader of *Mardi*, for it is the question that *Mardi* itself raises again and again. And Melville does not mitigate the complexity of this, his chosen theme. On the contrary, Volume One carries us from a purely factual world to a world wherein fact becomes subject to mind, demonstrating in the process the fragility of the mind when overburdened by the full weight of reality. And Volume Two of *Mardi* presents an exhaustive series of incidents dramatizing the antinomies of Volume One. From Maramma to Serenia, Taji and his companions continue their search for the perfect Yillah among the imperfect lands and peoples of Mardi. All of our historical aspirations to truth—religious, philosophical, and political—are satirized as failures; all of our future hopes for perfection are doomed by inherent and inescapable ignorance and divisiveness.

It is fairly easy to lose oneself in Volume Two of *Mardi*. Various thematic threads are picked up, dropped, and then picked up again, only to be dropped once more—all with little sense of developing pattern. Further complicating this seemingly random episodic structure are the digressive chapters containing the various commentaries, debates, and disquisitions by Taji and his companions on the events observed and on each other as observers. But amid this general tangle, a clear and relatively simple pattern does emerge. We are presented a world of events (as observed), and we are presented a good probing look at the observers themselves.

Given the values in Volume One, this dualism of "observer-observed world" immediately suggests some of the problems involved in interpreting the events of *Mardi*, for no two witnesses fully agree upon the meaning of what they have observed. We can state with some confidence, however, that Taji, Yoomy, Babbalanja, Mohi, and Media suggest the full range of human perception, sensibility, and response, and that *Mardi*, as it is presented, effectively suggests the totality of the world. This world of activity, by implication, is infinitely complex, just as the islands of the archipelago seem to multiply ad infinitum; nevertheless, we can perceive another structural principle operating that aids us in sorting out Melville's purposes. Briefly put, all the events of *Mardi* may be grouped under the headings of religious or political activity, the first dealing with our professed beliefs and motivations, the second with actual behavior. Again, it is not so much a flaw in Melville's execution of his theme as it is a revelation of that theme itself that he portrays observer

and observed as forever discrete, belief and behavior as inevitably disparate. And these are the conditions that lead to the unhappy, if not tragic,
end of *Mardi*.

The opening pages of Volume Two live up to the gloomy intimations
of Volume One. Maramma, the first island visited, is depicted as yet another anti-Eden. The central grove is dominated by "one gigantic palm
shaft, belted round by saplings" locked in "the serpent folds of gnarled,
distorted banians" (*M*, 107:330). The full implications of the banian become clear a few chapters later in Babbalanja's "nursery tale"; however,
Chapter 107 makes quite a forceful statement in itself through its carefully patterned imagery. Melville turns from the implicit values of the
banian-choked palm grove to the explicit description of manchineels
"with lustrous leaves and golden fruit" which would be "deemed ...
Trees of Life" except that "underneath their branches grew no blade of
grass, no herb, nor moss; the bare earth was scorched by heaven's own
dews, filtrated through that fatal foliage" (*M*, 107:330).

The idyllic beauty of Odo's tufted islet where Taji and Yillah happily
dwelled, even the lush beauty of Donjalolo's Willamilla—however restrictive of movement—seem as far removed as possible from this awful
land of perpetual, dreadful night, where "owls hooted from dead boughs;
or, one by one, sailed by on silent pinions; cranes stalked abroad, or
brooded in the marshes; adders hissed; bats smote the darkness; ravens
croaked; and vampires, fixed on slumbering lizards, fanned the sultry air"
(*M*, 107:331). This description, coming as it does at the beginning of
Volume Two, establishes the tone not only for the Maramma chapters,
but also for the rest of the voyage through Mardi. And, clearly, such a
beginning does not augur well for those in search of the fair Yillah.

There is very little original in Melville's attack upon the organized religion of Maramma. His cataloguing of the abuses of rigid, formulaic pay-
as-you-go religion has a literary history in English going back at least to
Chaucer and Langland. The revelation of the void at the center of Hivohitee's church is unequivocal and emphatic enough but doesn't really
lead to a deeper understanding of the religious sentiment as such. And
surely Melville is aware of the existence and the compelling power of
that sentiment, for it mirrors Taji's own compulsion to discover his own
meaningful relationship to the universe, albeit religion takes one out of
the world Taji seeks to plumb.

The religious question as Melville poses it is essentially philosophical
or, more narrowly yet, epistemological, just as the book's main quest is
in large measure interrogative: How and what do we know?—and what
authority does any human "knowledge" have?[8] These questions, of
course, dominate all Western philosophy from Descartes on, and Melville

reveals much of the bewilderment common to his age—one need only think of Coleridge and Emerson as epitomes of their respective intellectual cultures. But Melville, unlike Coleridge, does not shy away from artistic creation until he can work out his soul's uncertainties, and, unlike Emerson, does not grip fast to the belief "most consistent with our mind's hopes." Rather, in one of the most impressive acts of literary courage in the nineteenth century, Melville gives artistic form to humanity's highest dreams and worst fears—simultaneously. Searching every niche of his own complex mind and experience for some affirmation of an integrity of self within a meaningful world, he at the same time meticulously charts his own failures. Suggested quietly but strongly in the collapsed journeys of *Typee* and *Omoo*, this theme of perpetual failure, perpetual hope becomes almost strident in *Mardi*, and nowhere more so than in the Maramma portion of the book, in which the highest hope that religion traditionally offers is virtually annihilated.[9]

The religious aspiration, indeed, is presented in direct parallel with Taji's quest. Pani, the first person the searchers meet on Maramma, not only guides all pilgrims "in the dread name of great Alma" (*M*, 106:327), but also immediately promises "to discover sweet Yillah; declaring that in Maramma, if any where, the long-lost maiden must be found" (*M*, 106:326). Thus Pani, not Hivohitee, is the central figure in the Maramma episode, for it is he who claims to be the worldly guide to perfection.

Pani does not fare well at Melville's hands. He is rigid and peremptory: "What I ask, I demand" (*M*, 106:327). He is old, like Aleema, to the point of death, "with a beard white as the mane of the pale horse" (*M*, 106:326). And most significantly, he, like the wise men in the banian grove, is blind. His blindness typifies the problem of all who would "ascend lofty Ofo" (*M*, 106:327). The young pilgrim speaks for all, including Taji, when he says "There are many ways: the right one I must seek for myself" (*M*, 106:329). But with the experience of Peepi and Donjalolo fresh in our minds and the bewildering banian groves of Chapters 107 and 115 immediately in store, there seems little prospect for progress, and no prospect at all for confirmed success.

As Melville states the case in *Mardi*, the problem with this radical belief in the inner promptings of one's conscience is that there is no way to ascertain the "objective" validity of those "subjective" promptings. And however stimulating Jonathan Edwards might have found this philosophical poser, Melville found it devastating in its implications. For Melville, the freedom to err bore with it no compensating test by which one could recognize God's necessity. For him, the isolation of one's thoughts and emotions in a world presumed real but always beyond reach could only lead to a bedlam of pointless thoughts and acts. And thus, for Melville, this freedom of self-determination, the cornerstone of protestantism and the copestone of nineteenth-century romanticism, leads inevitably backward, not to the pure belief of the primitive Church, nor to the pure society of Eden, but to the antisocial chaos of savagery.

The absurdity of philosophical relativism is clearly underscored by Melville in his portrayal of the contradictory and mutually exclusive prayers offered up to the inferior deities of Maramma on Lake Yammo (in Chapter 111). By maintaining the concept of a God-ordered universe while scorning the efficacy of prayer and the reliability of faith, Melville does, indeed, depict a nightmare of the soul, the full horror of which is seen in the young pilgrim's fate. Another alter-ego to Taji (as is almost every significant character in the book by virtue of Taji's universal nature), the young pilgrim expresses a palpably ideal faith founded upon a Tertullianesque skepticism: "I love great Oro, though I comprehend him not" (*M*, 112:347). And he almost duplicates Taji's earlier, "We lived and we loved; life and love were united" with "I wonder; I hope; I love; I weep" (*M*, 112:347). But for all this he is called "impious boy" and seized "in the name of Alma [Christ]" and borne away as a sacrifice to the very image he "condemns" (*M*, 112:347).

Melville's satire is directed to something deeper than the imperfection of the Church, for, ultimately, Melville depicts the religious sentiment, powerful and admirable in itself, as having no working value in the world, just as he shows that it is only in this world that it could have value. There appears no point of meeting between the young pilgrim's inward-looking soul and the worldly, smooth-running hypocrisy of Pani and the Church. And upon Taji's departure from Maramma, all but the most casual readers are convinced that Yillah will not be found in Mardi at all.

Certainly the implications of the Peepi, Donjalolo, and Pani-Hivohitee episodes are clear: the inherent partiality and variability of the mind preclude our grasping truth in any absolute or even certain sense. Yet at the very moment of this inescapable conclusion, which by any rule of logic should have ended the quest and *Mardi*, we find Taji not downcast, but lifted to heights of ecstasy. In the oceanic rhapsodies of "Dreams" (Chapter 119), we see Taji as he was in his first golden vision of the Western Isles and as he will be when he finally turns defiantly "into the racing tide" (*M*, 195:654). Here, through the extended metaphor of dreams, Melville presents the power of Taji's imagination, endlessly creative as it annihilates time and space. It is in the dream world of imaginings that "Atlantics and Pacifics" undulate round Taji, lying "stretched out in their midst: a land-locked Mediterranean, knowing no ebb, nor flow" (*M*, 119:367). It is there that he listens to "St. Paul who argues the doubts of

Montaigne" and there that "divine Plato, and Proclus, and Verulam" become his counsel (*M*, 119:367).

Yet even in the romantic rhapsody of the world-conquering self—"so, with all the past and present pouring in me, I roll down my billow from afar" (*M*, 119:368)—Taji maintains the assumption of objective truth at the heart of a permanent reality. And there is the rub. Not dreams, but dream-perfect reality is what is sought—not Yillah afloat in an unfixed sea, but Yillah in the lands of Mardi. No wonder Taji's torment, which is the torment of all humanity as Melville conceives it.

This frustrating and frustrated search for a working, or at least workable, ideal clearly accounts for the predominantly satirical nature of Volume Two. It also accounts for the attacks being directed largely at institutions rather than at the sentiments underlying them. Thus, although Taji attacks the religious institutions of Maramma and the political workings of governments and nations, he does not attack religious sentiment and democratic ideals themselves.

Taji's ambivalence and the incongruity of such oceanic dreams in the face of Maramma's lessons obscure what is fairly explicit. Taji simply refuses to accept the implications of his own experience. His dream of attaining oneness with the universe is so intense that it blinds him to the facts of the world's recalcitrance. Melville wants us to see these dreams both as irresistible and impossible; thus defined, Taji's quest is as hopeless as it is necessary to his self-definition. It is this quality of antinomy that pervades the satire in the rest of the novel. The shortcomings of political and social reality are played off against an ideal of universal harmony defined as impossible by our own fractional, changeable nature.

This principle of antinomy is so consistent throughout Melville's political satire that an exhaustive analysis of his social commentary would be repetitious—even redundant; Melville's own decision to illustrate his case ad infinitum is probably the most glaring weakness of *Mardi*. But it is necessary to touch on the salient features of his argument to demonstrate just how far reality is removed from the ideal under Melville's critical gaze.

First, Melville makes clear that Taji and his companions are exploring all the known world. It is clear in Chapters 165–168 that in sailing "West, West! West, West!" (*M*, 168:551) Taji and his followers have taken in all of Mardi in their quest—leaving their "Wake around the World" and even then not stopping: "The universe again before us; our quest, as wide" (*M*, 168:555). Before asking where they go after circumnavigating the Mardian world, a question properly to be directed to the novel's conclusion, we must examine their main-travelled roads in Mardi.

The separateness amid unity that defines the Mardian archipelago is mirrored in the Mardians themselves, who like the Tapparians "secede from the rabble; form themselves into a community of their own; and conventionally pay that homage to each other, which universal Mardi could not be prevailed upon to render to them" (*M*, 127:399).

This instinct to value oneself above others and to assert one's sovereignty by secession "from the rabble" is only rhetorically different from Taji's own desire to attain his ideal in a corrupt world; both spring from the solipsism of the human mind and lead to the isolation of individuals within centrifugal societies. This concept of social isolation as a product of singular, incommunicable individual visions is so central to Melville's thinking on society that it virtually excludes all other questions for him. In short, humanism fails for the same reason that idealism fails: We see fractionally and cannot piece the shards of our visions into a whole; that golden bowl is forever broken.

Necessarily, then, Melville depicts all of the societies of Mardi at war—among themselves and with each other. The sorcerers of the isle of Minda are, in fact, lawyers, who are "employed in the social differences and animosities of that unfortunate land" (*M*, 144:462). But they aren't villains preying upon helpless innocents. The spells they cast "derived their greatest virtue from the fumes of certain compounds, whose ingredients—horrible to tell—were mostly obtained from the human heart" (*M*, 144:463). And this civil quarrelsomeness is not confined to Minda. The first Mardian society we encounter, on Odo, is haunted by "dismal cries, and voices cursing Media" (*M*, 63:191), and he, we recall, is presented as an ideal ruler. The last description we have of Odo is of a land in sedition and at war, Media making a gallant if futile stand. Virtually all of Mardian society stands on the uncertain foundations of slippery, shifting opinion.

Naturally enough, the relationships between societies are no more stable or fruitful. If within societies individuals are litigious, peoples of different societies are bellicose. The allegory of Hello and Piko is clear: "right well doth man love to bruise and batter all occiputs in his vicinity; he but follows his instincts; he is but one member of a fighting world" (*M*, 138:441). War is so instinctive in us that it becomes a game, a "festival" upon a down, beneath which lie "thousands of glorious corpses of anonymous heroes, who here had died glorious deaths" (*M*, 139:445). Archetype of all tyrannical rulers and paradigm of the aggressive self-interest in all men is King Bello, whose name suggests both the bombast of politicians and the elemental rapacity of barbarians. King of Dominora, which most immediately stands for England but ultimately suggests the origins of all nations, Bello illustrates the central thrust of Melville's political satire: in a world of mere opinions, many of which are bound to conflict, might, not right, is bound to rule. Bello thus relieves other nations of "their political anxieties, by assuming the dictatorship over them" (*M*, 145:468). And although he claims his authority is from "Oro," he does so while "shaking his javelin" (*M*, 145:468). Melville is not merely indulging in post-Revolutionary, post-1812 Anglophobia. Rather, he asserts the general proposition that "Bello was not alone; for throughout Mardi, all strong nations, as well as all strong men, loved to govern the weak" (*M*, 145:468).

In fact, it is necessary to revise an earlier statement and admit that Porpheero [Europe] is the one place not visited by Taji and his companions. The reason for this omission is rhetorically clear if somewhat suspect thematically. Melville is interested in devoting his main energy to the question of America, defined not simply as the new world but specifically as the antithesis to the old world—"last sought, last found, Mardi's estate, so long kept back" (*M*, 157:511). Melville's America at first sighting is scarcely different from Whitman's: "Ho! Mardi's Poor, and Mardi's Strong! ye, who starve or beg; seventh-sons who slave for earth's first-born—here is your home; predestinated yours; Come over, Empire-founders! fathers of the wedded tribes to come!—abject now, illustrious evermore:—Ho: Sinew, Brawn, and Thigh!" (*M*, 157:512). Very little to our surprise, however, this rhapsodic idealization of Vivenza [America] as stated by Babbalanja does not long survive close scrutiny. The legend of Vivenza, the living land of promise, might be founded upon the proposition that "In-this-re-publi-can-land-all-men-are-born-free-and-equal," yet "hidden away" in a corner is a "small hieroglyphic or two" which "after much screwing of his eyes, for those characters were very minute,... Mohi thus spoke—'Except-the-tribe-of-Hamo'" (*M*, 157:512–13). "Post-script" or not, the exclusion of Hamo's tribe nullifies the republican ideal as Melville states it, for it exemplifies the corruption found throughout Mardi—the power of might over right. And, indeed, Melville's satire on Vivenza hinges upon this common failing, captured in the absurd rhetoric of Alanno's speech to the assembly (*M*, 158:517–18), and upon that other failing common to all of us—the inability to see the world except through one's own eyes—darkly.

In a land where all men are kings (except for the tribe of Hamo), the conflicts of crossing visions are multiplied by permutations upon permutations. The great central Temple of Vivenza [Congress] is thus depicted as housing an absolute chaos of uncoordinated activities, where the riotous noise from the catacombs beneath the temple only heightens the din from theater (see *M*, 158:516), and where delirious speeches are delivered "while with an absence of sympathy, distressing to behold, the rest of the assembly seemed wholly engrossed with themselves" (*M*, 158:517). Peace comes only with adjournment, with the convocation dispersing "to their yams" (*M*, 158:518).

The "Voice from the Gods" in Chapter 161 presents a well-tempered and disinterested view of Vivenza, considered both ideally and realistically. Vivenza is described as "the best and happiest land under the sun," but primarily because her "origin and geography necessitated it" (*M*, 161:528). Freedom is thus attributed to space in a notable anticipation of Turner's frontier hypothesis: "Free horses need wide prairies: and fortunate for you, sovereign king! that you have room enough wherein to be free" (*M*, 161:526). And revolution or imperialism is seen as the inevitable outcome of that shrinking space and freedom (cf. *M*, 161:526).

The ultimate implication of "The voice from the Gods," and of the Vivenza portion of the book altogether, is that Vivenza must be considered a nation like any other, subject to the same old law of flux and reflux (*M*, 157:512). Such a dialectical theory of history might have been acceptable to the Whitman of "Passage to India," and it is certainly a commonplace in our age, but in the 1848–49 America of Thomas Hart Benton, with his optimistic belief in America's ever-expanding greatness, such a statement would appear unthinkable apostasy. The implications of Chapter 161 are clear: if Vivenza is, *sub specie aeternitatis*, like all nations of Mardi, and she is, then she is not fit home for Yillah. And she isn't: "though, as elsewhere, at times we heard whisperings that promised an end to our wanderings" (*M*, 162:531).

Even the West, that westering ideal of promise and future fulfillment that appealed not only to chauvinist politician, but also to mystical Whitman and that most "un-American" of American writers—sauntering Thoreau—appears no longer as a promised land of enchantment, but as a land of perverted thraldom to gold. The gold seekers of California are bitter parodies of Taji and his companions, for they too are "bold rovers" (*M*, 166:545), and they too seek an ideal to enrich their lives. But beneath the "gilded guise" there is "no Yillah there" (*M*, 166:547), and Yoomy's vision of America's Californian future presents merely "a golden Hell" where "thousands delve in quicksands; and sudden, sink in graves of their own making: with gold dust mingling their own ashes" (*M*, 166:547). Melville's satire of America is hard and uncompromising in that it is founded upon the characteristic polarity in *Mardi* of ideal and anti-ideal, and Vivenza, like Donjalolo's Willamilla valley and like Maramma, becomes an anti-ideal simply because it is not an ideal.

For Melville, it is clear that if the political, social ideal is not to be found in republican Vivenza it is not to be found anywhere, and he soon makes clear that Taji and company have, indeed, circumnavigated the globe without finding the ideal Yillah. In fact, for good measure Chapter 168 takes us almost round the world again according to a more conventional geography, from Asia to Africa and back to Europe. Yet even as we suspect that Melville's enthusiasm has outpaced his materials altogether, the novel reaches its climax. In Chapter 169, "Sailing On," Melville states explicitly what we have inferred all along: Mardi is an exploration of "the world of mind; wherein the wanderer may gaze round, with more of wonder than Balboa's band roving through the golden Aztec glades" (*M*, 169:557).

A notable feature of Melville's pronouncement of his grand theme is that it is made simultaneously with his awareness that he has failed: "the golden haven was not gained" (*M*, 169:557). The very magnitude of his own mind seems to have startled him into a recognition that the world of mind, unlike the real world, cannot be circumnavigated. Pressed to the unwelcome conclusion that the self cannot comprehend the universe, indeed cannot comprehend itself, Melville, instead of ceasing in his efforts to grasp the phantom secret of life, presses on "in bold quest thereof," buoyed up miraculously by a desperate motto: "better to sink in boundless deeps, than float on vulgar shoals; and give me, ye gods, an utter wreck, if wreck I do" (*M*, 169:557). Instead of placing an unfinished, "suggestive" *Mardi* on the shelves next to *Christabel, The Excursion, Hyperion, The Triumph of Life*, and *The Narrative of Arthur Gordon Pym*, Melville goes on to write another hundred pages, which serve not so much as denouement to the quest as an analytical postmortem of its fated end.

There are few, if any, better records of the death of Romantic idealism than the final hundred pages of *Mardi*, and, if for no other reason, this should ensure the book's lasting worth as a statement of nineteenth-century sensibility and mind. Melville's record of Romanticism's failure has preeminent authority simply because he is recording his own culture's failing vision in a courageous triumph of creativity over despair. Beginning in *Mardi*, this acutely conscious analysis of dying dreams leads him through the ever-darkening territories of *Redburn, White-Jacket, Moby-Dick*, and *Pierre*, until he reaches that very heart of darkness, *The Confidence-Man*, where like the visionary in Emily Dickinson's "I Heard a Fly Buzz," he can no longer see to see.

The search for Yillah throughout Mardi indeed takes Taji and his companions full circle; the inconsistency and, hence, unreliability of human personality and human perception mark the conclusion of the quest just as they signalled its beginning. The failures of Peepi, Donjalolo, Pani, and the nine blind men in the banian grove, in their efforts to establish and maintain a firm grip upon a solid reality, lead to Babbalanja's inevitable conclusion that "we have had vast developments of parts of men; but none of manly wholes. Before a full-developed man, Mardi would fall down and worship" (*M*, 180:593).

This Emersonian ideal of "manly wholes" that motivates Taji and his quest is seen here to be crushed by the weight of our inherent imperfection of mind. Babbalanja's conclusion is irresistible and historically secure: the Enlightenment's assertion of reason, and Romanticism's faith in intuition and imagination, sustained methodologies for defining perfection without providing any means of attaining it. Thus, as Babbalanja continues, although "giants are in our germs" eventually we become "dwarfs, staggering under heads overgrown"; taking so much to ourselves and upon ourselves "our measures burst. We die of too much life" (*M*, 180:593). The old dispensation—humanity specially created in the image of the Divine Maker and capable of attaining perfect salvation through His Grace—is revoked, and Eden is relegated to an everlasting past.

It is this bleak concept that informs the concluding chapters of *Mardi*, themselves an extended gloss upon the whole of the book. The formulation "Taji and his companions," which I have adopted to facilitate discussion of the central quest chapters, must now be abandoned, and what most readers recognize instinctively must be given clear expression: the relationship between Taji and his "other selves" is not firm, but tenuous, not necessary, but accidental. The minor carpings throughout the book between Yoomy, Mohi, Babbalanja, and Media reach their climax in the final twenty-five chapters, where the powers of imagination, memory, reason, passion, and will are shown to be forever discrete. Yoomy's nightingale song is stopped in mid-flight, leaving Mohi to ask for "the meaning" and Media for "the sequel" (*M*, 170:561). And Babbalanja complains, "Must nothing ultimate come of all that melody? no final and inexhaustible meaning?" (*M*, 170:561). Media, compelled by a regal power of will, "in dreams, at least, . . . deems himself a demi-god" (*M*, 172:565), but he appeals in vain for support from the others when dream turns to nightmare. Mohi, a dominant voice in the travelogue-satire portion of the book, which calls for historical amplification, in the end drops almost out of sight except as an image of an old man—and the chronicler of Media's fate.

Babbalanja, by contrast, not only gives voice to the book's guiding theme of multiplicity, but also takes multiple identities himself, possessed by Azzageddi and speaking for Bardianna and Lombardo. "Ten thoughts for one act was Bardianna's motto," (*M*, 177:585) says Babbalanja, and he himself lives in a world of "Ponderings," so withdrawn into himself in the form of Azzageddi that the others call him mad.

Taji himself virtually disappears in this portion of the book until Hautia's heralds appear after the voyagers leave Serenia at the end of Chapter 189. Or it might be more accurate to say that Taji's character can only be seen in the composite nature of his companions. Thus Taji, who in the early stages of the narrative is depicted as the great universalist, romantic dreamer, and consummate idealist, is defined in the falling action as desperately trying to hold his disintegrating self together in a disintegrating world.

And surely the world depicted in the chapters leading to Serenia is as madly disintegrating as the personalities of Taji, Media, Yoomy, Babbalanja, and Mohi. It is a world of opinions and opinions of opinions, satirically personified in Doxodox, ironically "surnamed the Wise One" (*M*, 171:562). This Doxodox, who claims to have "penetrated from the zoned to the unzoned principles" (*M*, 171:562), is a palpable fraud whose metier is a language, like that of Mardi, which begins with the "Interrogative" and ends with the "Dubious" (*M*, 171:563).

Caught in midnight calms (Chapter 173) and rent by midnight storms (Chapter 185), tantalized by Hautia's sirens and terrified by the fate that strikes their bowsman, at the very height of confusion and discord Taji and his companions land at the most unlikely island in all Mardi— Serenia. This island, whose name and character are largely self-explanatory, is altogether unbelievable in the total context of *Mardi*, for it is difficult to see how imperfect man in an imperfect world might produce a working model of Utopia.[10] Serenia, strictly speaking, does not stand as a practicable ideal, although the guide there certainly asserts a pragmatic idealism, and Serenia ultimately must be viewed as the last resort of the noble mind—a fantasy dream world not subject to the vicissitudes and uncertainties instinctive in both humanity and the actual world we live in. Only Babbalanja, of all the questers, opts to remain at Serenia, and he represents precisely the speculative, philosophical, and for all his skepticism, the idealizing mind.

As the others depart Serenia, Babbalanja in fact presents a commentary on the value of Serenia and its relevance to the "real" world. Media is admonished to return home in the hope, fond enough, that "these flowers, that round us spring, may be transplanted: and Odo made to bloom . . . like this Serenia" (*M*, 189:637). The rest of Babbalanja's advice to Media, the most worldly of the group, has a Polonian quality of facile self-contradiction: "Abdicate thy throne: but still retain the scepter. None need a king; but many need a ruler" (*M*, 189:637).

Babbalanja's remarks to Mohi and Yoomy are equally self-confounding. Babbalanja, the book's foremost spokesman for the multiplicity of vision and experience, counsels them to "bury in forgetfulness much that hitherto" he has spoken, but "let not one syllable of this old man's words be lost" (*M*, 189:637–38). Mohi is then counseled to live out his life (in the world of Mardi we presume) and to "die, calm-browed" (*M*, 189:638)—certainly an unlikely event given Babbalanja's view of Mardi, to say nothing of Mohi's. And after explicitly stating that Serenia offers the chance to "gain now, in flush of youth, that last wise thought, too often purchased, by a life of woe" (*M*, 189:637), he tells Yoomy, "Take all Mardi for thy home. Nations are but names; and continents but shifting sands" (*M*, 189:638).

Babbalanja's confusion reaches its zenith in his remarks to Taji. "Be sure thy Yillah never will be found," he begins, but he quickly moderates that to "or found, will not avail thee" (*M*, 189:638). Not stopping here, though, he goes on to complete a shift of mind that manages to contradict both terms of the opening contradiction: "Yet search, if so thou wilt; more isles, thou say'st, are still unvisited; and when all is seen, return, and find thy Yillah here" (*M*, 189:638).

Amid this spreading confusion, two things become clear. First, Melville preserves the concept of Serenia as the intellect's projected ideal, a desideratum of serenity consisting of self-satisfaction in a harmonious world. But Babbalanja's remarks and the others' responses to them, and to Serenia itself, make it painfully clear that Melville still, after almost two hundred chapters, sees no way of linking the ideal life of the mind with the factual life of the world and the self's experience of it. Certainly from Taji's point of view, Serenia is but one more, and perhaps the greatest, temptation to be resisted—a Unitarian cloister promising peace to the anguished soul, but only at the expense of reality.

With Serenia and all of Mardi behind him and Yillah nowhere to be found, there is left only the dark promise of Hautia—certainly one of the most fascinating characters in *Mardi*.[11] Taji has been avoiding Hautia for as long as he has been seeking Yillah, and it is clear to the reader that the fates of the three are inextricably bound. Although Hautia's identity and role are not made clear until the end of the voyage, she makes her first appearance in Chapter 61 as the "incognito" who visits Taji and Yillah on their third day at Odo. There she appears "enveloped in a dark robe of tappa, so drawn and plaited about the limbs; and with one hand, so wimpled about the face, as only to expose a solitary eye. *But that eye was a world*" (*M*, 61:186, my emphasis). As incognito, Hautia fixes that "fathomless eye" on Yillah "with a sinister glance," but to Taji "at last it seemed no eye, but a spirit forever prying into my soul" (*M*, 61:186).

On the next day, the fourth of their stay on Odo, Taji and Yillah are greeted for the first time by Hautia's three heralds. But it is their second appearance that is most significant: they appear on the very day of Yillah's disappearance. In fact, they signal Yillah's departure, as periodically throughout the quest they signal her absence. And thus at the end of the voyage, when Taji goes to face Hautia we anticipate that the quest might be ended if not completed.

Mardi ends, however, much as *Typee* and *Omoo* do, not with any resolution of the questions raised, but with a pointed restatement of them.[12] All of the mysterious and threatening forces connected with Taji's introduction to Yillah and his quest for her survive—still mysterious and still threatening. Hautia's heralds lead him to Flozella, the Acrasian bower of the bewitching Hautia: "her eye was fathomless" still, and the "same mysterious, evil-boding gaze was there, which long before had haunted me in Odo, ere Yillah fled" (*M*, 192:646). And still Taji asks the old question: "But how connected were Hautia and Yillah?" (*M*, 191:643). In fact, the chapters devoted to Hautia are filled with little but questions and doubts, and although Taji reveals an uncharacteristic shrewdness ("I thought to seem what I was not, that I might learn at last the thing I sought" [*M*, 192:646)]), he comes perilously close to drowning in Hautia's vortex.

Hautia's mystery and her ambiguous hold upon Taji reside primarily in her infinite promise and infinite mutability. She identifies herself as "the vortex that draws all in" (*M*, 194:650), and like La Belle Dame Sans Merci she freely promises what Yillah, as defined by Taji's failed quest, so palpably withholds: "Beauty, Health, Wealth, Long Life, and the Last Lost Hope of man" (*M*, 194:651).

As the pursuer of Taji, Hautia is the converse image of Yillah—the object of Taji's pursuit. As the symbol of fathomless creative power she serves as both inspiration and nemesis to Taji, and, by implication, to Melville, for as creative imagination she on the one hand offers the possibility of all things, while on the other hand she denies to all things any status other than that of possibility. And it is this ambiguity in Hautia that both attracts and repels Taji, for he desires Hautia's confirmation of idealism even though he is unwilling to be limited by the terms of her confirmation. In the end he must reject Hautia, simply because to accept her would be to deny Yillah's identity as an ideal to be realized in this world.

Although Taji does reject Hautia, he still finds Yillah beyond his reach. Gone forever is the Homeric linear morality by which the rejection of Circe frees Ulysses to return to Penelope; gone forever is the Spenserean belief that the Red Cross Knight can resist Duessa and Acrasia and, by so doing, take his rightful place with Una. Unable to wed dream and experience, Taji can possess neither Hautia nor Yillah, and his recognition of his own divided self leaves him philosophically nonplussed, with nowhere to go. The three pale sons of Aleema, who blighted his successful rescue of Yillah originally, indeed prove indestructible.

It is in light of these intractable realities that Taji's "abdication" must be interpreted. Divided within himself, Taji cannot attain the ideal harmony of his erstwhile dream. Faulty perception, shifting moods, and contrary desires, combined with the incomprehensible variety of experience have the power and inevitability of "the racing tide," seizing him "like a hand omnipotent" (*M*, 195:654). The amoral vision of Hautia is abhorrent, as a promise of life without meaning: "Better to me, oh Hautia! all the bitterness of my buried dead, than all the sweets of the life thou canst bestow; even, were it eternal" (*M*, 194:651). Unable, thus, to seize upon anything with certainty, he hugs tight to what he can of himself: "Now I am my own soul's emperor" (*M*, 195:659). And although his "first act is abdication" (*M*, 195:654), I don't think we are to take that as a "suicide." Rather, that desperate act reveals, with disarming honesty, Melville's awareness that he has asked questions he cannot answer—yet: "And thus, pursuers and pursued flew on, over an endless sea" (*M*, 195:654). It is a haunting promise that there is "more to follow."

The conclusion of *Mardi* should be viewed, therefore, as a suspended judgment on the central problem that arises within the book itself. Although in the near view this is what makes *Mardi* an endlessly tantalizing, endlessly frustrating book to read, in the far view it is also what makes it so significant. The division of the self and the alienation of that divided self within the natural and social world constitute the explicit themes of all Melville's fiction to come.

3

Redburn and *White-Jacket*: Unsentimental Journeys

Ah! what are our creeds, and how do we hope to be saved?
Tell me, oh Bible, that story of Lazarus again, that I may find
comfort in my heart for the poor and forlorn. Surrounded as
we are by the wants and woes of our fellow-men, and yet
given to follow our own pleasures, regardless of their pains,
are we not like people sitting up with a corpse, and making
merry in the house of the dead?

—*Redburn,* 37:184[1]

Mardi's conclusion is inescapable: humanity's insatiable longing to comprehend the infinite world can never be satisfied. There is no golden time nor golden clime, nor even golden dream in which one may repose on the bosom of the infinite. And although it is one of the unrelenting signs of our time that we can scarcely conceive of any intelligent person believing in even the possibility of such a dream, unless we accept the centrality of such a belief in Melville's early fiction, we shall never understand his art at all. In particular, we shall never understand the significance of Melville's laying bare what we in the late twentieth century seem to have known always, or at least have no recollection of ever having learned—that the individual lives isolated and alienated from an indifferent world. This is the shocking implication of *Mardi*'s conclusion, and it is Melville's unflinching acceptance of that implication that forms the basis for *Redburn* and *White-Jacket*.

Both *Redburn* and *White-Jacket* are conservative books in that they represent a retrenchment from the expansive romantic wanderings and yearnings of *Typee, Omoo,* and *Mardi.* But this retrenchment is not a total retreat. If anything, the narrowed focus of the two novels concentrates the terms of Wellingborough's and White-Jacket's quests. *Mardi's* prepossessing questions about time, space, free will, immortality, and God, its inquiry into the nature of perception, morality, and "being" are present in *Redburn* and *White-Jacket,* and the conclusions to those questions in *Mardi* might well be said to underlie the two following novels. But in recounting the events of their respective voyages Redburn and White-Jacket focus sharply, if not exclusively, upon their recognition of the infinite fragility of the mortal self. Death, which haunts the pages of both *Redburn* and *White-Jacket,* virtually subordinates and concentrates all other human limitations unto itself.

In their shrunken worlds, Redburn and White-Jacket seek little more than a modus vivendi. Redburn wants to be solvent financially and wants to be accepted into a community of tastes and values similar to his own. In like manner, White-Jacket seeks the freedom of his own mind and acts—and wants, in short, to get "home." Because both seek less, and because what they do seek is expressed in more moderate, believable terms, their failure to achieve their goals is perhaps even darker in implication than Tommo's and Taji's failures.

As the two novels unfold, it becomes more and more clear that the outstanding trait of Redburn and White-Jacket is their common sense of dislocation and alienation. They are, ultimately, strangers wherever they go, belonging nowhere and fitting in with no one. Both—by clothes, custom, and background—are odd men out on the ships that sign them on and among the crews with which they sail. In the end, Redburn has no future at home or away from home, and his "first voyage" is not so much an education in the world—as in the typical bildungsroman—as it is a point to pointless picaresque journey whereby he discovers the world as a vast orphanage.[2] Similarly, White-Jacket presents himself to us without antecedents, in medias res with a vengeance, and the home for which he is bound remains forever beyond the vague horizon of the book's ending. Whether at sea or in port, he too remains an Ishmaelian orphan, forever trapped by an incomprehensible present, with no past and no future.

Redburn

It is of telling significance that Melville's fourth book is the tale of a "first voyage": Melville thus resorts to the practice of all lost travelers—attempting to return to a known starting point and from there determine his present position. But journeys of the mind are more complex and unforgiving than those made by coach, and one can never literally return to an earlier state of mind, as Melville knew all too well. Thus, although

Redburn is the youngest of Melville's protagonists and is presented as a youth on his first voyage, the tale is actually told by a much older Redburn, a man of many voyages who can but imperfectly recollect his own initiation into life. Indeed, it is this split perspective we have of Redburn that gives the book much of its poignancy. We can never see the young Redburn quite in the full bloom of youthful innocence, nor can we listen to the older Redburn without feeling his weariness and disenchantment with a world that robbed him, first of innocence itself and then of its memory.

Redburn, then, is a reflection upon youth that can never quite become a reflection *of* youth. We never see Wellingborough in the way we see Conrad's protagonist in *Youth*. For Wellingborough at the beginning of the story has already lost many of the illusions that carry Conrad's hero through disaster and hardship and allow him to revel in his own preservation in a spiced, sunrise world. Redburn's story is one of "Confessions and Reminiscences of the Son-of-a-Gentleman, in the Merchant Service," and from the beginning we are aware that *Redburn*, rather than a song of innocence, is an anthem for doomed youth.

From the outset, Redburn's first voyage is ill-fated. His decision to go to sea at all is prompted by "sad disappointments in several plans" for his future life, coupled with "the necessity of doing something" for himself and "united to a naturally roving disposition" (*R*, 1:3). But his claim to a roving sea-disposition is clearly a misplaced romanticism that fades when he actually faces the reality of leaving home—promising his brother he will take care of himself.

It is difficult to imagine a youth less likely to take care of himself in the world Melville depicts. Fueled by "certain shadowy reminiscences" of early childhood, the young Redburn's imagination is inflamed by the fanciful word-dreams he can conjure up from a commonplace newspaper announcement about a "copper-fastened brig" (*R*, 1:4). As the narrator recalls it, his entire childhood seems to have been taken up with a series of "long reveries about distant voyages and travels" in which the actual experience is submerged in the thought of "how fine it would be, to be able to talk about remote and barbarous countries" (*R*, 1:5). In fact, his entire preoccupation with "foreign things" (*R*, 1:6) becomes an alchemical process of translating crude things into fine words and sentiments. "French portfolios," "pictures of Versailles," (*R*, 1:6), "a copy of D'Alembert in French," or even the word "'*London*' on the title-page" of a book is enough to breed in him "a vague prophetic thought, that [he] was fated, one day or other, to be a great voyager" (*R*, 1:7).

On the surface, these youthful dreams of romantic adventure are common enough, but Melville portrays Wellingborough's idealism as obses-

sive and dangerously divorced from reality. We might smile at the young
Redburn's dreamy interpretation of the sea pictures in his dining room,
but his bizarre response to his father's "old-fashioned glass ship" (*R,* 1:7)
goes beyond the ludicrous to the absurd. Melville, who can be the most
economical of writers when he cares to,[3] establishes the ship not merely
as an aesthetic ideal, but as a moral ideal freighted with the inherited
dreams of an illustrious family in a brave new world. That Wellingborough, namesake of a Constitutional congressman and son of a gentleman,
must ship out as a common sailor at all indicates at once the novel's
persistent theme that the Redburn family fortune is degenerating in time.
But Melville goes beyond this particular judgment to the general observation that the ideals of the past are universally inaccessible and uninher-
itable, and it is on this point that the entire book balances: the opposed
responses of the young Redburn and the old Redburn to this lost inheritance form the tragic pole around which the world of the novel turns.

The young Wellingborough is almost demented in his determination
to plunder the ship's hidden cargo, and his determination to repossess
his lost inheritance is the motivation and thematic thread that gives whatever unity there is to the disparate adventures of his first voyage. But it
is the elder Redburn's "recovery of reason," at some point subsequent to
the events related in the novel, that gives depth to the novel's statement
that ideals once lost can never be recovered.

We know irritatingly little about Redburn's life between his first voyage and his later account of it. We know that a good many years have
passed, that Redburn has had subsequent voyages—at least one on a
despised whaler, and that he has for one reason or another given up
his youthful fancies and dreams. His disenchantment is clear enough
throughout the narrative in the overtly mocking commentary on his own
youth and in the more subtle tone of ironic distance that prevails in the
narrative. But Melville takes no chance that we will miss his point. In this
opening chapter, the elder Redburn is defined explicitly by his changed
attitude to this glass ship—the dream object of his youth.

His youthful obsession that somehow dreams might be made real is
replaced in later life by an almost clinical awareness that dreams have
nothing to do with reality. In fact, the ship as described at the end of
Chapter 1 is best viewed as a barometer to Redburn's shifting attitudes
toward the world of dreams and the world of reality. Rather than sub-
duing the world, his dreams have succumbed to its relentless, patient
indifference. He still keeps the "shattered and broken" (*R,* 1:9) ship
in the house, he admits, but he "will not have her mended" (*R,* 1:9), nor
will he have the ship's figurehead "put on his legs again," (*R,* 1:9) until
he gets on his own.

The first chapter of *Redburn* exhibits precisely Melville's grasp of the world's ambiguity and the consequent confusion and alienation of the aspiring self. With a sophistication scarcely suggested in his first three books, Melville establishes an ideal that is at once credible and inaccessible. And therein lies the poignancy of Wellingborough's plight throughout the book.

Redburn thus shares with Melville's first three books the theme of a young man's search for a romantic ideal, but the intrinsic nature of Wellingborough's search differs markedly from the quests of Tommo, Omoo, and Taji. Melville's first three protagonists seek to explore new lands, new cultures, new experiences: constantly gazing upon and yearning for new horizons, both actual and metaphorical, their shared vision is relentlessly progressive and, as F. O. Matthiessen would say, in the optative mood. In direct contrast, Wellingborough's vision is reflexive, constantly turned back to the past—to his father and uncle and to his own thwarted expectations. And his experience is reflexive, too, for he travels not to the new world of Polynesia but to the old country, England. Surely the contracted world of *Redburn* and the regressive vision of its protagonist are integral to Melville's growing conviction, hard won in *Typee, Omoo,* and *Mardi,* that the world is not an Emersonian apple to be eaten in a dream, but the original Edenic apple, both cursed and irresistible.

The extent of Wellingborough's alienation from his world is clearly and emphatically depicted in the events leading up to his boarding the *Highlander* in New York. His departure from home is absolutely devoid of promise, thus counteracting his earlier dreamy images of "copper-fastened brigs" and parodying the romantic confidence of Melville's earlier questers. He leaves home on "a raw, cold, damp morning," and the "cold drops of drizzle" mingle "with a few hot tears" on his cheeks (*R,* 2:11). Clearly his dominant mood is not one of sentimental attachment to home and family, but one of bitterness at his hard and cruel fate. Alienated from world and self alike, Wellingborough dramatizes himself as a young boy upon whose young soul "the mildew has fallen . . . nipped in the first blossom and bud" (*R,* 2:11). Self-defeated as he begins, he walks on, convinced that "this indeed was the way to begin life, with a gun in your hand!" (*R,* 2:11).

On the boat trip to New York, his desperate self-pity mounts to virtual paranoia. The immediate cause of his distracted behavior is, of course, his poverty, but as we follow his adventures throughout the book, we discover that he is, indeed, out of step with virtually everyone he meets, at sea and ashore, rich and poor, young and old, family, friend, and stranger.

Wellingborough enjoys a momentary respite from his sense of fate's cruelty when he arrives in New York and is taken in by the family of his brother's college friend, but his sense of belonging is indeed short-lived, and he is indeed "taken in" by more than one person in New York. The young Redburn's dealings with the pawnbrokers and with Captain Riga reveal just how inept he is in gauging the world around him. But in that regard he is little different from his brother's fatuous friend, the first of several subordinate characters in the book who serve as alter-egos to Wellingborough. Habituated to the closed circle of the family, neither young man can conceive of a world in which his wishes are not received as hard currency. There is a crucial difference between the two young men, however. When all the negotiations for signing aboard the *Highlander* are completed, the collegian is free to return to home and family; Redburn must go to sea.

Young Wellingborough's naive foolishness in the face of Captain Riga's and the pawnbroker's duplicity is of course quite clear to the older Redburn telling the tale. Just as the narrator felt compelled to comment on Wellingborough's eccentric behavior on the boat to New York ("Such is boyhood" [*R*, 2:13]), he also points up the foolishness of his youthful attempt to gain leverage with Captain Riga by presenting himself as a youth of genteel background, and the sententious comment concluding the scene belongs by tone to the older, more reflective narrator: "Poor people make a very poor business of it when they try to seem rich" (*R*, 3:17).

A great deal of humor in the New York sequence of events derives from Melville's tactic of having the young Redburn's youthful foibles related by the older, skeptical Redburn, but it is a mistake to view the irony as operating only in one direction. For surely the world-weary skepticism of the narrator has been nurtured by the very incidents he relates, and thus the youth comments upon the man just as the man comments upon the youth.

Redburn's first voyage signals his absolute disinheritance. Forced into an uncaring world by the fallen fortunes of his family, Redburn finds that even the remnants of his patrimony are valueless. The fowling piece handed on to him by his brother is worth but $2.50, and the hunting jacket proves worse than useless to him, signalling to others his estrangement from their world. This utter estrangement of Redburn is dramatized most sharply as the *Highlander* departs from New York harbor. His wish that "instead of sailing *out* of the bay; ... [they] were only coming *into* it" (*R*, 7:33) alternates with his dark premonition that "some luckless day or other" he would "certainly fall overboard and be drowned" (*R*, 7:33). Wellingborough from the first has a real penchant for dwelling on death, his own and others', and here, just as he sets out to see the world, he envisions his worst fears: "I thought of lying down at the bottom of the sea, stark alone, with the great waves rolling over me, and no one in the wide world knowing that I was there" (*R,* 7:33).

The extremity of Wellingborough's imagined abandonment cannot be explained simply as the apprehension of a young man testing himself for the first time. Rather, his near hysteria proceeds from his acute awareness that he is taking an irreversible step away from his youthful dreams, once thought so secure and now seen to be in ruins, the old fort at the mouth of the narrows serving as an apt emblem of Wellingborough's state of mind. The fort is identified explicitly with Wellingborough's origins and with the authority of his father and family, with whom he had first visited this "very wonderful and romantic" spot (*R,* 7:35). Wellingborough's dreamlike experience is etched in his memory in vivid detail, and his recollection of the idyllic center of the fort, with its "cows quietly grazing, or ruminating under the shade of young trees, . . . and perhaps a calf frisking about" (*R,* 7:35) suggests in its pastoral indefiniteness all of Redburn's fond recollections of happy childhood and calls up in Wellingborough's mind the image of an inner sanctum of idyllic peace amid the dark confusion of the outer world.[4]

The ultimate significance of this passage, however, is Redburn's unwillingness to leave behind the past that he knows is dead. Even the older Redburn, for all his hard-purchased skepticism, cannot utterly forget his childhood dream. For him, the truth of his youthful idyll is fixed in time; for him the black goat "looking to sea, as if he were watching for a ship" looks "just the same as ever" (*R,* 7:35). And, the narrator goes on, "so I suppose he would, if I live to be as old as Methusaleh, and have as great a memory as he must have had" (*R,* 7:35). But the fond recollection of this child's playground amid the ruins calls up in the older Redburn an even more telling admission: "I should like to build a little cottage in the middle of it, and live there all my life" (*R,* 7:35).

The child's dream and the man's recollection of it have no power in the world of Redburn's first voyage, however, as Redburn himself realizes: "I must not think of those delightful days, before my father became a bankrupt, and died, and we removed from the city; for when I think of those days, something rises up in my throat and almost strangles me" (*R,* 7:36)

In fact, drowning and strangling are the two definitive images Redburn has of himself as the *Highlander* leaves New York harbor. And his sense of reality's intractable power is overwhelming: "I tried to think that it was all a dream, that I was not where I was, not on board of a ship, but that I was at home again in the city, with my father alive, and my mother bright and happy as she used to be. But it would not do. *I was indeed where I was, and here was the ship, and there was the fort"* (*R,* 7:36, my emphasis).

Disheartened, lonely, and filled with grim forebodings of the future, Wellingborough is the antithesis of Melville's previous ship-jumping heroes who are willing to face cannibals, jungles, civil authorities, and uncharted seas in their thirst for new experience. Redburn simply, but eloquently, feels "thrust out of the world" (*R,* 7:36) he knows into a world of frightening strangeness.

From the moment Wellingborough puts to sea, he is lost and out of place. If, as the mature Redburn reflects, sailors are "strayed lambs from the fold,... orphans without fathers or mothers" (*R,* 9:47), the young Wellingborough is an orphan among orphans. He is literally the odd man out after all the rest of the crew have been selected for the ship's two watches. And neither first nor second mate wants him. Thus Wellingborough finds himself unhappily thrust into a world both confining and inhospitable, holding no promise and offering no escape.

It is difficult to define the precise contours of Wellingborough's response to this world, for the narrative after Chapter 8 becomes a tangle of anecdotes, character sketches, small essays, and digressions. But the start and stop, fragmentary nature of the narrative is not without an ultimate direction; one might even argue that the indirections of *Redburn* are its direction. The pointless mental tackings of Wellingborough clearly mark his agonized wanderings through a pathless world without safe harbor. The voyage to England marks his growing disillusionment with the world and himself; his stay in England merely intensifies his disenchantment with the false dreams of his youth; and this disillusionment and disenchantment lead inevitably to Redburn's isolating disengagement from the ugly, sordid world he cannot change. Thus, Redburn's return voyage on the *Highlander* is fraught with despair, for it takes him not "home," but to a future he now knows is without promise.

There is nothing particularly subtle or unexpected about Wellingborough's disillusionment with life aboard copper-fastened brigs. Ill from hunger, he is put to the unseamanlike and unromantic task of cleaning pigpens and stowing shavings, learning in the process that "sea-officers never gave reasons for any thing they order to be done" (*R,* 6:29). Ill from food, his "mouth over the side, feeling ready to die" (*R,* 8:42), he succumbs to the sailors' heal-all tot of rum, and thus surrenders that portion of his land identity set down in the charter of the "Juvenile Total Abstinence Association" (*R,* 8:42). Cursed with bare feet and an aunt who died of consumption, he can scarcely believe the order to scrub down the decks with sea-cold water. Asked to loose the main-skysail in the dead of night, he is "awe-stricken and mute" (*R,* 16:78) in the midst of a terrible isolation.

Wellingborough's ineptitude and fright, of course, spring directly from his ignorance, which is to say from his fanciful expectations of what a voyage should be. The lack of boots to scrub decks in and a cup to drink coffee from are small items in the exhaustive register of Wellingborough's ignorance about the required skills and duties of a sailor. Left to his dreams and lulled by the swelling sea, he fancies himself "in some new, fairy world" (*R,* 13:64), but no longer able to "shut the ship out" (*R,* 13:64) he wakes to its strangeness as to "a barbarous country, where they speak a strange dialect, and dress in strange clothes, and live in strange houses" (*R,* 13:65).

What truly makes this an abominable voyage for Wellingborough is that he has no proper role to play at all. Clearly he is not the gentleman he would like to be, and having resigned himself, unwillingly, to his lost expectations, he finds to his chagrin that the intricate world of the sailor is closed to him as well. Valued only for the good will of his muscles and the use of his backbone, Wellingborough sets to his non-tasks of clubbing rust from the ship's anchor and picking oakum, whiling away the "tedious hours by gazing through a port-hole . . . and repeating Lord Byron's Address to the Ocean" (*R,* 26:122). Dead to the world of gentility, unborn to the elemental world of the sailor, Redburn remains forlorn, taking things, in the only pose left to him, "in the spirit of Seneca and the stoics" (*R,* 26:122).

The depth of Wellingborough's isolation aboard the *Highlander* is perhaps best seen in his pathetic attempt to establish a closeness with Captain Riga. Naturally, his efforts to make a father of Riga are met with ridicule by the crew and speechless rage by Captain Riga himself (*R,* 14:70). The lesson is not totally lost on the young Redburn: he recognizes for the first time that a man may smile and smile, and yet be a villain.

From this first hesitant admission that people and things are not always what they seem springs Wellingborough's growing skepticism throughout the book, the final product being the mature skepticism of the Redburn who tells the story. The crisis for Redburn comes in England, laden in his mind with its literary and historical image of pastoral peace and fraught with his expectation of retracing and somehow thus recapturing his father's former eminence. Wellingborough's link with England's past and his father's past glory is the "curious and remarkable" morocco guidebook, *The Picture of Liverpool* (*R,* 30:143). Wellingborough clearly identifies the "old family relic" (*R,* 30:143) given him by his father as a guide to "an unerring knowledge of Liverpool" (*R,* 31:152)—the last bulwark of his retreating faith. Yet the book proves worse than worthless, in part tantalizingly accurate, yet on the whole dangerously outmoded, no more fit to guide Redburn about the town

"than the map of Pompeii" (*R,* 31:157). Redburn's prosy stroll through
Liverpool—in search of the "Old Dock," Riddough's Hotel, the Abbey of
Birkenhead, and the Derbys' Mansion—is grounded on his assumption
that his father's guidebook will somehow "prove a trusty conductor
through many old streets in the old parts of town" (*R,* 31:157). Of
course it doesn't, and the chapter ends on a note of near-hysterical despair. The glorious past so jealously sought by Redburn seems to have
coyly and pointlessly withdrawn, to be succeeded by a banal and mundane present of custom houses and jails.

"Friendless and forlorn" (*R,* 31:154) in the unyielding present, cut off
from the self-effacing past, Redburn clings to one belief that "there is one
Holy Guide-Book . . . that will never lead you astray, if you but follow it
aright" (*R,* 31:157). Yet, within the context of disappointment and disillusionment associated with the old guidebook it is difficult not to agree
with Lawrance Thompson that Wellingborough's trust in the Holy Guide-
Book is intended ironically by Melville, if not necessarily by the young
Wellingborough.

The eleven chapters following Wellingborough's "prosy stroll" are a
clutter of observations, anecdotes, and musings on the hodgepodge dock
life of Liverpool. Through his eyes we see Liverpool as a doomed and
damned city, having more in common with Blake's London than with
Goldsmith's village. Even deeper disbelief and doubts are raised, however, when Wellingborough sees in the swarm of emigrants on the Liverpool docks the seed of America's glorious promise. His apostrophe to
the Western Hemisphere, where "all tribes and people are forming into
one federated whole" with a future "which shall see the estranged children of Adam restored as to the old hearth-stone in Eden" (*R,* 33:169)
sounds desperate, ironic, or both, coming where it does in the novel.
And indeed Redburn shortly afterward describes the seed-beds of Liverpool's "Rotten-row, Gibraltar-place, and Booble-alley" as "putrid with
vice and crime; to which, perhaps, the round globe does not furnish a
parallel" (*R,* 39:191).

If Liverpool is not uncompromisingly corrupt, it certainly is predominantly so. The chapters devoted to its description are burdened with
countless pictures of squalor, sickness, suffering, and ugliness—ending
only in death. Pressing through "masses of squalid men, women, and children," the young Redburn finds "poverty, poverty, poverty, in almost endless vistas" (*R,* 41:201). Although Wellingborough is pleased to reflect
that he "had never seen any thing like it in New York" (*R,* 41:201), his
sanguine pride in the uniqueness and superiority of New York and
America is soon shaken. He finds to his "continual mortification" that
Liverpool is "very much such a place as New York" (*R,* 41:202), with

"the same sort of streets pretty much; the same rows of houses with stone steps; the same kind of sidewalks and curbs; and the same elbowing, heartless-looking crowd as ever" (*R,* 41:202). The sameness of the Leeds Canal and the Erie Canal at Albany, of Lordstreet and Broadway, prompts Redburn to think that all talk about travel is humbug, "and that he who lives in a nut-shell, lives in an epitome of the universe, and has but little to see beyond him" (*R,* 41:203).[5]

The quietness of this pronouncement belies its deep significance. Irresistibly, it undermines not only Wellingborough's first voyage, but also the voyage of all those emigrants seeking America's new and promised land. Properly compared, England is not like America: America is like England. Not a predestined Paradise, "to be made so, at God's good pleasure, and in the fullness and mellowness of time" (*R,* 33: 169), America already reveals her fated end—as another of humanity's futile dreams. The predators of Europe, epitomized in "the pawnbrokers, inhabiting little rookeries among the narrow lanes adjoining the dock" (*R,* 40:195) have already taken flight to the New World and have established themselves in New York as readily as in Liverpool. Neither Redburn nor America can remain forever young, forever innocent. In the larger context of Melville's fiction, this "nutshell" image of the universe, with its implications of the imprisoned self, puts a quiet end to the lofty aspirations of *Typee, Omoo,* and *Mardi,* and the last half of *Redburn* presents a world not of limitless possibilities, but of rapidly constricting horizons.

The climax of Wellingborough's Liverpool experience is his discovery of the dying mother and children in the alley of "Launcelott's-Hey." The discovery marks his supreme disillusionment with the world and simultaneously forces upon him an awareness of his utter weightlessness in trying to shift the balance of "things as they are." All the squalor and harshness of a pitiless world are compressed into that alley of "midday ... twilight" where "not a soul was in sight" (*R,* 37:180). All the futility of humanity's ennobling self-conception is expressed in Wellingborough's determined but fruitless efforts to alleviate the misery of these dying strangers in a strange land. Above all, what Redburn sees in Launcelott's-Hey is death.

Mother and children define most dramatically what might be termed the central "psychology" of the book, for in *Redburn* there are only two "ages of man": that of innocence and that of hopelessness. The picture Melville paints of the death-embraced family is poignant and powerful in itself, but what gives depth to the scene is the fact that we see Redburn precisely at the crossroads of his own innocence and hopelessness. When he appeals to the ragpickers and policemen to do something to help the unfortunates, he is also appealing to them to save his own innocent belief in humanity. Furthermore, he is conscious of the crisis taking place in him: "I stood looking down on them [the dying], while my whole soul swelled within me; and I asked myself, What right had any body in the wide world to smile and be glad, when sights like this were to be seen? It was enough to turn the heart to gall; and make a man-hater of a Howard" (*R,* 37:181). Failing in all his efforts to aid the dying orphans and their mother, Wellingborough is himself brought to the desperate but "almost irresistible impulse to do them the last mercy, of in some way putting an end to their horrible lives" (*R,* 37:183–84).

There is unquestionably a great deal of explicit social criticism in this episode. Melville clearly is attacking the heartlessness and indifference of urban, industrial, modern society, which can produce cotton mills and cotton warehouses, ships and shipping lines, but can offer no solace to the people who work those mills, stock those warehouses, and man those ships. He is attacking "the law, which would let them perish of themselves [mother and children and, by extension, anyone] without giving them one cup of water, [and yet] would spend a thousand pounds, if necessary, in convicting him who should so much as offer to relieve them from their miserable existence" (*R* 37:184).

Ultimately, however, the depiction and arousal of social awareness is not the heart of Launcelott's-Hey and *Redburn;* this awareness but leads us down the stairs to pitiable, perishing humanity. It is when Redburn makes his final pilgrimage to the vault that the final truth is revealed. Finding "in place of the woman and children, a heap of quick-lime ... glistening" (*R,* 37:184), Redburn is shocked out of innocence forever. The dead are "at peace" with the world truly (*R,* 37:184), but theirs is the peace of annihilation that mocks existence and scoffs at resurrection and salvation.

The death and disappearance of the forlorn family form an ironic and grotesque parody of Christ's resurrection and thus define Redburn's absolute loss of faith. For three days Redburn visits the vault, always meeting "the same sight" (*R,* 37:184). It is only on the third morning that the smell from the vault indicates that its inhabitants have died. But they are not risen. Redburn finds the vault empty, but he cannot learn "who had taken them away, or whither they had gone" (*R,* 37:184).[6] He, in fact, tries to resurrect the dead: "again I looked down into the vault, and in fancy beheld the pale, shrunken forms still crouching there" (*R* 37:184), but fancy does not so well deceive: the dead are indeed dead, and in their place a heap of quick-lime glistens. Wellingborough despairs: "Ah! what are our creeds, and how do we hope to be saved?" (*R,* 37:184).

Redburn is a book that asks many questions, but none is more penetrating or far-reaching than this one. From the moment he leaves home, Wellingborough is in a perpetual puzzle over his relationship to an incalculably shifting world, but in Launcelott's-Hey the puzzle assumes its final definition. Here Redburn recognizes that his plight is the plight of all humanity. Here he comes to the unwilling realization that the sought for meaning of life is wrapped in the black enigma of death.

In the shock of his awareness he calls upon his "Holy Guide-Book" of last resort: "Tell me, oh Bible, that story of Lazarus again, that I may find comfort in my heart for the poor and forlorn" (*R,* 37:184). But his plea for resurrection is desperate and without hope. The chapter immediately preceding "What Redburn saw in Launcelott's-Hey" gives all too clear a picture of the impotence of the church and the inefficacy of prayer. The "Old *Church*" of Chapter 36 is literally built upon a "Dead House" (*R,* 36:178),[7] and although "pious sailors" pray to the church's "statue of St. Nicholas, the patron of all mariners," making offerings "to induce his saintship to grant them short and prosperous voyages" (*R,* 36:177), the answer to their prayers is to be found in the basement, "where the bodies of the drowned are exposed until claimed by their friends, or till buried at the public charge" (*R,* 36:178). There is no answer for Wellingborough in the church, where "undertakers, sextons, tomb-makers, and hearse-drivers, get their living from the dead; and in times of plague most thrive" (*R,* 36:179), and he concludes that we are all "like people sitting up with a corpse, and making merry in the house of the dead" (*R,* 37:184).[8]

This intimate contact with death in Liverpool clearly alters Wellingborough's life. He refrains from telling of the other things that befell him during his six-week stay in Liverpool, for "to tell of them, would only be to tell over again the story just told" (*R,* 38:185). But the trauma of his experience in Launcelott's-Hey cannot be that easily forgotten or ignored. Indeed, the elder Redburn's tale of his first voyage is haunted by the specter of annihilating, inexplicable death.

In telling the tale of his first voyage, the elder Redburn dramatizes a life hedged in by death. The young Redburn goes to sea at all only because of his father's death, and the voyage of the *Highlander* is defined beginning, middle, and end by death. In itself this is scarcely remarkable in the context of nineteenth-century trans-Atlantic sailing, but the deaths aboard the *Highlander* are noteworthy in two ways. First, all the deaths occur abruptly and dramatically, thus emphasizing the tenuous hold we have on life. Second, and more significantly, the lives of those who die are as impenetrably mysterious as their deaths. Thus Redburn, orphaned originally by the death of his father, finds himself orphaned again and again by all humanity.

The first death aboard the *Highlander* occurs virtually as the ship leaves New York harbor. Without warning, one of the sailors comes up from below deck and, shrieking, throws himself into the sea. Unlike the romanticized deaths in *Typee* and the mythicized deaths in *Mardi,* the death of the unknown sailor in *Redburn* is presented as unadorned fact. And it is a fact allowing for no interpretation, for although the crew lowers boats to search, "they never caught sight of the man" (*R,* 10:50). The fact in itself, however, is eloquent enough for the young Redburn. He rather ponderously speaks of the "wonderfully solemn and almost awful effect" (*R,* 10:51) that the death has on him and wishes himself home with his mother and sisters. But pompous moralizing is soon replaced by terror: "I found that the suicide had been occupying the very bunk which I had appropriated to myself, and there was no other place for me to sleep in" (*R,* 10:51).

This is the first instance of Redburn's self-conscious identification with the dead, and, to be sure, the situation is rather contrived. But the contrivance should not prevent our recognition that Redburn's "life story" is a death story, recounting his stronger and stronger identification with the dying and the dead. Redburn brushes death two more times on the voyage to England. In the first instance, "the great black hull of a strange vessel" (*R,* 19:92) appears out of the darkness and takes off part of the *Highlander*'s rigging. "The cause of this accident, which came near being the death of all on board" is clear enough: "the drowsiness of the lookout men on the forecastles of both ships" (*R,* 19:93), but the cause is clearly irrelevant for those who might have died. Redburn is reminded of a young man at home "who had left his cottage one morning in high spirits, and was brought back at noon with his right side paralyzed from head to foot" (*R,* 19:93), and he ponders how "some lordly men, with all their plans and prospects gallantly trimmed to the fair, rushing breeze of life, and with no thought of death and disaster, suddenly encounter a shock unforeseen, and go down, foundering, into death" (*R,* 19:94).

More than death itself, it is the unpredictability and accidental nature of death that disturb Redburn, for denied "plans and prospects," life loses form and meaning. Just as there was no reason for their near shipwreck, there is no reason for their escape. The *Highlander* might as easily have become the "water-logged schooner" (*R,* 22:103) they sight some few days after their near disaster. They, too, might have been left as they leave the schooner, "drifting, drifting on; a garden spot for barnacles, and a playhouse for the sharks" (*R,* 22:103).

Arrived "safely" in England, Wellingborough's experience in Liverpool, and particularly in Launcelott's-Hey, becomes, almost literally, a dead end. Although he is shocked into an awareness of death, his awareness does not enlighten his life. He has no more prospects in England than he had in New York, and there is nothing left for him but to return home, a sadder man to be sure, but scarcely the wiser. Consumed by his awareness that the culmination of life is the impenetrable fact of death, Redburn returns home, a blind man telling tales of darkness.

Wellingborough's dreams of personal greatness are linked in his mind with his vision of America's greatness, and his personal disenchantment is linked closely to his disillusionment with America's mythical identity as the "Promised Land." At the end of Chapter 33, when Wellingborough's confidence, optimism, and good feelings are at their peak, he unblushingly avers that America is "Earth's Paradise," albeit "not a Paradise ... now; but to be made so, at God's good pleasure, and in the fullness and mellowness of time" (*R,* 33:169). Wellingborough envisions "the world's jubilee morning" (*R,* 33:169) when our children's children "shall all go with their sickles to the reaping" (*R,* 33:169), when the curse of Babel shall be revoked, and the mystical fervor of Wellingborough's vision is compressed into his avowal that on that day "there shall appear unto them cloven tongues as of fire" (*R,* 33:169).

All the power of that prophetic chapter with its heightened hopes and heightened language are brought into chillingly sharp focus in Chapter 48, where "cloven tongues as of fire" do indeed appear to Redburn— long before any jubilee morning. The *Highlander* is only a few hours out of Liverpool when Redburn, along with the rest of the midnight watch, bears witness to Miguel Saveda's final, and awful, wordless comment on human mortality. As the crew gazes in "silent horror" at the living corpse, "two threads of greenish *fire,* like a *forked tongue,* darted out between the lips; and in a moment, the cadaverous face was crawled over by a swarm of *worm-like flames*" (*R,* 48:244, my emphasis).

Miguel's midnight message is one of death, not salvation. His death, occurring so dramatically at the beginning of Redburn's voyage home, is indeed an ill omen to Redburn and, of course, to his readers. But it is more than that. The tongues of fire that wrap Miguel's body sear and wither Wellingborough's last hope; they illuminate a reality that is a monstrous inversion of his dreams of a glowing future. When Miguel's body falls "with a bubble among the phosphorescent sparkles of the damp night sea, leaving a corruscating wake" behind it (*R,* 48:245), Wellingborough is thrilled "through and through with unspeakable horror" (*R,* 48:245). He sees, as do we, that the sinking corpse embodies his own dreams, so glittering yet so dead, leaving behind an emptiness, which in the world's palpable obscure finds expression only as a visible absence—a "wake."

From this point on in the narrative, death presses ever nearer to Redburn, and he feels ever more urgently the need to accommodate himself to this, the one ineradicable fact of existence, for failing to understand death, he cannot understand, nor live, life. And it is this radical alienation from his own experience that characterizes him in the falling action of the book's final fifteen chapters. In these chapters he becomes disengaged and objective in his observations and actions when once he had been eager, sentimental, even hysterical. He himself becomes, as it were, a living corpse, a "non-being" defined primarily by his inability to experience his immediate world. He becomes the fully dramatized living embodiment of the "abdicated self," intimated in Taji's pointless drifting at the end of *Mardi.*

Redburn's virtual disappearance from the center of action in the last fourteen chapters of the novel doesn't mean we don't see into his character; it means merely that his now essentially negative character is defined by Melville indirectly. Indeed, Melville's technique mirrors his theme, for Redburn's alienated self is revealed only in contrast to, and set apart from, the characters that dominate the closing chapters of the book. Thus Carlo, the young Italian emigrant, reflects the youthful innocence once possessed by Redburn; Harry Bolton serves as a correlative of Wellingborough's lost expectations and blighted future, and finally, there is Jackson, the most subtle and, in the end, the most powerful of Redburn's other selves. His is the most subtle reflection upon Redburn's character because Redburn himself is so committed to repudiating Jackson's blasphemous, soulless defiance of life and death. But there is cause to believe that Jackson's blood-freezing contempt for all things mortal and immortal, his spiteful "Everlasting No!," is the only choice left to Redburn, wandering lost and hopeless in the immense indifference of the universe.

Carlo is singled out from the rest of the emigrants and brought to our attention in the chapter immediately following "The Living Corpse." The emigrants as a group represent all those fond dreamers who believe in the promise of the future. They book passage for America, seduced by "tales of summer suns, that ripen grapes in December" (*R,* 40:193), but their passage in reality proves to be one of hardship, near starvation, and, for many, death. Himself an orphan in this world of woe, Carlo maintains an unshakable serenity and self-confidence throughout the voyage, however. Exposed to "all the ills of life," he greets them with a "careless endurance" (*R,* 49:245), buoyed up by the innocence of youth.

He lives in the enchanted world of his organ and its music, and in that old instrument, all "carved into fantastic old towers, and turrets, and belfries" (*R,* 49:250), are contained all the romantic world-conquering dreams of childhood. Gazing "fathoms down" into Carlo's "fathomless eye" (*R,* 49:250) and listening to him play, Redburn is lifted on the airy wings of music to the worlds of King Saul, Xerxes, Macbeth, and Beethoven. Wellingborough is not Carlo, however. Carlo's melodies are "dreams Elysian," bought at "street corners, for a single penny" (*R,* 49:251) and can bring only momentary distraction from the fever, fret, and sorrow of Redburn's world. Redburn is obsessed with the overwhelming reality of "an everlasting Asiatic Cholera [that] is forever thinning our ranks" (*R,* 58:289).

If Carlo calls up in Redburn bittersweet recollections of his own lost innocence, Harry Bolton painfully reminds him of his present fallen state. At first glance Harry seems a perfect English counterpart to Wellingborough: both are orphans, and both have outrun all expectations. Yet there seems to be an essential, if ill-defined, difference between the two young men. Although both Redburn and Harry have suffered setbacks, (*R,* 43:209), Harry is inconsolably desperate and unswervingly suicidal from the moment of his disinheritance, whereas Redburn persists in the midst of his desperation, even to the point of recording it in narrative. Ultimately, the contrasts between Harry and Redburn define the absolute nature of Redburn's disillusionment, for while in Harry we see the hopelessness of a young man who seeks the peace of death in preference to the horror of life, in Wellingborough we see the infinite hopelessness of a young man who can find no peace—in life *or* death, more and more weighed down by the anxiety and the moral paralysis of a man faced with two totally unacceptable options.

Redburn's dilemma is dramatized in his obviously sympathetic, but strangely passive, attitude to Harry from the beginning. He is strongly, almost physically, repelled by Harry's behavior at the Aladdin's Palace, yet he spends the evening there, all the while wishing he were "back in Liverpool, fast asleep in my old bunk in Prince's Dock" (*R,* 46:233). Finding Harry's behavior "unaccountable," (*R,* 46:233), he nevertheless casts his lot with him without reservation, and the two remain inseparable until the voyage's end.

Clearly, Harry's fall from a position of privilege and security to ignominy and death corresponds to Redburn's sense of his own unhappy fate. Redburn not only ends his tale with the account of Harry's death, but more to the point, he hears of Harry's death while he himself is "a sailor in the Pacific, on board of a whaler" (*R,* 62:312). But Harry's career is also the paradigm of all life in the novel, and ultimately it is this larger question that haunts Redburn—and Melville. By the end of the novel, life for Redburn is little more than a universal process of decay, leading to an everlasting winter, the deaths surrounding him but grim hints of his only future.

The *Highlander,* seen at once as an emigrant ship and as a death ship, is a clear emblem of Redburn's hopeless view of life and death in the later stages of the narrative. Frightened, appalled, and horrified in turn by his earlier brushes with death, Wellingborough faces with remarkable detachment the death of the emigrants from plague. We cannot take his coolness in "Many Passengers Left Behind" as one of "maturity" or "enlightenment," however. Rather, his response to the idea that "die by death we all must at last" (*R,* 58:289) is resignation in the Thoreauvian sense of "confirmed despair." The emigrant's dream of a new world and the *Highlander's* promise of fulfilling that dream perish together in the harsh realities of this world's plagues and Atlantic storms.

Redburn has a nice conscience about the deaths of the unfortunate emigrants, and he makes a plea for reforming the unbearable conditions on emigrant ships. But in the end he admits to a problem that plagues him throughout the rest of the voyage and throughout his written account of it, a problem that plagues Melville and dominates all of his fiction from this point on: the problem of the individual's inability to rationalize experience through language and thus communicate with others.

Redburn tries to bridge the gap between the "event" and his readers' understanding by "recounting the details of the Highlander's calamity" (*R,* 58:292), but his own understanding is one infinite step removed from the events recounted: hearing groans is not groaning, and seeing death is not dying. Redburn thus sees himself as speaking both for himself and for the rest of humanity when at the end of Chapter 58 he observes: "we are blind to the real sights of this world; deaf to its voice; and dead to its death" (*R,* 58:293).

There is one person aboard the *Highlander,* however, who is presented as both seeing and experiencing all the woes of humanity. That person is Jackson. From his first appearance until his death, Jackson fascinates Redburn and, not surprisingly, his readers. But it is not Jackson's "evil" nature considered abstractly that fascinates Redburn. Nor is it Jackson's mysterious hold upon the will of his crewmates that makes Redburn uneasy. Rather, Redburn sees, and fears, in Jackson the image of his own future self, should he ever succumb wholly to the despair that dominates his life. Jackson and Redburn, in fact, agree in the assessment of life's pointless terrors and meaningless end. Redburn's definitive comment on Jackson is that:

> He was a Cain afloat; branded on his yellow brow with some inscrutable curse; and going about corrupting and searing every heart that beat near him.
>
> But there seemed even more woe than wickedness about the man; and his wickedness seemed to spring from his woe; and for all his hideousness, there was that in his eye at times, that was ineffably pitiable and touching;

and though there were moments when I almost hated this Jackson, yet I have pitied no man as I have pitied him. (*R,* 22:104–5)

If we see Redburn's pity for Jackson as a form of melancholy sympathy or even self-identification, we can, I think, see into the deepest part of Redburn's soul, the part that he never opens consciously to his readers. What makes Jackson hideous in Redburn's eyes is his contempt for both life and death, viewed as equally lacking in purpose and meaning. And it is in Jackson's relentless vision of life's pointlessness that Redburn most sees himself—and most fears for his own future. In the aftermath of Miguel Saveda's death, for example, Redburn describes the general joylessness of the superstitious crew in the forecastle. But when he describes how the always-singular Jackson "would look toward the fatal spot, and cough, and laugh, and invoke the dead man with incredible scoffs and jeers" (*R,* 48:246), he adds one of the most unguarded self-revelations in the book: "He froze my blood, and made my soul stand still" (*R,* 48:246). Redburn's blood is frozen, his soul paralyzed, not because Jackson seems blasphemous or wrong in considering death a meaningless end to an equally meaningless life, but because to Redburn, Jackson has touched on an awful truth.

Although Jackson and Redburn agree on the futility of living, their responses to the human condition are profoundly different. Jackson seeks his own death relentlessly, sneering at the dead and scoffing at those who fear for their lives; at the height of panic among the plague-stricken emigrants Jackson is "elated with the thought, that for *him*— already in the deadly clutches of another disease—no danger was to be apprehended from a fever which only swept off the comparatively healthy" (*R,* 58:289). In fact, Redburn's comment on Jackson in these circumstances serves well as a motto to his character: "in the midst of the despair of the healthful, this incurable invalid was not cast down; not, at least, by the same considerations that appalled the rest" (*R,* 58:289).

The precise cause of Jackson's despair is never revealed and his life remains an enigma to the end. Although he clearly betrays the symptoms of syphilis, his death comes with a consumptive bursting of the lungs. His fall from the yardarm is silent; his voiceless benediction upon the "upward-gazing crowd" is grim: "some . . . were spotted with the blood that trickled from the sail, while they raised a spontaneous cry, so shrill and wild, that a blind man might have known something deadly had happened" (*R,* 59:296).

Jackson's end is dramatic to be sure, but it dramatizes the fate of all humanity, for, again in Redburn's words, "die by death we all must at last" (*R,* 58:289). The *Highlander* reaches its brave new world, but its passengers are decimated by plague and the survivors are spotted with blood. And there is no resurrection in sight. In yet another grim parody of Christ's resurrection, Redburn describes Jackson's rising from his "dark tomb in the forecastle ... like a man raised from the dead" (*R,* 59:295), but Jackson rises only to fall again "with a long seethe ... into the sea" (*R,* 59:295). And Redburn is but a Job's messenger, surviving to tell the tale (*R,* 59:296).

Redburn's response to the world represented by Jackson, the emigrants, the *Highlander,* and America ultimately might be described as one of absolute anxiety. At the end of the voyage he is a young man who has survived in spite of his inability to understand the world; the inheritor of an absolute will to believe, he has absolutely nothing to believe in. His momentary elation at returning "home," however heartfelt, proves to be all too fleeting, weighed down as it is by the chicanery of Captain Riga, the bleak prospects of Harry Bolton, and his own blighted dreams. In a world that demands "a little money to enjoy it" (*R,* 62:310), he has an "empty pocket" (*R,* 62:310). In search of security, Redburn finds himself "years after this" in the Pacific "on board of a whaler" (*R,* 62:312). Seeking a life of success, Redburn is doomed to record his own failure.

If *Redburn* represents Melville's attempt to return to his beginnings, to seek out and untangle the unresolved questions of *Mardi,* it is clear that by the end of the novel he has arrived at a point of no return. The limitations of time, space, mind, and experience—explored in his first three novels—are recognized in *Redburn* to be one with mortality itself. And this mortality is defined as the first, necessary, and final cause of all humanity's blighted aspirations and pained existence. That Redburn recognizes his loss is unquestioned; even more important is Redburn's persistence in the face of that loss—thus prefiguring a type of post-Romantic heroism that dominates Melville's next two novels.

White-Jacket

The opening chapters of *White-Jacket* reveal very quickly just how much Melville's vision of humanity's questing spirit has altered since *Typee.* Tommo and Omoo jump ship in strange, exotic lands and set off bravely in search of brave new worlds. Taji, more daring yet, abandons the *Arcturion* in mid-Pacific, confident in his westering vision of the Happy Isles. Redburn, much less confidently but only somewhat less hopefully, takes to the sea in flight from an indifferent world. Viewed in succession and as a sequence, the narrator-protagonists of the first four novels reflect Melville's growing sense of the intransigence of unpleasant reality; each protagonist in turn is pushed to more desperate action in an effort to find some other world more suited to his dreams. Melville's vision of humanity's diminished freedom and potential for achievement leads to the dark end of *Redburn,* and it is that dark end that becomes the starting point for *White-Jacket,* a novel in which the protagonist is truly "wandering between two worlds, one dead, the other powerless to be born." In a very real sense *White-Jacket* is both a postscript to *Redburn* and an extended preface to *Moby-Dick,* Melville's all-inclusive depiction of the archetypal wanderer, not bound to any haven ahead and rushing from all havens astern.

Although all the early novels begin in medias res, *White-Jacket* is the first book in which the protagonist does not set off in a new direction once the book is underway. One senses that Melville must have felt near the end of things as he wrote, for the book begins "toward the end of a three years' cruise" (*W-J,* 1:3),[9] and although the *Neversink* is homeward-bound, home is a harbor that is never reached in the narrative.

The narrator-protagonist of *White-Jacket* doesn't even introduce himself at the beginning of the narrative, beginning rather with a self-effacing comment on his jacket—"NOT a *very* white jacket, but white enough, in all conscience, as the sequel will show" (*W-J,* 1:3). Even in *Typee,* Melville depicts the loss of identity as one of our most agonizing fears, and the multiple names of Tom-Tommo-Omoo, the assumed identity of Taji, and the split identity of Wellingborough-Redburn, reveal his continuing acute awareness of the uncertainty of identity in a shifting world. But White-Jacket's effacement is almost complete: he is never named throughout the book. He is known *only* by his outer garment, a piece of Carlylean clothes-philosophy of some significance.

In its broadest outlines *White-Jacket* presents a nameless protagonist caught up in a pointless voyage to a destination that is never reached— a clear reiteration and intensified statement of the narrator's essential situation at the end of *Redburn.* Picking up where *Redburn* left off, *White-Jacket* is a novel about the self's alienation in a world that is both unaccommodating and unalterable. Yet there are essential differences between the two books. There is a decidedly progressive quality to the narrative in *Redburn,* although, as we have seen, the progressive changes in Redburn's attitude and condition are for the worse. In contrast, the narrative in *White-Jacket* is essentially static, at times oppressively so, and the narrator seems to end where he began—in the doldrums of indecision and isolation.

A more important difference between *Redburn* and *White-Jacket* is to be noted in Melville's changing treatment of the satirical elements in the two books, particularly as they center in the isolated, alienated protagonists. In *Redburn,* the narrator's satire is founded essentially upon the young Wellingborough's persistent but futile efforts to find a world that conforms to his ideal expectations, and the satire in the novel leads to Redburn's total disengagement from a world he has explored and found lacking. But White-Jacket begins his narrative in this state of radical disengagement, and the implications of his isolation penetrate deeply into the book's core. White-Jacket's satire is directed at a world he does not—and does not want to—belong to.

White-Jacket's critical remarks on the Articles of War, on naval regulations in general, and on life aboard the *Neversink* in particular, are absolute. They spring from a mind and heart blighted by the injustice and imperfection of the world as it is, a mind and heart unappeasable in their demand for a wholly different world to live in. Although the satire in the book is affective because it is uncompromising, to some degree it is ineffective for the same reason, much as Part Four of *Gulliver's Travels* lacks the sharp force of Parts One and Two. White-Jacket seems so wholly alienated from his world that we question the relevance of his displeasure with it.

It is indicative of Melville's ever-darkening vision in *White-Jacket* that the *Neversink* itself totally dominates the narrative. White-Jacket's man-of-war world is a confining and oppressive microcosm, as there scarcely seems to be a world outside the ship, Melville holding White-Jacket to his declaration that "my man-of-war world alone must supply me with the staple of my matter; I have taken an oath to keep afloat to the last letter of my narrative" (*W-J,* 54:226).

The essence of the *Neversink*'s world is the absolute authority vested in the rigid hierarchy of U.S. naval custom and law. The result is not limited freedom for its individual members, but virtually no freedom at all. With a few exceptions, the lives of the crew are governed absolutely by the will of those in command—in typical military pecking order, enforced by the threats of flogging, keel-hauling, imprisonment, or hanging. Melville's opposition to the Articles of War in Chapter 70 is self-evident enough and familiar enough to allude to merely in passing. The polemics of this chapter and of the equally outspoken chapters on flogging are persuasive no doubt, but more persuasive is the indelible picture of life without freedom that relentlessly emerges, chapter by chapter, throughout the long narrative. The men of the ship are *always* accountable to their superiors. They are assigned numbers and stations for every possible action of the ship (see Chapters 3 and 67); they are called to quarters for everything from floggings to a church service (Chapters 33 and 38); indeed, they play checkers (Chapter 42), shave (Chapter 85), and finally are buried—"by the numbers" (Chapter 81).

Crushed constantly beneath the weight of absolute authority, the "people" aboard the *Neversink* lose all identity. Not only White-Jacket, but also all the ship's company seem to become part of the ship's fixtures. "Bandage," "Wedge," "Sawyer," "Pounce," "Bungs," and "Bland," "Priming," "Cylinder," and "Old Combustibles," not to mention the nameless troglodytes who burrow below decks, are little more than the moving parts of the *Neversink* machine. True, White-Jacket admits that without naval regulations the "man-of-war's crew would be nothing but a mob" (*W-J*, 3:9), but he makes it quite clear that absolute authority is the cause of the men's riotous nature, not vice versa. For example, he tells us explicitly that the excesses of the crew while on liberty in Rio are "the lamentable effects of suddenly and completely releasing '*the people*' of a man-of-war from arbitrary discipline" (*W-J*, 54:227). The operative word here is *arbitrary,* and ultimately it is the arbitrary nature of naval discipline that makes life on the *Neversink* unbearable. Not to put the case too finely, Melville staffs the *Neversink* with an incompetent commodore, a drunken, ignorant captain who almost sinks the ship off Cape Horn, a medical officer who is a butcher, and a master-at-arms who is a thief. The *Neversink* represents a world in which self-interested power is vested in privilege, custom, and chance rather than in inherent ability.

White-Jacket admits the virtue, even the necessity, of authority when it is founded in inherent superiority of ability; he sees in Collingwood's mastery of the "most desperate characters" of the British Navy "the influence wrought by a powerful brain, and a determined, intrepid spirit over a miscellaneous rabble" (*W-J*, 36:148). But no such brain or spirit is present in Captain Claret of the *Neversink,* who perforce, then, must exert his mindless will by the mindless sadism of flogging, a process that subverts humanity by subordinating it to mindless regulation.

The injustice of this arbitrary power haunts White-Jacket throughout the voyage, but even more terrifying to White-Jacket is the unpredictability of power wielded without responsibility or purpose. Because power exerted at random reduces life to a game of merest chance—without freedom and without meaning—the *Neversink* is intrinsically perverse, and its voyage becomes a tangle of contradictions. The *Neversink* is a warship in a time of peace, sailing half-way around the world for no known reason. It carries a commodore with no fleet and a captain with no capacity for command. It fights no battles but suffers numerous casualties. It summers out its Christmas at the Equator and winters out the Fourth of July "not very far from the frigid latitudes of Cape Horn" (*W-J*, 23:89). A naval ship without rum, it approaches its final port manned by a beardless crew. Truly it is a ship with "sealed orders," and life aboard her, from beginning to end, is a fathomless mystery.

At the center of the mystery stands the teller of the tale, wrapped in his jacket, "white, yea, white as a shroud" (*W-J,* 1:3). And if it is the *Neversink* that dominates his world, it is his response to that world which dominates our attention. From the beginning to the end of his narrative, White-Jacket finds himself in a state of virtual impasse, much like that of Redburn at the conclusion of his narrative. Closed in by the rigid, yet unpredictable and meaningless world of the *Neversink,* barred from all escapes save death, with its equally unpredictable yet absolute consequences, White-Jacket seeks in vain for a meaningful self-definition. Throughout the narrative he stands as a man divided, unwilling to accept the world's definition of himself, yet unable to set free or even find the self that lives within the jacket. Finding peace neither within the world nor apart from it, White-Jacket is Melville's sustained image of mortal humanity's total dislocation in an alien and hostile world. This disjunction between the inward life of White-Jacket's mind and the exterior life of his experience remains unbridged, and the conclusion of the novel is irresolute and inconclusive.

White-Jacket is imprisoned by the unsinkable reality of his man-of-war world, with no parole save death. He is oppressed by the arbitrary discipline of the *Neversink*'s officers, just as the rest of the crew is; every waking moment he lives in terror of being flogged or, almost as bad, being called to "witness punishment" of others, during which "not to feel scarified to the quick ... would argue a man but a beast" (*W-J,* 33:138). And White-Jacket knows all too well, by observation and experience, that even in the ordinary running of the ship, officers "scruple not to sacrifice an immortal man or two, in order to show off the excelling discipline of the ship" (*W-J,* 46:197). Indeed, White-Jacket sleeps according to regulations, oppressed by the officers' unrelenting pursuit of order at the expense of comfort. True, White-Jacket views comically the "most arbitrary" and "most rigorous edicts" that lead to the "extraordinary neatness, and especially this *unobstructedness* of a man-of-war" (*W-J,* 22:87), but his humor does not hide the grim reality beneath absurdity: "it may be safely laid down that, when you see such a ship [an over-neat vessel], some sort of tyranny is not very far off" (*W-J,* 22:87).

White-Jacket finds nothing to mitigate the perversions of power within the U. S. Navy. Indeed, the fact that the *Neversink* is an American ship intensifies his despair. In *White-Jacket,* as in *Redburn,* America represents the philosophical and political ideals categorically opposed to privilege, arbitrary power, and human subjugation, and White-Jacket's polemical argument is openly founded upon an appeal to the U. S. Constitution, the Declaration of Independence, and underlying both, the Law of Nature (see Chapter 35 in particular). But the published ideals of America are shown to have no relationship to the American reality. Although White-Jacket affirms that "our institutions claim to be based upon broad principles of political liberty and equality," he ruefully concludes that "it would hardly affect one iota the condition on shipboard of an American man-of-war's-man, were he transferred to the Russian Navy and made a subject of the Czar" (*W-J*, 35:144).

The argument makes for strong satire, but at the same time it reveals White-Jacket's open dissatisfaction with the "American experiment." For White-Jacket, the clearest and most disheartening indication of America's faltering idealism lies in the fact that the hateful Articles of War exist "by virtue of an enactment of Congress" (*W-J*, 35:143). By enacting the Articles of War, Congress has perverted the "genius of the American Constitution" (*W-J*, 35:143) that gave it life, and White-Jacket finds himself truly a man without a country, trapped between the ideal, but dead, world of the Constitution and the nightmare, and all too real, world of the Articles of War.

Alienated from the abstract concept of justice and equality contained in the American Constitution, White-Jacket is equally alienated from his fellow men. Although throughout the narrative he reiterates any number of times the democratic aphorism that all men are created equal, his own almost total isolation is one of the most striking features of his life aboard the *Neversink,* a categorical manifestation of Melville's central theme that the individual is alone in a frightening world.

From first to last, White-Jacket sees himself as an isolato. The very jacket that gives him his identity aboard ship is the source of difficulty for him from all directions. Among the otherwise anonymous crew it singles him out for the officers, largely because of it he is ostracized from his original mess, and ultimately he becomes a "Jonah" in the mess of Jack Chase. Burdened by his unwanted, self-restricting identity, he tries to swap his jacket with a crew-mate, he tries to auction it off, and he meditates "giving it a toss overboard" (*W-J*, 29:121). These variations on the narrator's own metaphor of his jacket identity make palpable enough the "identity crisis" he endures throughout the book. But to focus clearly on the precise nature of that crisis we must look at the few companions White-Jacket does have aboard the *Neversink.* In *White-Jacket,* as in his earlier novels, most notably in *Mardi* and *Redburn,* Melville defines his narrator-protagonist by contrasting his situation and response with the situations and responses of his friends. Thus in *White-Jacket* it is Jack Chase, Lemsford, Nord, Ushant, and Shenly who provide the most extensive commentary on what White-Jacket is and what he is not.

White-Jacket is "not at all singular in having but comparatively few acquaintances on board" (*W-J*, 13:50); his own relative isolation constantly suggests a universal loneliness in the man-of-war world. But White-Jacket does admit to carrying his "fastidiousness to an unusual extent" (*W-J,* 13:50), and consequently the men he singles out as his "friends" represent the best that can be thought, said, and done in the world of the *Neversink.*

There is little doubt for most readers, and no doubt for White-Jacket himself, that Jack Chase represents the heroic ideal of life in a man-of-war world. A "frank and charming man" (*W-J,* 4:13) and a "gentleman" (*W-J,* 4:14), Jack Chase is "universally regarded as an oracle" (*W-J,* 4:13) by the crew, who mount the main-top as "pilgrims" seeking "to have their perplexities or differences settled" (*W-J,* 4:13). It is Jack Chase who makes room for White-Jacket in "Mess No. 1" when he is ostracized by his own messmates, Jack Chase who gains liberty for the crew in Rio by sweet-talking the Commodore, and Jack Chase who saves White-Jacket from a flogging by speaking up on his behalf.

There is no reason to question White-Jacket's or the crew's admiration of Jack Chase. But the mists of hyperbole surrounding his oracular main-top do not blind White-Jacket and should not blind us to the fact that the main-top is but the highest point in a *man-of-war* world. Thus, at best Chase can be viewed as a tragic figure (although undeveloped as such), embodying heroic ideals in a world that denies heroism. At worst, he stands as a kind of hero-*manqué,* snatching petty victories in the midst of overwhelming defeat. Either way, as an ideal he represents for White-Jacket merely the best that can be hoped for in an essentially objectionable world.

In view of Chase's clearly established preeminence on the *Neversink,* it might seem inexplicable that he should accept as unalterable the flaws and abuses of naval discipline. Yet this "inexplicable" contradiction between Chase's inherent virtue and his acceptance of the inherent viciousness of the world is the very essence of his character, and it must be weighed carefully if we are to grasp Melville's purposes in the book.

In an almost Platonic sense, Chase represents our best, most ethereal self, weighed down by the material world. In the most literal terms, he is, after all, the Captain of the Main-top who nevertheless spends most of his time on and beneath the decks of the *Neversink.* And this image of "fallen" man accompanies him throughout the narrative. A "stickler for the Rights of Man, and the liberties of the world," Chase deserts the *Neversink* "to draw a partisan blade in the civil commotions of Peru; and befriend, heart and soul, what he deemed the cause of the Right" (*W-J,* 5:17). Yet his absolute devotion to absolute justice is crushed in a moment, when the Peruvian sloop of war on which he serves is hailed by the *Neversink.* As Jack tells his Peruvian commander, Don Sereno, "there is no resisting the frigate" (*W-J,* 5:19). And there is not a breath of resistance in his greeting of Captain Claret: "Your most devoted and penitent Captain of the Main-top, sir; and one who, in his very humility of contrition is yet proud to call Captain Claret his commander" (*W-J,* 5:19). Indeed, the entire scene constitutes an emblem of moral ideal-ism's subjugation to the unyielding power of authority, and this image of subjugated, even servile, moral idealism consistently accompanies Jack's appearances throughout the novel. A monarch in the main-top, reciting Camöens to his admiring disciples, on the quarterdeck Jack is much like any other tar suing for favors in the harsh man-of-war world. True, he gains "liberty" for the crew in Rio, but at what expense of truth?—"'Valiant Commodore,' said he [Jack], at last, 'this audience is indeed an honor undeserved. I almost sink beneath it. Yes, valiant Commodore, your sagacious mind has truly divined our object. Liberty, sir; liberty is, indeed, our humble prayer'" (*W-J,* 51:215)

Were the diction less ludicrous, it would be blasphemous, yet even as a parody of prayer, Jack's appeal to the Commodore illustrates the sub-jugation of virtue to power. Even Jack's intervention on behalf of White-Jacket, when he is about to be flogged, is tainted by his sharp sense of impotence. Only after a corporal of marines speaks on White-Jacket's behalf does Jack step forward, offering in "a manly but carefully respect-ful manner" the rather innocuous comment that "he had never found . . . [White-Jacket] wanting in the top" (*W-J,* 67:281).

Perhaps the most memorable instance of Jack's impotence is his ac-quiescence to "the great massacre of the beards" (Chapter 85). Again the scene wavers between farce and ritual as Jack absolves the barber-executioner his sin, but one can't overlook the fact that it is Jack who leads the crew into a willing acceptance of arbitrary power. And if we take at all seriously the many and manifest suggestions that Jack is a "Christ figure" (his initials, his descent from the main-top to be with "the people," his intercession on behalf of the crew with the world's rulers, his oracular wisdom, and his saving of White-Jacket from sin and death), then we must conclude that Melville conceives of Christ as impotent in the affairs of this world. He is an idea without substance, an ideal without force. Jack Chase thus embodies the essential dilemma of Melville's dog-ged inquiry into the nature of perfection and his hardening conviction that perfection is unattainable in this life. Accepting Chase as an ideal but at the same time rejecting him as a model of behavior in the man-of-war world, White-Jacket signals clearly his own voluntary exile from the world.

As we move toward the two climactic scenes of the book that fix White-Jacket's character as an isolato (his arraignment and his fall from the yardarm), it is helpful to bear in mind White-Jacket's other "chums" and "heroes" aboard the *Neversink,* for they cast a clear, albeit reflected, light upon his motivations and upon his dilemma. So different in many regards, Nord, Lemsford, Ushant, Landless, and Shenly taken together share an unwillingness to accept the world's definition of themselves, and consequently, they also find themselves unable to establish any kind of meaningful life within the world as they find it. Each of them reflects a facet of White-Jacket's complete and complex disengagement from the world.

Nord, the "man-of-war hermit" of Chapter 13, represents the most radical sort of alienation from the *Neversink*'s world, his determination "so to conduct himself as never to run the risk of the scourge" making him a "wandering recluse" even among the "man-of-war mob" (*W-J,* 13:51). Baffled by Nord's ability to "preserve his dignity, as he did, among such a rabble rout" (*W-J,* 13:51), White-Jacket is, indeed, self-baffling, for he unequivocally identifies himself with Nord, confessing, "my heart yearned toward him; I determined to know him" (*W-J,* 13:51). Of all the similarities between the two hermits of the *Neversink,* the most striking is their refusal to admit to any past. White-Jacket complains of Nord that he "was barred and locked up like the specie vaults of the Bank of England" (*W-J,* 13:52), but White-Jacket, too, is a "remarkable man" (*W-J,* 13:52), sprung full blown from the head of adversity and set adrift in the man-of-war world.

Nord is scarcely mentioned after his introduction, and it is safe to assume that the two hermits do not make fast friends, not even with each other. But they do share a friend in Lemsford, the poet, who shares many of White-Jacket's qualities—"wit, imagination, feeling, and humor in abundance" (*W-J,* 11:41). White-Jacket immediately seizes upon him as having a spirit "akin to his own" (*W-J,* 11:40), and in Lemsford we see reflected the secret self that White-Jacket in his isolation must hide.

The very center of Lemsford's being is his poetry; indeed, one might even say that Lemsford *is* his poetry, taking his identity from it much as White-Jacket takes his name from his coat. And in his poetry Lemsford leads a precarious, isolated life, shared only with White-Jacket and "certain select friends" (*W-J,* 11:41). His threatened manuscripts serve as an effective image of the rich and complex self shared by Lemsford and White-Jacket, a self which must remain hidden to survive in a man-of-war world. The rigid regulation of life so inimical to the secret poetic self of Lemsford (and White-Jacket) finds expression in "the deadly hostility of the whole tribe of ship-underlings—master-at-arms, ship's corporals, and boatswain's mates,—both to the poet and his casket" (*W-J,* 11:41), and the ship's underlings are right: Lemsford's poetry and White-Jacket's narrative are subversive to the regulative and prohibitive principles of the Articles of War.

Because the world of the *Neversink* is both unbearable and unyielding, it is perhaps surprising that White-Jacket never seriously contemplates escape. Such a solution would have been irresistible for all of Melville's earlier protagonists. Bad food, bad conversation, and boredom are sufficient reasons for Tommo, Omoo, and Taji to set off in search of new worlds. Even young Redburn temporarily escapes the *Highlander,* although in his case it was an old world he sought. But there are no old worlds for White-Jacket, the man without a past. Nor are there any new worlds for him. In the marvellously ambiguous terms of the book's metaphor, White-Jacket is "homeward *bound."* In this, his fifth novel, Melville closes the circles of world, time, and space, trapping the self within unbreakable bonds. White-Jacket cannot escape the world of the *Neversink* simply because it is the only world there is, and life in this world is viewed as the gradual but irreversible process of dying, and death itself is viewed as total annihilation.

Because death and the threat of death are virtually omnipresent in White-Jacket's narrative, it would be a thankless as well as an unnecessary task to catalogue the countless allusions, images, and direct statements that define the *Neversink* as a ship of death. It suffices to say that all life aboard the *Neversink* is subject to the proscriptions of the Articles of War, the transgressors of which "shall suffer death" (see Chapter 70), adding only that this story is told by one whose identity lies wrapped in a jacket "white as a shroud," a jacket that nearly proves a literal shroud on two occasions: first, when White-Jacket is almost shot down from the rigging when mistaken for a ghost by his superstitious crewmates, and second, when he falls from the yardarm as the ship approaches home.

The entire crew of the *Neversink,* from the nameless sailors of the hold to the "matchless" but sorely compromised Jack Chase, are breathing monuments to the living death of the man-of-war world. But two incidents in the book stand out particularly as exemplifying this inexorable erosion of the self by time and the world. The first, and perhaps most memorable because of its grotesque humor, centers in the surgical operation performed on a wounded top man by the Surgeon of the Fleet, Cadwallader Cuticle, M.D. The second, much more subtle but no less significant, focusses upon the inexplicable death of Seaman Shenly, messmate and friend to White-Jacket.

The three chapters devoted to Surgeon Cuticle, his cronies, and their combined efforts to bring about the premature death of the wounded sailor are familiar enough to readers of the novel, and the none-too-subtle satire on official incompetence and scientific inhumanity is self-evident in these chapters.[10] It is still worth repeating, however, that the tableau of doctors and patient captures in emblematic form all that is moribund in White-Jacket's world. The wounded man serves as another minor, but not insignificant, alter-ego to White-Jacket. He is a fore-top man and a messmate of White-Jacket's, but more important, he shares White-Jacket's love of freedom and of rebellion under constraint. In sum, his end shows forth clearly the fate of all those who would give open expression to their inner resentment and rebellion, for although he survives the wound he receives from the ship's sentry, he cannot survive the cure he receives from the Surgeon of the Fleet.

If the good-natured and well-intentioned killing of the fore-top man by the Surgeon illustrates how fruitless are humanity's attempts to seek liberty in a tyrannical world, the Surgeon himself illustrates, most ironically, that there is no victory to be gained through submission to that world, either. Although Cuticle stands as an example of perfect conformity to the dictates of his world, death moves toward him just as certainly, although not so suddenly, as it moves toward the patient on his operating table. Unlike the sailor, who carries the mark of the world's curse in the form of a "small, ragged puncture" in the thigh (*W-J,* 60:247), Cuticle carries all the marks of the world's approval. But for all his dignity and honors, Surgeon Cuticle, "a curious patch-work of life and death, with a wig, one glass eye, and a set of false teeth" (*W-J,* 61:248), moves toward the same end that awaits his dying patient. With such a patient and such a surgeon, the operation itself appears as a macabre dance of death, an arabesque of intertwining ironies, a spectacle "better than a churchyard sermon on the mortality of man" (*W-J,* 63:259). The theme of White-Jacket's churchyard sermon is that "life is more awful than death," for although "to-day we inhale the air with expanding lungs, and life runs through us like a thousand Niles; . . . to-morrow we may collapse in death, and all our veins be dry as the Brook Kedron in a drought" (*W-J,* 63:260).

White-Jacket, like Redburn before him, is indeed obsessed with death from the beginning to the end of the narrative. But whereas death comes upon Redburn as an unwelcome and unexpected intruder into the garden world of his youthful dreams, to White-Jacket death is an intimate and constant companion, the antithesis to life which, nevertheless, defines life's boundaries. If *Redburn* records Melville's version of humanity's fall from innocence, *White-Jacket* depicts his vision of life in an unregenerate world. Redburn's persistent but relentlessly diminishing faith—in himself, in America, in the future—is utterly extinguished, and White-Jacket finds himself living in a world of darkness wrapped in the blackness of death.

It is precisely this image of life and death that emerges in White-Jacket's account of Shenly's death. The chapter title itself, *"How Man-of-war's-men Die at Sea"* (Chapter 79), emphasizes the universality of Shenly's fate. But a double emphasis is placed on Shenly's death in that once again White-Jacket tacitly, but forcefully, identifies himself with his dying messmate. Unlike the top-man who dies dramatically and grotesquely on Cuticle's operating table, and unlike the other top-man, Baldy, who falls "with a horrid crash of all his bones, . . . like a thunderbolt, upon the deck" (*W-J,* 46:196), Shenly dies quietly, but no less surely, from the simple attrition of life as lived on a man-of-war.

There is no ostensible cause for Shenly's death, but this seeming vagueness becomes purposeful when viewed in conjunction with White-Jacket's description of Shenly's last moments of life—confined in the "heated furnace" below decks (W-J, 79:336). Shenly dies quietly and slowly from the same oppression that kills Baldy and the wounded top-man outright. Neither derelict in duty nor rebellious to authority, Shenly in death symbolizes the best that can be hoped for in a man-of-war world. White-Jacket keeps a vigil all night by the "dreamless sleeper" at his side, turning away the relief watch and sitting by the corpse "till daylight came" (*W-J,* 79:337). In terms of the book's metaphorical statement, however, there is no relief for White-Jacket, and no daylight; the picture of him sitting in darkness, next to a corpse and waiting for daylight, is an apt emblem of the book's complex statement of the insoluble dilemma of life.

Throughout the book, but certainly more emphatically in its closing stages, White-Jacket is depicted as a man without options, a man trapped in a world he cannot understand and with no place else to go. For White-Jacket, rocking in his "Pisgah top" (*W-J,* 93:397), heavenly shores and harbors are but dreams, seen with but the mind's eye—never reached. His voyage and his narrative end with the ship still "on the sea—still with the land out of sight—still with brooding darkness on the face of the deep" (*W-J,* 93:396).

White-Jacket, like the previous novels, ends with its protagonist at sea, literally and metaphorically, but it defines more clearly than the earlier novels what being at sea in the world really means to Melville. White-Jacket's essential plight in this regard is once again reflected in two minor characters—Landless and Ushant. Although each represents a radical, even simplistic response to the complex world of ship, sea, and shore, taken together they suggest the complex struggle taking place in White-Jacket in his efforts to find his place in the world. Furthermore, the respective fates of Landless and Ushant define the absolute hopelessness of White-Jacket's efforts.

Both Landless and Ushant are introduced late in the narrative, thus adding even more emphasis to their already remarkable characters. Landless's perfect and good-natured acceptance of his man-of-war life, almost enviable at first glance, is bought at the price of reality, for his zest for life springs not from a wide-ranging mind and imagination, but from no mind at all. To White-Jacket, Landless epitomizes a mindless experience of the world, recorded on his unflinching back, "cross-barred, and plaided with the ineffaceable scars of all the floggings accumulated ... during a ten years' service in the Navy" (W-J, 90:383). And, thus, he epitomizes for White-Jacket an absolute resignation to that Gehenna within Gehenna—a mindless, meaningless world.

Ushant is the direct antithesis of Landless. Captain of the Forecastle and thus representing all the "people," we first sight him "slowly coming down the rigging from the foretop" (W-J, 86:363) and identify him with the lofty ideals of Jack Chase and with White-Jacket's democratic principles. Ushant is, to Jack Chase and White-Jacket, the original sailor, Chaucer's Shipman incarnate. Flogged and imprisoned for refusing to shave his beard, Ushant bears himself with an unearthly dignity and self-composure that signals his imperturbable separation of his mind and will from the facts of his experience.

Landless and Ushant together stand as the polar opposites running through the heart of White-Jacket's world. Neither Landless's unreflective, mindless acceptance of the world's fact nor Ushant's self-containing, world-excluding will and mind can lend stability to White-Jacket. He demands nothing less than meaningful experience *in* the world. And it is precisely this fusion of mind and experience, meaning and fact, that the novel as a whole denies. In the Articles of War and the American Constitution, in Captain Claret and Mad Jack, in Jack Chase, Lemsford, Nord, Shenly, Landless, and Ushant, we see the unbridgeable gap between the world as dreamed and the world as lived. In White-Jacket himself, we see the anxiety and paralysis of one who must live with that difference.

The most direct definition of White-Jacket's character and his plight are found in the chapters describing his arraignment at the mast (Chapter 67), his fall from the yardarm (Chapter 92), and his farewell speech to "shipmates and world-mates, all round" (Chapter 94—*The End*). Although each of these scenes seems fairly straightforward in itself, taken together they form a fairly complex statement on the ineluctable dilemmas of White-Jacket's life.

For White-Jacket, the prospect of being flogged and humiliated, unjustifiably at that, confirms his own worst expectations in a man-of-war world. But even his most scathing attacks upon the Articles of War and the abuses of naval discipline don't prepare us adequately for his immediate resolve to throw himself with his accuser over the side, "to drag Captain Claret from this earthly tribunal of his to that of Jehovah, and let Him decide between us" (*W-J,* 67:280).[11]

Even White-Jacket is confused about his motivations to commit murder and suicide. He does not fear for his "man's manhood," which he feels is "bottomless" (*W-J,* 67:280); rather, he feels "swung" by "the instinct diffused through all animated nature, the same that prompts even a worm to turn under the heel" (*W-J,* 67:280). In this extremity, however, White-Jacket's judgment and convictions are uncertain. He quickly shifts the origins of this "instinct" from God to "Nature"—which "has not implanted any power in man that was not meant to be used" (*W-J,* 67:280) and then just as quickly moves to the assertive but dubious conclusion that "the privilege, inborn and inalienable, that every man has, of dying himself, and inflicting death upon another, was not given to us without a purpose" (*W-J,* 67:280).

The shift to the passive voice, the double negative construction, and the painfully indefinite "purpose" all point clearly to White-Jacket's complete ambivalence about his own motivations and the significance of his life and death. Considering murder and suicide "the last resources of an insulted and unendurable existence" (*W-J,* 67:280), a precise description of his own existence in the man-of-war world, White-Jacket nevertheless responds to his "reprieve" with "tears of thanksgiving" (*W-J,* 67:281).

White-Jacket's absolute ambivalence toward himself and his world, life and death, is presented to us in intensified dramatic form in the scene describing his fall from the yardarm (Chapter 92). Virtually every detail of the scene carries with it a wealth of metaphorical significance, carefully accumulated throughout the first ninety-one chapters of the novel— a rhetorical method Melville is to use with overwhelming skill and power in the closing chapters of *Moby-Dick.* Consistent with the novel's central theme of the self's frustrated aspirations and tragic limitations, White-Jacket's fall from the main-top occurs just as the *Neversink* approaches America's shores, "gliding toward our still invisible port" (*W-J,* 92:391). White-Jacket never sees this port, and he doesn't allow us to see it, either. The dreamy quarter-watch talk in the top "about the shore delights into which they intended to plunge" (*W-J,* 92:391) is never realized. Instead, White-Jacket is wakened once again to an awful reality.

White-Jacket's midnight task of setting the main-top-gallant-stun'-sail is itself an intricate figure of his attempts to solve the riddle of the man-of-war world, but it is his own plumb-line fall, "straight as a die, toward the infallible center of this terraqueous globe" (*W-J,* 92:392) that gives the true measure of White-Jacket's precarious and unsupported life. The cause of his fall, too, illustrates just how unforgiving reality is to those who ignore it. Tossed about by the inexplicable "sudden swells of the calm sea" (*W-J,* 92:392), White-Jacket mistakes his own "muffling" jacket for the ship's sail, and holding onto himself, as it were, plunges "into the speechless profound of the sea" (*W-J,* 92:392).

Metaphorically, this fall is a subconscious suicide, a desperate plunge out of an alienating reality. And, thus, the fall restates the conditions and motivations of White-Jacket's conscious determination in Chapter 67 to be annihilated. White-Jacket's descent into the "purple and pathless" depths of the sea is accompanied not by terror or frenzy, but by a "deep calm" (*W-J,* 92:393). In fact, it seems to be the most peaceful moment in White-Jacket's life as he yields "in a trance," sinking "deeper down with a glide" (*W-J,* 92:393). The thought of his own death evokes not so much fright as curiosity: "I wondered whether I was yet dead, or still dying" (*W-J,* 92:393). But death itself, not the thought but the fact, revolts him, immediately and instinctively: "of a sudden some fashionless form brushed my side—some inert, coiled fish of the sea; the thrill of being alive again tingled in my nerves, and the strong shunning of death shocked me through" (*W-J,* 92:393).

Just as earlier White-Jacket had given way for the moment to an "instinct" for self-destruction, he now gives way to an "instinct" for self-preservation. Central to Melville's conception of White-Jacket's plight is the idea that White-Jacket himself is incapable of understanding or governing his own existence. He hangs "vibrating in the mid-deep," listening passively to the "wild sounds" of life and death—"one . . . a soft moaning, as of low waves on the beach; the other wild and heartlessly jubilant, as of the sea in the height of a tempest" (*W-J,* 92:393). Poised in this perfect balance of life and death, of soft moaning waves and heartlessly jubilant sea, White-Jacket's survival or annihilation, so far as he can understand either, depends on the merest chance. Although there are mysteries in the deep, there are no revelations: "the life-and-death poise soon passed; and then I found myself slowly ascending, and caught a dim glimmering of light" (*W-J,* 92:393).

It is popular to view White-Jacket's eventual emergence from "the speechless profound of the sea" as a spiritual rebirth,[12] but such an interpretation appears reductive when held up to the specific details of White-Jacket's poised existence between life and death. If anything, White-Jacket's emergence from the sea is a vivid metaphor for his literal birth, mysterious and incalculable; and this, the deepest experience of his life's voyage, remains for White-Jacket totally ambiguous, as he enters the world he must live in but can never comprehend.

White-Jacket does survive, but at the expense of the jacket that throughout the novel has been both his "self" and his "shroud." This persistent ambiguity of the jacket is irreducible, and, indeed, as White-Jacket cuts himself free from its prisoning folds we are not sure whether we are witnessing a suicide or an apotheosis. White-Jacket's description—"I ... ripped my jacket straight up and down, as if I were ripping open myself" (*W-J*, 92:394) seems strangely at odds with his immediate exclamation—"Sink! sink! oh shroud! thought I; sink forever! accursed jacket that thou are!" (*W-J*, 92:394).

It is this firmly balanced and unresolved ambiguity that forms the conclusion proper to the narrative. White-Jacket "survives" only to return to the same man-of-war world that he left so precipitously, not at all the best of possible worlds, but simply the only world he has. Captive to his own instinct for survival, White-Jacket must play out his role in a world he neither loves nor understands, a world that offers no meaning to life, merely a momentary stay against annihilation.

It is with this portrait of care-ridden, death-enveloped man in a careless world that the narrative of White-Jacket ends. Chapter 93, with its suppositions and indecisions, and Chapter 94, with its self-confounding surmises, are perhaps the clearest expressions of White-Jacket's appalled reflections upon the inescapable conclusions of his own experience and thought. In the Pisgah top of his imagination White-Jacket can dream the vision of "holy soil" (*W-J*, 93:395) and "blessed clime" (*W-J*, 93:396), but Camöens's "shadowy shore" (*W-J*, 93:396) is never reached in this world. The promised land remains "far inland" (*W-J*, 93:396), to be reached only when "we have seen our last man scourged at the gangway; our last man gasp out the ghost in the stifling Sick-bay; our last man tossed to the sharks" (*W-J*, 93:396).

Although one might take the novel's last chapter (94) as a postscript "testament of acceptance," I find it a very fragile fulcrum to use in lifting the immense weight of the novel. Indeed, this last chapter's ambiguous title—"*The End*"—is itself an example of "conflicting and almost crazy surmisings" about "the precise harbor" for which we are bound (*W-J*, 93:395). White-Jacket seems absolutely incapable of relinquishing his belief in a final harbor, and yet, at the same time, he can find absolutely nothing in his experience to justify that belief. Given the central and persistent metaphorical values in the novel's attack upon naval laws and personnel, I find little comfort in White-Jacket's description of God as the "Lord High Admiral" who will yet "interpose ... though long ages should elapse, and leave our wrongs unredressed" (*W-J*, 94:400).[13] And I see no comfort at all in his description of life's voyage: "The port we sail from is forever astern. And though far out of sight of land, for ages and ages we continue to sail with sealed orders, and our last destination remains a secret to ourselves and our officers; yet our final haven was predestinated ere we slipped from the stocks at Creation" (*W-J,* 94:398).

This image of chartless, compassless voyaging to a destination unknown does not resolve life's ambiguities so much as it paints them in the most vivid colors. Thus the ending of *White-Jacket* presents us not with a conclusion, but with an impasse. White-Jacket, that is to say all humanity, is ambivalent and adrift in an ambiguous world—desiring a world he cannot reach, imprisoned in a world he cannot bear.

In his first five novels, Melville relentlessly probes at our best efforts to find some other world than that of our incomplete, disappointing experience. The very substance of Melville's art rests upon his ability to portray convincingly this passion of humanity's yearning for an enchanted land where mind and act, self and world, are one, and the unique power of his art rests upon his unblinking honesty in anatomizing the reasons for our failure to realize those dreams.

The inherent contradiction between humanity's ideal conception of absolute truth, justice, freedom, and immortality, and its necessary worldly experience of expediency, oppression, and mortality is, of course, the goad at the heart of all Western philosophy from at least Plato onward. From 1847 to 1850, Melville's active and acute mind grappled with that contradiction and its implications, and in his first five novels he presents a progressively darkening vision of disillusionment shared by many of his Romantic predecessors and contemporaries. The Romantics' disillusionment was cataclysmic, founded as it was on the shocked and unwilling recognition that the ideal realm, however formulated in the mind, is forever inaccessible to human experience. Recognizing the impossibility of an integrated self in a coherent world, the disillusioned Romantic was all too acutely aware that he was witnessing the demise of two thousand years of Western thought and aspiration. What makes Melville virtually unique among his many disillusioned contemporaries is that he sees beyond the shattered dreams and has the courage to chart with uncompromising care the awfulness of his new-found world. And it is with this act of courage, in facing directly the tragic truths of the human condition, that Melville bestows his greatest legacy to our age.

CHAPTER

4

Moby-Dick: An Utter Wreck

> Before I launch out into those immense depths of philosophy,
> which lie before me, I find myself inclin'd to stop a moment in
> my present station, and to ponder that voyage, which I have
> undertaken, and which undoubtedly requires the utmost art
> and industry to be brought to a happy conclusion. Methinks I
> am like a man, who having struck on many shoals, and having
> narrowly escap'd ship-wreck in passing a small frith, has yet
> the temerity to put out to sea in the same leaky weather-
> beaten vessel, and even carries his ambition so far as to think
> of compassing the globe under these disadvantageous
> circumstances.[1]

From the first page of *Moby-Dick* it is clear that the false starts, frustrations, and inevitable failures of Tommo, Omoo, Taji, Redburn, and White-Jacket have taken their toll on Melville's conception of the quest. In view of the diminishing worlds and constricting visions of Melville's first five novels, it is expressive of his resilient mind that he conceives one last and greatest quest for a whole vision of a whole world. But Melville was not one to leave any question unasked, and however desperate the conclusions to his first five novels, in *Moby-Dick* he manages to call up the energy for a sustained and comprehensive depiction of humanity's tragic plight.

Although Ishmael sets out on what proves to be a circumnavigating quest after the world's deepest and most fiercely kept secret, his motives and expectations in setting out are radically different from those of the hero-protagonists in the earlier fiction. Looking backward from *Moby-Dick*, we can perceive a perceptible if gradual change in Melville's con-

ception of his questing heroes. The naive and apparently groundless belief in happy valleys, noble savages, and golden isles shared by Tommo,
Omoo, and Taji had, as we have seen, dimmed greatly in Redburn and
White-Jacket. But even Redburn has his deep-rooted memories of romantic glass ships and French coasts, and he holds before him always the
prospect of recapturing his father's greatness—of returning from his enforced adventures to tell wonderful tales, over port, to admiring family
and friends. And White-Jacket is sustained through all the miseries of the
Neversink's cruise by the thought, however misplaced and ultimately
denied, that he is homeward bound to the milk-and-honeyed land of liberty, fraternity, and equality. To Ishmael, as we shall see, these memories,
these dreams and prospects are naught. From the first, his soul is all a
"damp, drizzly November" (*M-D*, 1:12);[2] his going to sea is the last alternative of a desperate man—a "substitute for pistol and ball" (*M-D*,
1:12). And if, in the overview, the voyage of the *Pequod* is Melville's
boldest quest in search of that "certain significance [that] lurks in all
things" (*M-D*, 99:358), the utter wreck of its ending depicts with the
emblematic simplicity of a parable Melville's horror at the fathomless and
ineluctable mystery of the world's hard reality.

We don't have to read far to see somewhat into the causes of Ishmael's
"hypos."[3] First, he is no green youngster like Redburn, nor even so young
a man as Tommo or White-Jacket, and he carries within him the accumulated frustrations and failures that characterize and define the life
experiences of Melville's younger protagonists. Second, he is virtually
penniless. He goes to sea as a sailor rather than as a passenger or a commodore because, he says whimsically, "they make a point of paying me
for my trouble. . . . And there is all the difference in the world between
paying and being paid" (*M-D*, 1:15). Behind the good humor of his explanation lies the hard truth of his life, that the world has yielded him
the most meager sustenance, and that only grudgingly. His penniless
state, however, is but a material sign of his deeper and more general
alienation from life, and he is, to be sure, a proper Ishmael—an isolato
and an outcast.

The opening pages of the novel define Ishmael's decision to go to sea
as the act of a desperate and outcast man, but when we read "The Counterpane," that strangely quiet, haunting chapter, we discover the true
horror at the heart of Ishmael's life. The chapter begins quietly enough
as Ishmael wakes about daylight in the Spouter-Inn, with Queequeg's arm
thrown over him "in the most loving and affectionate manner" (*M-D*,
4:32). But the patchwork quilting of the counterpane, coupled with the
"interminable Cretan labyrinth" (*M-D*, 4:32) of Queequeg's tattooed
arm, serves to carry Ishmael back to the mazed center of his own proper

being. Ishmael's story of his childhood punishment is the most unguarded and unmannered statement he makes about himself in the entire
novel, and for that reason it is also the most revealing single statement
we have of his true character.

The triggering cause of Ishmael's punishment is relatively insignificant,
but the punishment itself, which was for him to be "packed . . . off to bed,
though it was only two o'clock in the afternoon of the 21st June, the
longest day in the year in our hemisphere" (*M-D,* 4:32), has stamped
Ishmael for life. His experience on that longest day of the year, one might
say the longest day of his life, was so traumatic that he admits, even as he
writes, that he "never could entirely settle" whether his experience was
"a reality or a dream" (*M-D,* 4:32). Entombed in his "little room in the
third floor" (*M-D,* 4:32), he is thrice removed from the light and life
outside his prisoned self; he is the outcast waiting for the "resurrection"
(*M-D,* 4:32) that never comes. Motherless to begin with, he is twice
orphaned by a harsh and unforgiving stepmother. In the very midst of life
he lies imprisoned, "the sun shining in at the window, and a great rattling
of coaches in the streets, and the sound of gay voices all over the house"
(*M-D,* 4:32–33).

All these things conspire to define the essential Ishmael—outcast
among men. The essence of his nightmare lies in his waking to a room
"wrapped in outer darkness" in which "nothing was to be seen, and nothing was to be heard; but a supernatural hand seemed placed in mine"
(*M-D,* 4:33). The "nameless, unimaginable, silent form or phantom, to
which the hand belonged" (*M-D,* 4:33) brings neither resurrection nor
comfort to Ishmael, however. A horrible inversion of the comforting
mother Ishmael so longs for and cannot find, this nameless silent phantom serves as the very image of his pain and grief.

The horror of the young Ishmael's isolation and the greater horror of
his being able only to imagine a comforting hand held out in darkness
haunts the entire narrative. Indeed, for the narrator-Ishmael, all the terrors of the whale hunt and the catastrophe of the *Pequod*'s voyage do
not compare to his early traumatic recognition that he is utterly alone in
this world: "for several hours I lay there broad awake, *feeling a great
deal worse than I have ever done since, even from the greatest subsequent misfortunes*" (*M-D,* 4:33; my emphasis).

Seeing Ishmael as we do at the beginning of his narrative—ageing,
penniless, unwanted, and totally isolated in the world, it is perhaps surprising that he is willing to accept a substitute for pistol and ball. But in
fact, the business of whaling is so linked in Ishmael's mind with images
and portents of death that at times it seems not a substitute for suicide
so much as a means of accomplishing it.[4] Ishmael is no less quick than

we are in making linked analogies between the larger world he inhabits and the Spouter-Inns and Peter Coffins of his immediate environment. New Bedford to him is a city of dreadful night; it is "Gomorrah" and "Tophet," lit only here and there by "a candle moving about in a tomb" (*M-D*, 2:18). He realizes, just as we do, that pondering the marble tablets in Father Mapple's Whaleman's Chapel is just another expression of his habit of "pausing before coffin warehouses, and bringing up the rear at every funeral" (*M-D*, 1:12) he meets.

In these opening chapters devoted to Ishmael's character there is a singularly fine distinction made between suicide and going whaling—between death and life; in Ishmael, Melville depicts a man who lives, yet has nothing to live for. Pondering the inscribed tablets of death in the Whaleman's Chapel, Ishmael sees in them the "deadly voids and unbidden infidelities ... that seem to gnaw upon all Faith, and refuse resurrections to the beings who have placelessly perished without a grave" (*M-D*, 7:41); yet he concludes, "Faith, like a jackal, feeds among the tombs, and even from these dead doubts she gathers her most vital hope" (*M-D*, 7:41). It is this faith born of despair that defines Ishmael's tenacious, yet tenuous hold upon life; thus he ends this chapter of tombstones and death with an affirmation: "three cheers for Nantucket; and come a stove boat and stove body when they will, for stave my soul, Jove himself cannot" (*M-D*, 4:41).

An unwanted child in an alien world, clinging to his fragile mortality, just as at the end of the voyage he will cling to Queequeg's life-buoy coffin, Ishmael not too surprisingly sees himself at the mercy of "the invisible police officer of the Fates" (*M-D*, 1:15). But his ruminations in "Loomings" on the Fates and the "grand programme of Providence" (*M-D*, 1:16), and his later philosophizing in "The Mat-Maker" on "chance, free will, and necessity" (*M-D*, 47:185), do more than define Ishmael's sense of powerlessness. They also define his all-important response to that powerlessness. Given the nature of Fate and Providence, Ishmael's general response is one of necessary acceptance, but more explicitly, Ishmael assumes for himself the role of inquisitor—looking into the "springs and motives" (*M-D*, 1:16) of the universe to uncover its fated, providential plan and, thereby, to discover himself.

Unlike all Melville's earlier questing heroes, who sought a good, better, or even a best world, Ishmael perforce takes the world as it is and dives into it with a desperate curiosity. No Edenic valleys nor golden isles for Ishmael: only "the overwhelming idea of the great whale himself" (*M-D*, 1:16). With no new worlds to dream, Ishmael sets out for this world's "wild and distant seas," seeking out "the undeliverable, nameless perils of the whale," and "a thousand Patagonian sights and sounds" (*M-D,* 1:16). Accepting what he cannot change, Ishmael proposes for himself a limited hope, and even that is conditional upon the Fates: "I am quick to perceive a horror, and could still be social with it—would they let me—since it is but well to be on friendly terms with all the inmates of the place one lodges in" (*M-D,* 1:16).

All of Melville's romantic, questing heroes have been isolatoes, their dissatisfactions with conventional society leading them in search of other places, other times. But in *Moby-Dick,* Melville is unequivocal in revealing the certainties and the securities of conventional belief as illusions, the self-delusions of those who wilfully ignore the Patagonian sights and sounds of the world. Thus, in the opening chapters of the novel Ishmael is set apart from his fellow men, not by his condition, which all humanity shares, but by his heightened awareness of that condition. Ishmael confronts his destiny, while "crowds of water-gazers" merely stand, "fixed in ocean reveries" (*M-D,* 1:12). The unconscious compulsion that drives them to "get just as nigh the water as they possibly can without falling in" (*M-D,* 1:13) in Ishmael is carried to a higher pitch: he goes whaling.

The land-sea dichotomy introduced in Chapter 1 pervades the novel, but that dichotomy is not reduced to mere opposition: security-danger, peace-fright, calm-tempest, life-death. In Ishmael's numberless comparisons between life at sea and life on land, he stresses time and again an essential similarity, not difference. To cite but two striking examples, Ishmael concludes his notable discussion of the intricate dangers of the whale line thus: "if you be a philosopher, though seated in the whaleboat, you would not at heart feel one whit more of terror, than though seated before your evening fire with a poker, and not a harpoon, by your side" (*M-D,* 60:241). An even better example of the links between land and sea life emerges from Ishmael's analysis of his monkey-rope connection with Queequeg. Struck by the danger of his position, Ishmael initially feels that his "free will had received a mortal wound" and that "another's mistake or misfortune might plunge innocent me into unmerited disaster and death" (*M-D,* 72:271). He concludes, however, that "this situation of mine was the precise situation of every mortal that breathes; only, in most cases, he, one way or other, has this Siamese connection with a plurality of other mortals" (*M-D,* 72:271).

In these two examples, and in countless others, the critical distinction between life at sea and life on land is that the peril of imminent disaster and death is merely more obvious at sea. And even this distinction is blurred yet further by the fact that all the "land" people in the novel are intimately connected with whaling. They are ex-whalers—like Peleg,

Bildad, Peter Coffin, and Father Mapple; relatives of whalers—like the widows and wives in Mapple's congregation; or, more to the point, whalers between cruises—like Queequeg and Bulkington.

This sameness of land life and sea life in the novel underlies the book's universal appeal, by which we recognize that life aboard the *Pequod* conveys the essential terms of the human condition and is not merely a semi-documentary account of nineteenth-century whaling conditions. Nevertheless, in terms of the book's metaphorical statement, there is a recognizable land "mentality," which consists primarily of a refusal to recognize these universal, if unpleasant, truths that Ishmael, and all whalers, and we, can only know by diving in the deep. Appropriately, given the mid-nineteenth-century setting and writing of the novel, Melville singles out optimistic Christianity and optimistic materialism as the two most appealing, and thus most deluding, rationalizations of his time, and his treatment of both is no less severe for its being so subtle. Indeed, Melville's genius for dramatic irony, which we tend to associate with later works like "Benito Cereno" and "Bartleby," reaches its first full expression in his depiction of Father Mapple and Captain Bildad.

Almost all readers would agree that Father Mapple's sermon is a paradigmatic rendering in parable form of the Calvinistic, or broadly Protestant, doctrine of redemption, although critical opinion is evenly divided on whether Melville intended to uphold a Christian norm or, through irony, point out that norm's shortcomings. In the predictable, almost formulaic tradition of Protestant homiletics, Mapple describes "the sin, hard-heartedness, suddenly awakened fears, the swift punishment, repentance, prayers, and finally the deliverance and joy of Jonah" (*M-D,* 9:45). Thus, however pessimistic the stages of Jonah's soul journey, the result is unequivocally optimistic, and for Mapple the even more optimistic (and utterly unorthodox) application of his text and doctrine is that everyone may attain the multifoliate delight of salvation (see Chapter 9, pp. 50–51).

Perhaps the familiarity of this doctrine and the homiletic tradition behind it blinds us to Melville's subtle, but devastating, undermining of both. If we read the sermon with an "equal eye," that is, neither as Christian nor "anti-Christian" readers, we find it to be nothing more than a tangle of evocative rhetoric, pointless abstractions, and empty verbal flourishes. As an exercise in salt-sea metaphor the sermon is a diverting tour de force, but that shouldn't deter us from noting the ravelled ends of its "two-stranded lesson" (*M-D,* 9:45).

The first strand of the "lesson to us all as sinful men" (*M-D,* 9:45), for example, leads rather tortuously to the conclusion: "Sin not; but if you do, take heed to repent of it like Jonah" (*M-D,* 9:49). Now it is

puzzling to contemplate how sinful man can avoid sinning, but it is virtually self-confounding to contemplate how man at the height of his sin
might take heed "to repent of it like Jonah,"—even though self-contradiction and monumental question-begging might be the inevitable products of a lesson founded so confidently on the opaque dogma that "all
the things that God would have us do are hard for us to do . . . and hence,
he oftener commands us than endeavors to persuade" (*M-D*, 9:45). This
presumptive doctrine leads Mapple to the inescapable Calvinistic inference that "if we obey God, we must disobey ourselves; and it is in this
disobeying ourselves, wherein the hardness of obeying God consists"
(*M-D*, 9:45).

There are more frightening monsters yet beneath the surface of
Mapple's sea sermon. God's command to the disobedient Jonah, to
"preach the Truth to the face of Falsehood!" (*M-D*, 9:50), is, of all the
commands Mapple's God might have given, the one that every fiber and
sinew of *Moby-Dick* point to as being impossible to obey—be we ever
so willing. Thus Mapple's sermon serves as an ironic preface to the world
of the novel, where "Truth" is seen always as through a glass, darkly.

In the "Battering Ram," Ishmael offers a significant gloss on this central
doctrine of Father Mapple's sermon when he proclaims that "clear Truth
is a thing for salamander giants only to encounter" (*M-D*, 76:286), but
we needn't go so far asea to discover the inherent irony and incongruity
of Mapple's sermon. We need only look at his own agonizing attempt to
preach truth to the face of falsehood—and thereby sustain his own precarious faith. Preaching self-denial, Mapple is obsessed with the state of
his own soul, his mountain of woe reaching a peak in the admonition-
confession: "woe to him who, as the great Pilot Paul has it, while preaching to others is himself a castaway!" (*M-D*, 9:50).[5] Preaching the identity
of Truth and God, by submission to which we attain salvation, Mapple
reaches the confounding conclusion, "Woe to him who would not be
true, even though to be false were salvation!" (*M-D*, 9:50). Preaching
the insignificance of this world and the eternal wonder of God's heaven,
Mapple winds his way to an inconclusive end: "eternal delight and deli-
ciousness will be his, who coming to lay him down, can say with his final
breath—O Father!—chiefly known to me by Thy rod—mortal or immortal, here I die. I have striven to be Thine, more than to be this world's, or
mine own. Yet this is nothing; I leave eternity to Thee; for what is man
that he should live out the lifetime of his God?" (*M-D*, 9:51).

"What is man at all?" is the question ultimately raised by Father
Mapple's sermon, and it is Melville's bitterest irony that Mapple provides
the answer even as he asks the question: man is an Ishmael and a
Jonah—outcast, alone, questioning, inexorably drawn toward death. The

chapel, the congregation, the service, and Father Mapple himself combine to form a complex emblem of this life and this death, which all the glozing rhetoric of the sermon cannot hide.

The "Whaleman's Chapel," which supposedly offers comfort to "moody fishermen, shortly bound for the Indian Ocean or Pacific" (*M-D*, 7:39), provides cold comfort indeed for moody Ishmael. The storm-battered chapel can scarcely be said to house a "congregation" at all, for "each silent worshipper seemed purposely sitting apart from the other, as if each silent grief were insular and incommunicable" (*M-D*, 7:39). These "silent islands of men and women," who sit "steadfastly eyeing several marble tablets, with black borders, masoned into the wall on either side of the pulpit" (*M-D*, 7:39), look up to Father Mapple, ex-sailor and harpooner, as he stands, flanked by memories of the drowned, preaching the "hope" of salvation. As a text of hope to sailors and sailors' widows, his tale of "the kelpy bottom of the waters; sea-weed and all the slime of the sea" is numbing in its misdirection, and leaving behind the twisted sea-words of Father Mapple's sermon, Ishmael must go to sea for himself—"to see what whaling is ... to see the world" (*M-D*, 16:69).

Compared to Father Mapple's "spiritual withdrawal ... from all outward worldly ties and connexions" (*M-D*, 8:43), Peleg's and Bildad's immediate and complete involvement in the *Pequod*'s voyage appears at first glance to signify their acceptance of the world's harsh reality. Like Father Mapple they have sailed distant seas, but although they too are "landsmen" now, they have a quick sense of the terrors of whaling, unmitigated by any optimistic rhetoric. Even Peleg's most violent rhetoric about stove boats and jumping down a live whale's throat does not match the reality of the *Pequod*'s ill-fated voyage, however, as Ishmael discovers, and the reality of that voyage casts a retrospective shadow of irony upon the blustery high spirits of Peleg and Bildad, who view whaling as a profitable "business."

Peleg's and Bildad's materialistic self-interest is nowhere more obvious than in their determination of Ishmael's "lay," notwithstanding Bildad's mumbling of convenient Biblical rhetoric, and his pious concern for "the other owners of this ship—widows and orphans, many of them" (*M-D*, 16:75). This commercial Christianity—or pious materialism—so clearly dramatized in Bildad is further exemplified in the fitting out of the *Pequod* by his sister, fittingly named Aunt Charity. Reducing the half-remembered terrors of whaling to a ledger of profit and loss, supporting this simplistic view of life with that oldest but most workable self-delusion—"that a man's religion is one thing, and this practical world quite another" (*M-D*, 16:72), Bildad epitomizes that nineteenth-century materialistic optimism that made "people in Nantucket invest their money in whaling vessels, the same way that you do yours in approved state stocks bringing in good interest" (*M-D*, 16:71).

Melville's exposure of that misplaced optimism is manifest in virtually every ensuing page of the novel, for clearly there is little of Aunt Charity's "safety, comfort, and consolation" (*M-D*, 20:90) in whaling, or in life, and, as far as the *Pequod*'s voyage goes, there is no profit either. Bildad's and Peleg's most careful calculations of the ship's needs, both in provisions and crew, and their most careful instructions to Ahab and his mates are nothing to Ahab's overwhelming purpose and Moby Dick's overwhelming power. The preacher who extols the wonders of the deep to widows and orphans of drowned sailors, and those same widows and orphans who invest in further whaling voyages, provide little or no solace to Ishmael in his "hypos," nor are they answers to the rest of the *Pequod*'s crew, who are also "Isolatoes"—"not acknowledging the common continent of men, but each *Isolato* living on a separate continent of his own" (*M-D*, 27:108).

There is no mistaking Melville's point: the truth that lives in the deep can be confronted only in the deep, and only by those courageous enough to forsake the "common continent" of conventional opinion. Thus, the *Pequod*'s crew is aptly termed an "Anacharsis Clootz deputation from all the isles of the sea, and all the ends of the earth, accompanying Old Ahab in the Pequod to lay the world's grievances before that bar from which not very many of them ever came back" (*M-D*, 27:108). In Ishmael and the rest of the *Pequod*'s crew, and in Ahab, the guiding, driving force of the *Pequod*'s voyage, Melville defines once and for all the conviction that has been growing since *Typee*, the conviction that we are eternal outcasts, alone and unloved in an alien world. At the same time, that crew, that captain, and that voyage dramatize the heroism and tragedy of our unsuccessful yet unyielding efforts to confront that alien world.

"The Lee Shore," that small "six-inch chapter" (*M-D*, 23:97) so concentrated in image, captures the essence of Melville's conception of this reckless and resolute quest for truth. The "treacherous, slavish shore," with its sirens' promise of "safety, comfort, hearthstone, supper, warm blankets, friends, all that's kind to our mortalities" is, indeed, "the ship's direst jeopardy" (*M-D*, 23:97). Bulkington, who stands at the helm "when on that shivering winter's night, the Pequod thrust her vindictive bows into the cold malicious waves" (*M-D*, 23:97), epitomizes for Ishmael that "mortally intolerable truth; that all deep, earnest thinking is but the intrepid effort of the soul to keep the open independence of her sea"

(*M-D,* 23:97). Yet even he gives us no cause to believe, or even hope, that the quest for truth will be successful, for the chapter that immortalizes Bulkington is, after all, his "stoneless grave" (*M-D,* 23:97).

At the very beginning of the *Pequod's* voyage, humanity's heroic search for truth is thus defined both as necessary and impossible. With the ill-fated experiences of Tommo, Taji, Redburn, and White-Jacket behind him, Melville no longer conceives of truth abiding in happy valleys, golden isles, fatherlands, or home; he has searched all the haunts of humanity and found no abiding truth. In *Moby-Dick,* the "highest truth" resides "in landlessness alone . . . , shoreless, indefinite as God" (*M-D,* 23:97), an assertion radically different from the assumptions underlying the earlier quests. As we discover in the rest of the novel, truth is thus conceived as transcendent to this world, forever beckoning to us all, forever eluding our grasp.

In the end, we can neither control nor understand our world, can neither control nor understand ourselves. The bold quest for truth, pursued so bravely in *Mardi,* does indeed come to an utter wreck in *Moby-Dick;* nevertheless, we have no better record of that quest or its failure than *Moby-Dick* itself. As Ishmael puts it in his eulogy to Bulkington, "better is it to perish in that howling infinite, than be ingloriously dashed upon the lee, even if that were safety!" (*M-D,* 23:97–98). When Ahab, Bulkington, Ishmael, and the rest of the *Pequod's* isolato crew set out from Nantucket, they leave behind them all those who "would craven crawl to land,"—and thus abandon all hope of finding a social, communal, "usable truth."

At the center of the *Pequod's* voyage and at the focal point of Ishmael's vision stands Ahab. If Ishmael embodies common humanity pushed to the extremity of survival, Ahab expresses the elemental, violent response of that "cornered" humanity. Surely this is the significance of his desperate, futile rage at all things that "task" and "heap" him, and just as surely it is the crew's recognition of their common cause with Ahab that makes them such willing agents to his "mad" purpose.

This identification of crew with Ahab, which so many readers seem to forget or wilfully overlook, includes Ishmael as well, and although Ishmael is unable to explain Ahab's hold upon the crew, he certainly is conscious of it and finds himself irresistibly drawn by the same force, like a "skiff in tow of a seventy-four" (*M-D,* 41; 162–63). Ishmael's explicit identification with Ahab's purpose calls into question those interpretations of the novel that see Ishmael as some kind of antithesis, or even antidote, to Ahab's monomaniacal imbalance. It is true that in "A Squeeze of the Hand" Ishmael can, at least for the moment, "forget all about our horrible oath" (*M-D,* 94:348), and he can even wish that such moments of peaceful squeezing of sperm were an eternity. But it is a mistake to confuse Ishmael's wishes here with the reality of his world. Ishmael himself is aware of how *un*common the "sweet and unctuous duty" (*M-D*, 94:348) of squeezing sperm is, and Ishmael himself terms this most pleasant of avocations "a strange sort of insanity" (*M-D*, 94:348).

It is in this context that we must read Ishmael's admonition to "squeeze ourselves universally into the very milk and sperm of kindness" (*M-D*, 94:349). Ishmael's dreams of "attainable felicity" are, as the narrative clearly demonstrates, no more accessible to Ishmael than they are to Ahab. Ishmael's dream of love, hope, and charity is rendered ludicrous by his nighttime vision of "long rows of angels in paradise, each with his hands in a jar of spermaceti" (*M-D*, 94:349), nor does Ishmael let us forget how "dearly purchased" is this whale that gives so much joy to him and his mates. This is the whale killed by Stubb on that fateful day when Pip is abandoned to the "heartless immensity" of the open sea (*M-D*, 93:347). Indeed, all Ishmael's philosophizing on the desirability of forever squeezing sperm follows directly upon his solemn recognition that Pip's fate prefigures his own "like abandonment" (*M-D*, 93:347).

The reverbrations of irony in the sequence of chapters beginning with "The Castaway" and ending with "The Try-Works" are complex and manifold. Captured whales and abandoned sailors, blue skies and drowned souls, squeezed hands and amputated toes all point to a world rich in promise but frighteningly careless of human wishes. The ambiguous world of "The Cassock," in which the whale phallus serves as an ironic reminder of shrunken vitality, calls into doubt Ishmael's appealing optimism in the previous chapter and casts an ambiguous, uncertain light upon his "conversion" in the chapter that follows—"The Try-Works." Those who find some conventional affirmation in the novel see in Ishmael's sermonette on darkness and the face of fire, with which he concludes the chapter, a rejection of Ahab's monomaniacal quest. But surely Ishmael's "conversion" is no more believable or persuasive than Father Mapple's exhortation—with which it forms a direct parallel. Ishmael's newfound wisdom is as fraught with inconsistency and is as untrue to his own experience as Mapple's earlier stated Christian ideals are.

The try-works chapter, which does indeed mark a significant point in the development of Ishmael's character, is in fact best seen in relationship to both "The Sermon" and "The Counterpane," the two chapters that help define his character at the beginning of the narrative. "Wrapped . . . in darkness," which perversely allows him to see more clearly "the redness, the madness, the ghastliness of others" (*M-D*, 96:354), Ishmael dozes off into another of those fitful, truth-giving dream states similar to that described in "The Counterpane." Again he awakes with a consciousness of "something fatally wrong": he is paralyzed by "a stark bewildered feeling, as of death" (*M-D*, 96:354). No longer a child, Ishmael attempts to rationalize his experience; "Look not too long in the face of the fire, O man!" he counsels in the very tone and rhetoric of a sea-going Mapple (*M-D*, 96:354), admonishing all men to "believe not the artificial fire, when its redness makes all things look ghastly" (*M-D*, 96:354).

Yet Ishmael's original gloss upon his experience is not satisfactory—even to him. His initial conviction that "to-morrow, in the natural sun, the skies will be bright" is first dimmed by his admission that "the sun hides not Virginia's Dismal Swamp" and then obscured totally by his recognition of "all the millions of miles of deserts and of griefs beneath the moon" (*M-D*, 96:354–55). What emerges from the dialectic of Ishmael's uncertain argument is the conclusion that "'All is vanity.' ALL" (*M-D*, 96:355). Ishmael at the end of "The Try-Works" is exactly where he was at the beginning: he is aboard the "rushing Pequod, freighted with savages, and laden with fire, and burning a corpse, and plunging into that blackness of darkness" (*M-D*, 96:354) that leads to Moby Dick. And insofar as the *Pequod* is "the material counterpart of her monomaniac commander's soul" (*M-D*, 96:354) Ishmael is as inextricably bound to Ahab's purposes as he ever was, however much he might wish otherwise.

This inescapable bonding between Ishmael and Ahab, at least unto death, is in fact the central paradigm of the book. The necessity of each to the other is absolute, for Ishmael is the historian of the *Pequod's* voyage, and at the center of that history stands Ahab. Their respective roles as actor and narrator define Ahab's and Ishmael's essential relationship throughout the novel, and the novel fittingly concludes with Ishmael stepping forth to tell us what he saw Ahab do. It is worth stating this central relationship between Ahab and Ishmael so directly because the overall complexity of the novel tends to prevent us from looking for anything straightforward in it, and it is easy to overlook or forget, or treat as unimportant, anything that we *can* understand.

Virtually every chapter in the novel either directly or indirectly consists of Ishmael's description of someone doing something. Even the expository chapters like "Cetology" and "Cutting In" and the meditative chapters like "The Whiteness of the Whale" and "The Pacific" perpetuate the book's central distinction between thought and the objects of thought. Thus, our knowledge of whales consists of accounts set down from firsthand experiences (rightly or erroneously remembered and reported), and reality itself seems to take its form from human perceptions.[6] Throughout *Moby-Dick* this polarized distinction between the report of an act or an object (Ishmael's function) and the act (Ahab's function) or object (Moby Dick's function) reveals Melville's persistent preoccupation with *the* philosophical quandary of Western thought from Kant on: how do we know what we know, and how do we know that what we "know" is "true?"

Melville's formulation of this perplexing and far-reaching philosophical question is, of course, most clearly seen in the chapter, "The Doubloon." The entire chapter takes the form of the thinly veiled philosophical question, "What is truth?" The chapter begins with the assumption that "some certain significance lurks in all things, else all things are little worth, and the round world itself but an empty cipher" (*M-D,* 99:358), and it ends with Pip's wry twofold conclusion: "I look, you look, he looks; we look, ye look, they look. . . . And I, you, and he; and we, ye, and they, are all bats . . . (*M-D,* 99:362).

Expressing on the one hand the self's highest ideals and on the other its bitterest disillusionment, this chapter brings to sharp focus the dynamics of Melville's tragic vision. The Enlightenment assumption that there is "some certain significance" in all things is undermined and finally brought down by Melville's post-Romantic conviction, based on bitter experience, that the individual has no certain avenue to that significance. In a world of infinite wonder we are imprisoned by our own ignorance and inherent limitations.

The doubloon, with all its rich emblazonings, from the first suggests all the things of this world. But scrutinized from every angle of vision, by Ahab, Starbuck, Stubb, Flask, the Manxman, Queequeg, Fedallah, and finally Pip, the coin does not give up its certain significance. It stands "untouchable and immaculate," beyond any interpretation, and every sunrise finds the doubloon where "sunset left it last" (*M-D,* 99:359).

In his treatment of humanity's attempts to perceive "reality," Melville owes a great deal to the eighteenth-century Enlightenment, and he leaves our own age a rich legacy, but his conception of humanity's tragic condition is distinctively of the nineteenth century.[7] Melville does not accept Kant's assumption of the consistency, and therefore reliability, of perceptions: Ahab, Starbuck, Stubb, and the others—each sees something radically different in the doubloon. But neither does Melville recognize the relativistic and symbolistic assumptions of our century. For all the renderings of the doubloon by Ahab and the others there is "but still one text. All sorts of men in one kind of world, you see" (*M-D,* 99:362).

The individual interpretations of the doubloon suggest the complete spectrum of human understanding as it attempts to grasp its world, and clearly Melville sees human understanding and response as varied—even contradictory. The coin, the whale, the world cannot be both what Ahab says they are and what, for example, Flask says they are. Thus the painful riddle of human life for Melville consists of the individual self's inability to determine whether one particular vision of reality is right or wrong. In a sardonic parody of Emerson's "Circles," Melville puts the chapter's and the book's riddling thesis in Ahab's mouth: "this round gold is but the image of the rounder globe, which, like a magician's glass, to each and every man in turn but mirrors back his own mysterious self" (*M-D*, 99:359). Melville's dramatization of the multiplicity of human responses to this mirroring, mysterious world is as varied and rich as his conception of character allows, but ultimately the spectrum of human response undergoes a double refraction into the novel's two dominating characters—Ahab and Ishmael. And it is upon them that we persistently focus our attention.

In "Moby Dick" and "The Whiteness of the Whale" we see side by side (a favorite rhetorical device of Melville's), Ahab's and Ishmael's responses to Moby Dick—the central mystery of this mystery-wrapped world. In "Moby Dick," we learn the history of "that murderous monster" that drove poor Ahab mad. So far as it is stylistically possible, Melville presents to us through Ishmael's narrative Ahab's direct experience with Moby Dick. Thus we see Moby Dick as Ahab the hunter would see him—a peculiar snow-white wrinkled forehead, and a high, "pyramidical white hump" with a deformed "sickle-shaped lower jaw" (*M-D*, 41:159). And Ahab's reaction to the "unexampled, intelligent malignity" of this largest of all prey is that of "inflamed, distracted fury" as he dashes at the whale, "blindly seeking with a six inch blade to reach the fathom-deep life of the whale" (*M-D*, 41:159).

Ahab's initial physical engagement with Moby Dick defines his character throughout the novel. Ahab comes to identify with the whale "not only all his bodily woes, but all his intellectual and spiritual exasperations" (*M-D*, 41:160). His "torn body and gashed soul" bleeding into each other, Ahab is made mad. Ahab's "monomania" is characterized not by an idea but by a commitment to action: he sails upon the *Pequod* "with the one only and all-engrossing object of hunting the White Whale" (*M-D*, 41:162). This murderous singleness of purpose characterizes Ahab throughout the narrative; every word he utters goads the crew in their unknowing but willing pursuit of Moby Dick, and his every act is seen as a step toward the ultimate confrontation with his "Job's whale."[8]

Ahab's dramatic dimensions are grand—even overwhelming—and it is easy to forget that his character is essentially unadorned. Ishmael's "poor old whale-hunter," still moving before him in "all his Nantucket grimness and shagginess," (*M-D*, 33:130), is elemental "man acting," stripped of complex motivations. Ahab's singleness of purpose defines both his grandeur and his madness. The man who can say "the path to my fixed purpose is laid with iron rails, whereon my soul is grooved to run" (*M-D*, 37:147) holds an irresistible attraction for those facing so many paths to so many questionable purposes. He attracts the crew of the *Pequod* And he attracts us. But the chapter in which Ahab speaks of his iron way contains the equally powerful image of the "Iron Crown of Lombardy" (*M-D*, 37:147). This crown, with its "far flashings" of dazzling, confounding power, suggests just how dear a price Ahab must pay for his single-minded dedication. Committed to his iron way, Ahab is neither spurred by sunrise nor soothed by sunset; committed wholly to one purpose, Ahab finds all other purposes meaningless: he is "damned, most subtly and most malignantly! damned in the midst of Paradise" (*M-D*, 37:147).

Throughout the body of the narrative Ahab maintains his unswerving pursuit of his nemesis. He gives up his pipe, that thing "meant for serene-ness, to send up mild white vapors among mild white hairs" (*M-D*, 30:114). He pores over his charts, plotting the course of Fate, prefiguring in his dreams his final confrontation with Moby Dick. Sleeping "with clenched hands" and waking "with his own bloody nails in his palms" (*M-D*, 44:174), Ahab is, indeed, self-crucifying—sacrificing his common humanity to his soul-devouring purpose.

In many ways Ahab's obsessive quest for his nemesis might be viewed as a protracted suicide. Seeking what all others flee (one thinks instantly of the Town-Ho story, of Captain Boomer, and of the *Rachel*), Ahab is whittled away to the very rudiments of his manhood. At times, as in "The Candles," he seems little more than vivified apparatus, cursed with a sense of his own wearing down. But Ahab is not "technological man," and Melville is not depicting the death struggle between doomed Nature and self-destructive technology. Quite to the contrary, as the *Pequod* approaches the ocean home of Moby Dick, Ahab becomes more and more primitive in his weapons, more and more naked in his defenses.

The scenes of Ahab with Perth, the carpenter, do not subdue, but rather intensify our sense of Ahab's naked mortality. Perth, the Carpenter-God, can give Ahab only what "chisel, file, and sand-paper" allow (*M-D*, 108:392). A perverse parody of the god Ahab both curses and worships in "The Candles," Perth is a "pure manipulator," working "by a kind of deaf and dumb, spontaneous literal process"—"living without premedi-tated reference to this world or the next" (*M-D*, 107:388). As such, he cannot comprehend, let alone satisfy, Ahab's order for a "complete man."

Ahab's ideal man answers to his own sense of what he lacks. Being old, crippled, and weak, he envisions a man "fifty feet high in his socks" with a chest "modelled after the Thames Tunnel" (*M-D*, 108:390). A seaman all his life, he longs for "legs with roots to 'em, to stay in one place"

(*M-D,* 108:390). Most important, his ideal man would have "no heart at all, brass forehead, and about a quarter of an acre of fine brains"—no eyes to see outward, but "a sky-light on top of his head to illuminate inwards" (*M-D,* 108:390). Lacking all these, Ahab prophetically concludes, "By heavens! I'll get a crucible, and into it, and dissolve myself down to one small, compendious vertebra. So" (*M-D,* 108:392).

On at least this one issue Ahab and Starbuck see eye to eye. In "The Quadrant" Starbuck reinforces this image of the crucible with his own observation on Ahab: "Old man of oceans! of all this fiery life of thine, what will at length remain but one little heap of ashes!" (*M-D,* 118:412). And it is this compression of Ahab's character into the lowest common denominator of selfhood that gives such intensity to his final confrontation with Moby Dick. Ahab's compression of self into one all-including act of revenge compresses his entire world. Between his first meeting with Moby Dick and his second, time for Ahab does not exist. Between the place of their first meeting and their second there is no space. And thus, insofar as we identify with Ahab, the three-day chase that concludes the novel's narrative action has all the density of life itself, with its myriad unspoken truths implicit in every breath, every move. Everything we know, imagine, and surmise about Ahab is instinct in his maddened harpooning of Moby Dick. In a literal sense there is only this *one* action in *Moby-Dick:* Ahab's harpooning of the white whale and being towed to his death. The will to this one act dominates Ahab's every motion, and in turn Ahab commands the *Pequod*'s every tack. It is not only fitting therefore, but also dramatically necessary, that the *Pequod* and her crew follow Ahab—to be wrapped in "the great shroud of the sea" (*M-D,* 135:469).

"One did survive the wreck," of course—Ishmael, the teller of the tale: the desperate young man of the three-hundredth lay who set out whaling to see the world comes back to report his findings. There is little simple about Ishmael's narration however, for Ishmael's "telling" proves to be a protracted, painful exercise in self-discovery—a digging with words at the roots of his own experience. In essence, Ishmael discovers what happened to him on the voyage only as he writes, and among other effects, this reflective-creative process accounts for the great sense of immediacy we feel in reading of events we know happened some time ago.

Ishmael clings tenaciously to humanity's impossible dream of knowledge—of good and evil. Ishmael goes to sea in an effort to discover and understand his world, and although Ishmael's motives and goals are not nearly so dramatic as Ahab's, they are no less compelling. And they are certainly as significant in their implications, for if Ahab's madness and failure to avenge himself upon Moby Dick dramatize the futility of all human endeavor and the fragility of all human purpose, Ishmael's persistent inability to understand his world—let alone relate it to us—dramatizes our incapacity for reaching any agreement with the "Fates" that anonymously rule the world.

This grim conclusion finally overwhelms Ishmael as surely as if he had literally drowned with the rest of the *Pequod*'s crew. The cruel irony of Ishmael's position is that he cannot cease in his efforts to explain the inexplicable. When he fails to grasp the "certain significance" that he asserts must lurk in all things, he cannot stop himself from sifting and resifting his evidence in search of some hint or clue that would at least explain his failure.

The *locus classicus* of Ishmael's approach and response to his world is "The Whiteness of the Whale" (Chapter 42). It immediately follows "Moby Dick," which states "what the whale was to Ahab" (*M-D,* 42:163), and in it Ishmael attempts to explain "what, at times, he was to me" (*M-D,* 42:163). Even in this opening statement Ishmael places a condition upon his knowledge, and the chapter proves to be little more than a catalogue of his confusions, misapprehensions, and doubts.[9] Even as Ishmael states the intensity of his feeling about the "rather vague, nameless horror" of Moby Dick's whiteness (*M-D,* 42:163), he despairs of "putting it in a comprehensible form" (*M-D,* 42:163). The rhetoric of suggestion and indirection is not a copy-book exercise, however, but a necessary outgrowth of Ishmael's philosophical predicament. As he ingenuously puts it: "how can I hope to explain myself here; and yet, in some dim, random way, explain myself I must, else all these chapters might be naught" (*M-D,* 42:163).

Ishmael's being—as well as his narrative—is at stake here, for his identity hinges upon his ability to perceive and express his world in terms of propositional certainty. Determined to find such certainty, Ishmael instead finds the whiteness of the whale—that "dumb blankness, full of meaning" (*M-D,* 42:169) that invites the closest scrutiny even as it blinds.

The central rhetorical device of this device-laden chapter is antithesis, which accurately reflects the inherent difficulty of Ishmael's search for some certain significance. As the chapter progresses, each of Ishmael's propositions gives rise to a contrary, yet seemingly valid proposition. The whiteness associated with "the innocence of brides, the benignity of age" (*M-D,* 42:163) is immediately balanced by the "ghastly whiteness" of the "white bear of the poles, and the white shark of the tropics" (*M-D,* 42:164). The "divine spotlessness and power" of its most august religious associations are countered by the "transcendent horrors" of the "white-shrouded bear or shark" (*M-D,* 42:164). "Subtlety appeals to subtlety" throughout the chapter as we strain to follow Ishmael to a conclusion. Yet, like Prufrock's, Ishmael's is a tedious argument leading to an overwhelming question. The chapter in which Ishmael would explain the whiteness of the whale, thereby explaining Moby Dick, his world and, therefore, our world, collapses in his inability to find constancy in his perceptions and feelings. Sublimity and terror, terror and sublimity intermingle, join, and give birth, not to certainty, but to "indefiniteness" (M-D, 42:169).

Ishmael has no way to resolve the antitheses of his own fertile mind. The chapter does not ultimately direct us to a choice between sublimity and terror, but rather directs us to the impossibility of such a choice. The whiteness that symbolizes a harlot Nature is "the visible absence of color, and at the same time the concrete of all colors" (M-D, 42:169). Not one or the other of these definitions, but both of them together make up the "colorless, all-color of atheism" from which Ishmael shrinks (M-D, 42:169). And the very indefiniteness of that colorless, all-color "shadows forth the heartless voids and immensities of the universe, and thus stabs us from behind with the thought of annihilation" (M-D, 42:169).

In the book's central paradigm, as it appears to us in "The Doubloon," the world is all kind of things to all men, but one thing unto itself. Imprisoned by personal perceptions, will, and ego, the individual self cannot test the authority of what Emerson calls an original relationship to the universe. In this context it is the agonizing and ultimately futile search for the self's original authority that Ishmael represents, and we don't find Ishmael in "The Doubloon," for example, simply because the chapter in its entirety defines Ishmael's condition: he is, finally—to paraphrase Emerson again—"man looking."

Ishmael's original, persistent, and final identity in the novel is that of perceiving, reflecting, inquiring, imaginative humanity. He does some things to be sure, but his function as member of the crew is infinitesimal compared to his function as historian of the voyage. Thematically he is, finally, Ahab's other self. He signs aboard Ahab's ship, he mans an oar in Ahab's boat the final day of the chase, and the tale he tells is Ahab's tale. He is Ahab's consciousness, and the two in their separate, but linked, pursuits of Moby Dick dramatize the self's attempt both to act in, and comprehend, the world's drama.

The whale that Ahab would destroy Ishmael would understand, yet these impulses are not contradictory, but complementary. Although Ahab can and does act against Moby Dick, he "comprehends" neither his adversary nor himself. Ishmael, endeavoring to comprehend his world, peers into the dark world of the Pequod's voyage, yet remains on the periphery of that world's activities and, finally, understanding neither

Ahab nor Moby Dick, is left revolving in a vortex of uncertainty and doubt. After the collapse of Ahab's quest and the sinking of the *Pequod* Ishmael looks out upon a world in which indeed, "all things are little worth, and the round world itself but an empty cipher" (*M-D*, 99:358).

Befitting his name, Ishmael throughout the novel is abandoned, adrift, isolated in some fashion or other from the world he would understand. He loses himself in mast-head reveries, the "problem of the universe" revolving in him (*M-D*, 35:139), while below on the quarterdeck mad Ahab steers his undeviating course. He holds the monkey rope for Queequeg, but it is Queequeg who stands ankle deep in blood, his own sharp spade and the sharks flashing round his floundering feet.

Even as one of many isolatoes aboard the *Pequod*, Ishmael stands out. When he, along with the rest of Starbuck's whaleboat crew, is lost at sea on the occasion of their very first lowering for whales, it is Ishmael who is the "most" lost. Starbuck, who usually appears as almost hysterical, remains calm and contrives to light the lamp, and Queequeg holds the lantern all through the night. But to Ishmael, even at this first lowering, the sea is an "almighty forlornness," the lantern an "imbecile candle," and Queequeg "the sign and symbol of a man without faith, hopelessly holding up hope in the midst of despair" (*M-D*, 48:195).

Even when Ishmael seems intimately involved in the activities of the *Pequod*, he stands truly apart from the rest of the crew, his separateness revealed in his inability to engage in any activity and take his identity from it. After he and the rest of Starbuck's crew are rescued by the cruising *Pequod*, Ishmael views the universe as a "vast practical joke" (*M-D*, 49:195), but his "desperado" vow to take a "cool, collected dive at death and destruction, and the devil fetch the hindmost" (*M-D*, 49:197) has more of hysteria than philosophy to it (the chapter is entitled "The Hyena"). Placing this chapter along side "A Squeeze of the Hand," we sense just how changeable Ishmael's "philosophy" can be, and if we examine all of the chapters in which Ishmael figures prominently, we find much less development and coherence than we do contradiction and confusion. The euphoria of "A Squeeze," the terror of "The First Lowering," the nihilism of "The Hyena," the musing abstraction of "The Mast-Head," the smug sermonizing of "The Try-Works" all go to make up Ishmael's divided mentality. In search of himself, Ishmael reaches for all beliefs, but reaching for all, he holds none—his peculiar intellectual position being "somewhat illustrative of that sagacious saying in the Fishery,—the more whales the less fish" (*M-D*, 37:328).

In "The Grand Armada," from which this last observation is taken, Ishmael presents what is probably the clearest picture we have of his self-conception and his relationship to the world. Surrounded by a herd of pursued and frightened whales, Ishmael is quick to compare his current predicament with his perennial condition. The circle upon circle of the whales' "consternations and affrights" correspond in his mind to the "tornadoed Atlantic" of his being. And the "peaceful concernments," the "dalliance and delight" of the "inscrutable creatures" at the center of the gallied herd, correspond to the "eternal mildness of joy" he finds "deep down and deep inland" within himself (*M-D*, 87:326).

It is attractive to think of a "mute calm" deep down and deep inland within the self, but as "The Mast-head" provides an image of a vertical fall into hard reality, so "The Grand Armada" presents the picture of a lateral boundary of horror: the revolving planets of unwaning woe are given immediate and all too palpable substance in the "universal commotion" of the gallied whales who are thrown into panic and fright by the thrashings of a harpoon-entangled whale. The composite portrait of Ishmael presented to us in "The Mast-Head" and "The Grand Armada" is that of man trapped—virtually paralyzed—in the midst of an inimical world. This Ishmael, man, is but a refugee in this world, dreaming of another.

Mast-head reveries of "sublime uneventfulness" do not etherealize the hard deck and the unforgiving sea, nor do mute calm musings alleviate the threat of a constricting, crushing world. In fact, dreams, reveries, and musings add to Ishmael's danger, for they distract him from an ever-insistent reality. No less certainly than Ahab, Ishmael has been wounded by his experience, and no less certainly than Ahab, Ishmael has his fixed purpose, although it runs on different rails than Ahab's. Ishmael looks for nothing less than the "certain significance" that *must* "lurk in all things."

Beset by "the overwhelming idea of the great whale himself" (*M-D*, 1:16), wanting to "see what whaling is" and to "see the world" (*M-D*, 16:69), Ishmael soon discovers his own limitations, for, he confesses, "there is no earthly way of finding out precisely what the whale really looks like" (*M-D*, 55:228). Ishmael's attempts to present us with a tolerable idea of the whale's living contours, beginning with the chapter "Cetology," are frustrated by our almost perfect ignorance of whales. In a brief burst of self-revealing irony Ishmael admits that his is "no easy task": "the classification of the constituents of a chaos, nothing less is here assayed" (*M-D*, 32:116–17). Diving into the same "unfathomable waters" as his predecessors, Cuvier, Hunter, and Lesson, Ishmael surfaces with the same "incomplete indications" that "torture us naturalists" (*M-D*, 32:117). The chapter in fact is a masterpiece of evasion. Because, he says, he will enlarge upon the sperm whale elsewhere, in this chapter he deals only with its name. The right whale too will be dealt with "elsewhere." Little is known of "Whalebone whales" (*M-D*, 32:122), and nothing is known of the razor back whale except his name. Sulphur bottoms are "seldom seen" and "never chased," (*M-D,* 32:123), of the killer whale "little is precisely known to the Nantucketer, and nothing at all to the professed naturalist" (*M-D,* 32:125), and "still less is known of the Thrasher than of the Killer" (*M-D,* 32:126).

Ishmael's inquiry into whales begins with the disclaimer "I promise nothing complete" (*M-D,* 32:118) and ends with the self-rationalizing assertion "God keep me from ever completing anything" (*M-D,* 32:128). But beneath the modesty of the first and the defensive assertion of the second statement lurks the true basis of Ishmael's uncomfortable discovery that "any human thing supposed to be complete, must for that very reason infallibly be faulty" (*M-D,* 32:118). Most briefly put, from Ishmael's standpoint all human endeavor is incomplete simply because we are mortal. These "incomplete indications" of truth with which mortals deal are ultimately the measure of our failure, not success, and as for "clear Truth," in Ishmael's eyes that is "a thing for salamander giants only to encounter" (*M-D,* 76:286).

In the course of his narrative Ishmael recounts various attempts to lift the veil and penetrate to the deep reality of the whale's ocean world. But again the central motif of his inquiries is our ignorance. The whale—considered anatomically, biologically, historically, pictorially, literarily, mythically, and religiously, is—for all that—a "portentous and mysterious monster" indifferent to puny human efforts. All pictures of all whales are "all wrong" (*M-D,* 55:225)—for a very good reason: "the living whale, in his full majesty and significance, is only to be seen at sea in unfathomable waters" (*M-D,* 55:227). In the very process of delineating everything that has been thought and said about whales, Ishmael affirms "that the great Leviathan is that one creature in the world which must remain unpainted to the last" (*M-D,* 55:228). Thus, the "Etymology" of the whale with which Ishmael opens his tale is not a record of progressive human enlightenment about the whale but a record of persistent ignorance.[10] Neither painter's tint nor writer's word can capture Leviathan.

Clearly Melville is presenting a grimly pessimistic picture of human aspiration and achievement: we recognize this even when we cannot define its causes or extent. But Melville is interested precisely in defining the causes and extent of our tragic nature. And strangely enough, the character to whom we must turn for an answer to this most far-reaching of questions is Pip, the lowly cabin boy. Pip is not on stage often during the course of the drama, but if we are to understand Ahab and Ishmael, we must understand Pip, the one person aboard the *Pequod* with whom both Ahab and Ishmael are identified. In a novel filled with elemental characters and "representative men" Pip is the most elemental of all and the most representative of the essential human condition. His stature, his color, his name, his age, his position aboard the *Pequod* all conspire to define Pip as Melville's "unaccommodated man"—a "poor, bare, forked animal."

Pip bears a family likeness to all the *Pequod*'s crew. It is he, we remember, who has the final, definitive word in "The Doubloon," articulating our blind, powerless gropings for significance while "God goes 'mong the worlds blackberrying" (*M-D*, 99:363). It is Pip in "Midnight, Forecastle," who prays: "Oh, thou big white God aloft there somewhere in yon darkness, have mercy on this small black boy down here; preserve him from all men that have no bowels to feel fear" (*M-D*, 40:155). Pip's concluding comments in "Midnight, Forecastle" and "The Doubloon" are glosses and intended to lead us to the truth. We are meant to see, if Pip doesn't, that the drinking, dancing, singing, and fighting among the crew spring explicitly, if unconsciously, from bowels of fear. And by the time we reach "The Doubloon," we are all mad enough to see the divine sense of Pip's paradigm of human perception: "I look, you look, he looks; we look, ye look, they look" (*M-D*, 99:362).

At the end of that chapter Pip goes on to point out that "I, you, and he; and we, ye, and they, are all bats" (*M-D*, 99:362). That is, we are both mad and blind in the brightest light the world has to offer. But Melville does not content himself with a mere encyclopedia on the vanity of human wishes. His ultimate purpose is to make a definitive statement on the root cause behind the futility of all human endeavor. This takes us back to the central characters of Ahab and Ishmael and rushes us to the novel's conclusion; and it is through Pip, seen as the elemental self, that we measure the implications of Ahab's death and Ishmael's survival. It is fearful, mind-shattered Pip who provides us with the necessary insight into the novel's conclusion, for from the broken shards of his experience and vision we can construct a likeness of Melville's awful purpose in this, his comprehensive statement on the human tragedy.

There is no more important chapter in all of *Moby-Dick* than "The Castaway." The entire novel is laden with hints, suggestions, foreshadowings, prophecies, and premonitions—the prefigurements of earlier chapters yielding the resolutions of later chapters, with a consequent "rhetorical resonance" that builds to the breaking point of the novel's conclusion. But "The Castaway" is not just another chapter of prefigurement. It is unique in that it contains an explicit depiction of both Ahab's and Ishmael's destinies, the lowly Pip providing "the sometimes madly merry and predestinated craft with a living and ever accompanying prophecy of whatever shattered sequel might prove her own" (*M-D*, 93:344).

The long paragraph at the beginning of the chapter that describes Pip's innocent, bright nature and the effects of whaling upon it might well be taken as Ishmael's definition of essential humanity, and the chapter in its totality depicts the fall of humanity not according to Christian myth, but according to Melville. In Melville's conception, there is neither myth nor religious doctrine to cushion our fall, it being, rather, the necessary condition of existence that we fall—inexplicably, inevitably, and irretrievably.

Pip's innocence, which would illuminate all life as a celebration and a holiday, is "most sadly blurred" by the "panic-striking business in which he had *somehow unaccountably become entrapped*" (*M-D*, 93:345; my emphasis). The Pip who "had once enlivened many a fiddler's frolic on the green" and "with his gay ha-ha! had turned the round horizon into one star-belled tambourine" (*M-D*, 93:345) at sea becomes Father Mapple's castaway among castaways. Abandoned by Stubb to the sea, Pip finds the "intense concentration of self in the middle of such a heartless immensity" (*M-D*, 93:347) more than he can bear. No longer a "star-belled tambourine" the "ringed horizon began to expand around him miserably" (*M-D*, 93:347) and although in the end he is "saved," "the sea had jeeringly kept his finite body up, but drowned the infinite of his soul" (*M-D*, 93:347).

Stated in these general terms, Pip's fall from innocence and his drowned soul do constitute a "living and ever accompanying prophecy" of the *Pequod*'s and her crew's "shattered sequel." But more explicitly, Pip's two misadventures in Stubb's whaleboat prefigure precisely what happens to Ahab and Ishmael on the fatal third day of the chase. In the first instance, in the "involuntary consternation of the moment" of the whale's being struck (*M-D*, 93:345), Pip leaps from the boat, entangling himself in the lethal line Melville so carefully describes in Chapter 60. Although Ishmael describes the incident in some detail and although we are allowed to ponder over its significance, he insists that "all passed in a flash. In less than half a minute, this entire thing happened" (*M-D*, 93:346). Although Pip on this occasion is saved, and Ahab, at the conclusion of the novel, isn't, we see in Pip's speechless, blue, choked face, close up and in time-suspended detail, the end of Ahab, some forty-two chapters later. Then Ahab too is caught round the neck by a flying turn of line and "*voicelessly* as Turkish mutes bowstring their victims, . . . shot out of the boat, ere the crew knew he was gone" (*M-D*, 135:468; my emphasis).

Melville reasserts the identity of Pip and Ahab in "The Cabin." Ahab admits openly to Pip that "there is that in thee, poor lad, which I feel too curing to my malady" (*M-D*, 129:436), and Pip's protestation of loyalty and faithfulness make Ahab exclaim, "If thou speakest thus to me much more, Ahab's purpose keels up in him" (*M-D*, 129:436). What is at stake here is Ahab's humanity. It is not that Ahab lacks humanity; on the contrary, he consciously sacrifices it in order to face the inhuman and heartless immensity of the sea.[11]

Ahab's uncharacteristic recognition of his own humanity in "The Cabin" prompts his further reflections upon life and humanity in "The Symphony"—the scene of Ahab's anguished anagnorisis before the tragic catastrophe of the hunt. Here, three chapters after "The Cabin," Ahab calls up memories of his own "green land" and "bright hearth-stone" (*M-D*, 132:444). But Ahab has suffered through "forty years on the pitiless sea!" (*M-D*, 132:443), and as Ishmael observed of Pip, "the panic-striking business in which he had somehow unaccountably become entrapped, had most sadly blurred the brightness ... " (*M-D*, 93:345), and he too was "destined to be luridly illumined by strange wild fires, that fictitiously showed him off to ten times the natural lustre" (*M-D*, 93:345).

The Ahab we see in "The Symphony" is bewildered, fallen *man*. The serene world of inseparable sea and sky (that reminds him of his own lost youth) surrounds Ahab, but does not include him. The "immortal infancy, and innocency of the azure," the "sweet childhood of air and sky," are "oblivious ... of Ahab's close-coiled woe!" (*M-D*, 132:442). It is a "step-mother world" that can only recall in Ahab memories of a past innocence: it cannot carry him back to that innocence. Thus, this moment's respite from "forty years of privation, and peril, and storm-time" has as much pain to it as joy. Ahab sees, for the first and last time, what he had "only half-suspected, not so keenly known ... before" (*M-D*, 132:443). He has lived in a "masoned, walled-town of a Captain's exclusiveness" (*M-D*, 132:443), cut off from sympathy with the "green country without," isolated from the young girl whom he widowed when he wed (*M-D*, 132:443). Seeing himself in "the magic glass" of Starbuck's human eye, Ahab sees himself as a "forty years' fool,"—as a wearied "Adam, staggering beneath the piled centuries since Paradise" (*M-D*, 132:444).

"The Symphony" dramatizes Ahab's tragic recognition of his own fallen nature: "like a blighted fruit tree he shook, and cast his last, cindered apple to the soil" (*M-D*, 132:444). But Melville's concept of the fall has no accommodating Christian doctrine to rationalize it and make even cindered apples palatable. Ultimately, Melville has, and can offer, no explanation for Ahab. Ahab himself puts the question bluntly and unanswerably: "'What is it, what nameless, inscrutable, unearthly thing is it; what cozening, hidden lord and master, and cruel remorseless emperor commands me ...?'" (*M-D*, 132:444–45). Ahab's anguished question,

"Is it I, God, or who, that lifts this arm?" (*M-D*, 132:445), remains unanswered to the very end of the book.

The best gloss we have to Ahab's character is found in the blue, choked face of a cabin boy named Pip. Melville dramatizes in Ahab's action the voiceless absolute of fact. Will, aspiration, motive, opinion, desire, dream, and dread are all drowned in the annihilating moment of event. In *Moby-Dick*, all events and human acts—not just that greatest human event, death—constitute that "undiscovered country, from whose bourn no traveler returns." Ahab's recognition, even as he prepares to dart the harpoon, that his pursuit of Moby Dick has *no* "certain significance" makes his final act great and tragic; his simultaneous recognition that nothing conclusive ever can or will be said about that act gives his final utterance poetic substance: "Thus, I give up the spear!" (*M-D*, 135:468).

Not all coffins do sink and "one did survive the wreck" ("Epilogue": 470), but Ishmael's survival is something quite other, although not less, than what most readers make of it. Ishmael's survival at the end of the novel can be considered "salvation" only in the grimmest, most ironic sense. He knows little more of the *Pequod*'s captain and his mad aspirations, little more of whales and whaling than he did when he announced to Captain Peleg "I want to see what whaling is. I want to see the world" (*M-D*, 16:69). To view the ending from another perspective, the young sailor who is rescued at the end of the book by the "*devious-cruising Rachel*" ("Epilogue":470) becomes the wandering, forlorn sailor who at the beginning of the novel asks us to call him "Ishmael." He is doomed, like the Ancient Mariner, to repeat his tale again and again, counting over the beads of his life, looking for someone to tell him what they mean.[12]

Again we turn to Pip's experience in "The Castaway" for enlightenment. If Pip's first experience in Stubb's boat forms a close analogue to Ahab's end, his second experience is a finely wrought prefigurement and gloss upon Ishmael's end. Even as Ishmael tells us of Pip's misadventures, he focusses the reader's attention upon himself by observing that "in the sequel of the narrative, it will then be seen what like abandonment befell myself" (*M-D* 93:347).

The parallels between Pip's and Ishmael's abandonment at sea are indeed many. The second time Pip jumps from the whaleboat, Stubb is "but too true to his word" (*M-D*, 93:346), and Pip is left behind on the open sea. In like manner, Ishmael is "tossed out" of Ahab's boat on the last day of the chase and "dropped astern" ("Epilogue":470). Further, what is to become the most traumatic experiences for both Pip and Ishmael takes place in a mockingly beautiful and serene world. When Pip jumps, it is a "beautiful, bounteous, blue day; the spangled sea calm and cool, and flatly stretching away, all round, to the horizon, like gold-beater's skin hammered out to the extremest" (*M-D*, 93:346), an image of serenity and innocence echoed in Ahab's description of the morning of the third day's chase: "were it a new-made world, and made for a summer-house to the angels, and this morning the first of its throwing open to them, a fairer day could not dawn upon that world" (*M-D*, 135:460). Emphatically, both Pip and Ishmael are castaways in Eden, irrevocably cut off from that which they most desire, tortured by the unreachable nearness of their almost remembered dreams.

This seeming beautiful world becomes but a "heartless immensity" to Pip and Ishmael, cast away and drowning in an "intense concentration of self." But here Melville makes a fine and crucial distinction between the isolated selves of Pip and Ishmael, one that has the greatest significance for our understanding of Ishmael's role as narrator. Pip in his isolation is "carried down alive to wondrous depths," and witnesses "God's foot upon the treadle of the loom" (*M-D*, 93:347). In that brief but powerful poetic dive at the truth that underlies the book's reality, Melville evokes all that Ahab learns but can never tell as he is towed to pieces by "that damned whale." In contrast, although Ishmael responds to and describes Pip's experience, he himself never penetrates those depths.

Cast upon the same sea as Pip and Ahab, Ishmael responds in a far different way. To the end, Ishmael is an observer of life's drama, not an actor in it. The salient feature of his "Epilogue" is that it reveals Ishmael's radical separation from the essential, climactic event of the narrative. Thrown from Ahab's boat, Ishmael is left "on the margin of the ensuing scene," and although he is "in full sight of it" ("Epilogue":470) he is not part of it. Although in "The Grand Armada" Ishmael proclaims that amid the "tornadoed Atlantic" of his being he is able to "centrally disport in mute calm" (*M-D*, 87:326), by the end of the book we are forced to assess the price of Ishmael's detachment. Forever on the margin of things, Ishmael is with neither his captain nor his crewmates when they meet their ends, and the most remarkable event of this most remarkable voyage remains for Ishmael merely a scene. "Like another Ixion" ("Epilogue":470), Ishmael revolves round the axis of his drowned world, and from that world's "vital centre" ("Epilogue":470) springs the only reality he will ever know—a coffin lifebuoy.

Melville takes great pains to emphasize the gratuitous, pointless, and most certainly inexplicable nature of Ishmael's survival. Surely no one would question the apocalyptic pessimism of the first English edition of the novel, which concluded without benefit of epilogue, and whatever reasons Melville might have had for including the "Epilogue" in the first American edition, it is wholly in keeping with the tragic mood of drowning aspiration that prevails at the end of "The Chase—Third Day."

The epigraph from Job identifies Ishmael with the messengers of doom in that bleakest of all Biblical stories—messengers who survive the general wreck of Job's world solely in order to tell him of his losses. So far as I know, no Biblical commentators consider those disaster-shrouded messengers as symbolic of continuing faith, hope, and charity; in reading Job, one can scarcely refrain from identifying the messengers with despair itself, which makes us marvel all the more at Job's persistent belief. If, indeed, there is an analogue to Job himself in the "Epilogue" to *Moby-Dick*, it lies in those readers who are unswervingly committed to some saving, positive vision—no matter the oceans of evidence to the contrary.

Melville, in fact, goes out of his way in the "Epilogue" to tell us that Ishmael's survival is one not of purpose but of accident: "*it so chanced*" that it was Ishmael "*whom the Fates ordained to take the place of Ahab's bowsman*" ("Epilogue":470). It does even less for one's sense of Ishmael's purposive survival to be told that "Ahab's bowsman" was Fedallah, for this identification of Ishmael with Fedallah points to death, not life. A prophet of death throughout the book, Fedallah last appears to prefigure the imminent death of Ahab, the sinking of the *Pequod*, and the drowning of her crew.

Although the hearse that is Ahab's and the hearse that is his crew's are not for Ishmael, the ironies of his "salvation" are incalculable, for he is saved by a coffin. He is saved, yes, but the terms of his survival are so minimal that they moot the meaning of existence itself. If we look back through the novel to the various rescues at sea, we become all too aware of how tenuous life is. But how much more fortuitous is his rescue by the *Rachel* in the "Epilogue"—the Rachel who, "weeping for her children, because they were not" (*M-D*, 128:436) "*in her retracing search after her missing children, only found another orphan*" ("Epilogue":470).

It is this orphan who tells the tale, *Moby-Dick*. It is this Ishmael, the surviving orphan, who is condemned to ponder, reflect upon, and attempt to explain events that he can't possibly understand. And we should not be fooled. Although Ishmael from time to time in *Moby-Dick* proclaims his commitment to the "attainable felicity" of "the heart, the bed, the table, the saddle, the fire-side, the country" (*M-D*, 94:349), in fact, the only references in the narrative that show us Ishmael after the events of the *Pequod*'s voyage show him as a whaler, not a landsman.[13]

In "A Bower in the Arsacides" (Chapter 102) there is a passing reference by Ishmael to being aboard a whaler when "a small cub Sperm Whale was once bodily hoisted to the deck for his poke or bag, to make sheaths for the barbs of the harpoons, and for the heads of the lances"

(*M-D,* 102:373). One might argue, in fact, that the very casualness of this allusion gives weight to our vision of Ishmael as a continuing, if unwilling, whaler. But we needn't belabor the point. In the preceding chapter, "The Decanter," Ishmael describes a "fine gam" at midnight "somewhere off the Patagonian coast" between the crew of his ship and the crew of the *Samuel Enderby*—"long, very long after old Ahab touched her planks with his ivory heel" (*M-D,* 101:370). There is camaraderie here to be sure, as they drink flip "at the rate of ten gallons the hour" (*M-D,* 101:370). But there is little of the attainable felicity of hearth, bed, fireside, table, and country. When a squall hits, all hands are called to reef topsails, during the course of which, as Ishmael recalls, "we ignorantly furled the skirts of our jackets into the sails, so that we hung there, reefed fast in the howling gale, a warning example to all drunken tars" (*M-D,* 101:370).

Ishmael's tragic commitment to understanding his world and Ahab's tragic commitment to acting out his own will in the world together form the essence of Melville's tragic vision. The fearful idea that haunted the darker pages of *Typee, Omoo, Mardi, Redburn,* and *White-Jacket* is brought to full light in *Moby-Dick:* we can fully understand neither ourselves nor our world, and are doomed to live in ignorance and to die in ignorance. Ahab's pursuit of that great white whale remains "something other" than what any of us can make of it, and we are all orphans clinging to our coffins in perilous seas, waiting for some devious-cruising *Rachel.*

This is Melville's vision in *Moby-Dick,* and it is blinding in its brightness. There is no comfort here for the transcendentalist, for whom idea, act, and reality are one. But there is not much comfort for the existentialist or the phenomenologist, either; in *Moby-Dick,* human acts are pointless, not self-defining, and acts of consciousness are opaque, not self-justifying. Equally, there is little comfort for the literary critic committed to rationalizing Melville's world and presenting it "whole." That is something Melville himself could not do. And there, I suggest, lies the least comfort of all—in Melville's own mind. The man who defined the boldest aspirations of humanity somehow found the unique courage to define their utter wreck. In *Moby-Dick,* neither the irresistibility of those aspirations nor the inevitability of our failure to realize them is in any way muted. And that is what makes it the profound work of tragic art that it is.

CHAPTER

5

Pierre: Drowned Souls

In tremendous extremities human souls are like drowning
men; well enough they know they are in peril; well enough
they know the causes of that peril;—nevertheless, the sea is
the sea, and these drowning men do drown.

—*Pierre*, XXII, iii:303[1]

The appearance of *Pierre* in 1852 is perhaps the most astonishing
event in Melville's publishing career. Having produced six long, intellectually demanding novels in five years, he scarcely paused before
throwing himself into the self-consuming furnace of *Pierre*. The bold
quest for "Truth" that began with *Typee* and led Melville unflinchingly,
although not painlessly, to the awful realizations of *Moby-Dick* had
brought him face to face with the utter wreck he had fearfully foretold
in *Mardi*. Rather than retreat into silence in 1852, rather than rationalize
the undesired and undesirable conclusions of *Moby-Dick* into more palatable formulations, in *Pierre* Melville surveys all their most horrifying
implications, providing a blueprint for the tales of darkness and disillusionment that follow. In this sense *Pierre* is a most important work to
study, for in spite of all its obvious shortcomings as a work of art, it is the
link between Melville's two careers as a writer. It is on the one hand the
post mortem and epitaph to Melville's heroic vision, and on the other it
is the first chapter to Melville's extended anatomy of a nightmare world
devoid of certainty, justice, and truth, a world lit not by light, but rather
darkness visible.

Following immediately upon *Moby-Dick, Pierre* historically has suffered critically by the inevitable comparisons. But because these simplistic comparative judgments are so inevitable and so strong emotionally and aesthetically, it is all the more imperative that the serious reader of Melville try to see beyond them, to make some judgments about why Melville wrote a book like *Pierre* after *Moby-Dick*, and why, after *Pierre*, Melville's fiction adopts forms, themes, situations, and characters that are radically different from those in the earlier fiction.

In virtually every regard *Pierre* is radically different from Melville's earlier novels. The exuberant romanticism of *Typee* and *Mardi* has given way to the puerile sentimentalism of Pierre, soon to be metamorphosed into his despair and grim misanthropy. The metaphysical quests of *Mardi* and *Moby-Dick* have yielded to Pierre's psychosexual, self-maddening inquiry and Plotinus Plinlimmon's self-negating, pseudo-transcendental pamphlet concluding with "If—." The open expanse of sea in *Moby-Dick*, however frightening in its mystery, provided scope to humanity's thirst for achievement and discovery, but *Pierre* is a landlocked and claustrophobic book, the relative expanse of Saddle Meadows giving way quickly to the inexorable narrowing walls of the New York City streets, the Apostles' garret, and finally the cramped prison cell that also serves as charnel house. Notably, the dominant images of *Pierre* are the Memnon Stone, with its threat of crushing weight, and the Enceladus Rock, trapped by the earth in a gesture of futile defiance and aspiration. In *Pierre* the near deaths, metaphorical deaths, alter-ego deaths, and spiritual deaths of the earlier fiction become absolute. Isabel, Lucy, Pierre, Pierre's mother, his cousin—indeed, the entire Glendinning family line— at the end of the book are all dead.

The culminative tragic vision in *Moby-Dick* is that of man forever at odds with himself, set apart from his fellow man, and cast adrift in a pitiless world that he can never understand; in *Pierre*, there is no mysterious whale, no vengeful god, no mad captain, no demon Parsee, no villain at all, properly speaking. There is only Pierre himself to blame for his dismal end, and if his "singularly developed character and most singular life-career" (*P*, I, iv:12) is tragic at all, it is a tragedy that Melville asserts we all share.

These marked changes are not gratuitous or casual. *Pierre* and its protagonist turn in upon themselves precisely because Melville's bold attempt in *Moby-Dick*—to fathom all nature, all human experience, all meaningfulness in the universe—collapsed upon itself. The essential incoherence of the variable self, and the consequent blindness of the self to the implications of action, which underlay the engulfing tragedy of *Moby-Dick*'s conclusion, become the explicit starting point of *Pierre*, and the full depth of Melville's tragic vision in *Moby-Dick* is sounded in the working out of Pierre's fate.[2]

Although these changes are certainly significant, perhaps the most far-reaching innovation in *Pierre* is Melville's abandonment of the first-person protagonist-narrator for a third-person voice that is at once omniscient and personal, akin in many ways to the narrative voice in George Eliot's *Middlemarch*—sympathetic, yet critical, worldly wise, yet powerless to affect the world he describes.[3] The narrator's voice is so dominant in controlling our responses to *Pierre* that, like the narrator in *Middlemarch*, he virtually becomes the central figure in the novel. However disembodied he might be, his opinions and judgments are authoritative, and the massive, sometimes heavy-handed, irony that pervades the narrative springs from the narrator's seeing through, and allowing us to see through, Pierre's illusions and disillusionments. All Melville's earlier works raised the question of what lay behind the appearance and illusions of this world: *Pierre* begins with the assumption that there is nothing in this world but appearance, and no appearance in this world that is not illusion.

The opening chapters of *Pierre* strike one as rather badly written, sentimental pastoralism. The archaic, overly formal and hyperbolic exchanges between Lucy and Pierre seem, and are, excessive, and Melville falls embarrassingly short in his attempt to create a neo-Spenserean mood of sensuous, yet spiritual, love. Melville seems out of his element in attempting to create the rapture of young love, and the narrator's extravagant paean to Love in Book II, Chapter iv does little more to persuade us of his conviction. In the very act of describing for us "the choicest drop that Time has in his vase" (*P*, II, iv:32) the narrator points to the instability of love that "begins in joy," but "may end in grief and age, and pain and need, and all other modes of human mournfulness" (*P*, II, iv:33). Pierre's and Lucy's laugh-filled love ride in the country carries them not to the "immutable eternities of joyfulness...in this dream-house of the earth" (*P*, II, v:36), as Pierre envisions, but rather to the first "foretaste...of endless dreariness" (*P*, II, v:37), that leads them ultimately to prison and death.

From the very beginning of the novel the narrator casts doubt upon Pierre's and Lucy's "mutual reflections of...boundless admiration and love" (*P*, I, i:4). His voice is persistently ironic, if not actually sardonic, as he regularly reminds us of what the world holds in store for youthful enthusiasts and idealists. In some ways the narrator's position in *Pierre* seems much like that of the narrator in *Redburn*, who, recounting the adventures of his own first voyage, sees through his youthful illusions and mistakes. But the implicit continuity between the younger and the older Redburn has no counterpart in *Pierre*. The narrator sounds as though he were forever old, and the distance between his perspective and Pierre's, so great at the beginning of the novel, by the end of the novel seems infinite. Pierre, unlike Redburn, does not learn from his experience and become a wiser, though sadder, man. He is simply annihilated by his mistakes.

The narrator hints at Pierre's dark future when he describes Pierre standing on the "noble pedestal" of enthusiasm and self-confidence and asks whether "Fate hath not just a little bit of a small word or two to say in this world" (*P*, I, iv:12). Again, in describing Pierre's "ruddiness, and flushfulness, and vain gloriousness of . . . soul," the narrator immediately points to the "foreboding and prophetic lesson taught, not less by Palmyra's quarries, than by Palmyra's ruins," which "Time seized and spoiled" (*P*, I, ii:8). Blessed with a noble family name, with wealth, position, and authority, with a strong body and "a delicate and poetic mind" (*P*, I, ii:5), Pierre is indeed "a noble American youth" (*P*, I, iv:13), "the complete polished steel of the gentleman, girded with Religion's silken sash" (*P*, I, ii:7). Yet he is on a collision course with ruin from the very first page of the novel.

This radical inconsistency between Pierre's great advantages and his compulsive pursuit of disaster has made many readers shrink from the book as a futile exercise in perversity and faulty motivation. Yet early in the novel the narrator warns "any man" from dreaming "that the last chapter was merely intended for a foolish bravado, and not with a solid purpose in view" (*P*, I, iv:12); and if we step back from the book long enough and far enough to see its essential composition, we see this "solid purpose" clearly.

The initial problem in *Pierre* is clear: the vision of life given to Pierre by his mother, his father, his family traditions and advantages, does not conform to the world as Pierre finds it. His mother—"a singular example of the preservative and beautifying influences of unfluctuating rank, health, and wealth" (*P*, I, ii:4)—certainly has not prepared Pierre in any way for the moral decisions he finds thrust upon him. Her relationship with Pierre is explicitly and consciously founded upon self-deception and delusion and is wholly dependent upon Pierre's remaining ignorant and consistently "docile." In his "glide toward maturity" (*P*, I, ii:6) Pierre gets no more help from his father than from his mother. Dying when Pierre was twelve, Mr. Glendinning is, in Pierre's recollection, "without blemish, unclouded, snow-white, and serene; Pierre's fond personification of perfect human goodness and virtue" (*P*, IV, i:68).

The only thing wrong with these cumulative ideals passed on to Pierre by his parents is that they are false, as the narrator constantly reminds us. The pride of family lineage and accumulated property is for the narrator the "unimaginable audacity of a worm that but crawls through the soil he so imperially claims!" (*P*, I, iii:11). The narrator makes clear that Pierre's idealization of his father springs from an accident of time and place. Pierre is twelve when his father dies, and "at that period, the Solomonic insights have not poured their turbid tributaries into the pure-flowing well of the childish life" (*P*, IV, i:68). By a similar accident of fate Nature planted Pierre in the country and, thus, "secludedly nurtured, Pierre, though now arrived at the age of nineteen, had never yet become so thoroughly initiated into that darker, though truer aspect of things, which an entire residence in the city from the earliest period of life, almost inevitably engraves upon the mind of any keenly observant and reflective youth of Pierre's present years" (*P*, IV, i:69). The narrator's asides, allusions, and assertions define Pierre as a twelve-year-old boy trapped in a nineteen-year-old body, and the lessons of Pierre's parents and the ideals of his childhood are the worst possible preparations for his life as an adult, simply because these lessons and these ideals do not prepare him to make moral decisions.

The moral crisis, the all-desolating and withering blast for Pierre, is the discovery of Isabel, who claims to be the illegitimate daughter of Pierre's father and, hence, the missing sister who heretofore had seemed to Pierre the "one hiatus" in the "illuminated scroll of his life" (*P*, I. ii:7). Perhaps nothing is more mysterious in *Pierre* than Isabel's easy, virtually uncontested, possession of Pierre: one look, one letter, and one conversation are all that is required to make him hers unto death. The Pierre who sets out for his fair Lucy's, buoyed by the conviction that "it is a flawless, speckless, fleckless, beautiful world throughout; joy now, and joy forever!" (*P*, III, iii:60), turns round at her gate and, on a vague presentiment, returns home with the letter in his hand that will seal his fate.

The letter Isabel sends Pierre is shamelessly sentimental and only semi-coherent, but neither, nor both, qualities prevent Pierre's implicit belief in its contents. Nor, having recollected the mysterious history of the chair portrait, as presented to him by his Aunt Dorothea, does Pierre doubt or question the full story of Isabel's early life as she presents it to him, although it is rambling, vague, and at least half mad.

Although this early characterization of Isabel is clumsy and unconvincing, there is an energy contained in the depiction of these two star-crossed lovers that transcends Melville's rather inept appropriation of a threadbare literary convention and points to the "solid purpose" of the novel. In being forced to choose between fair-haired, blue-eyed Lucy and dark-haired, olive-cheeked Isabel, Pierre must choose between the familiar and the strange, the social and the sexual, the predictable and the inexplicable—in short, between all that is conventional and acceptable and all that is original and, therefore, threatening to his society. The seeming gulf between the domestic melodrama of the first half of the

vs. convent

novel and the dark satire of the last half is bridged by this thematic consistency. Pierre, as rebellious son and as earnest young writer, is one in his determination to find, and go his own against, the prevailing currents of opinion and behavior.

Pierre's initial trauma springs from his conclusion that his father, the saint, had been a social and sexual hypocrite, revealing his own true self only to Isabel's mother and, briefly, to the artist-friend who painted the chair portrait. But the ambiguities of his father's situation are visited upon Pierre as well, and his greatest trauma results from his volatile and ambivalent feelings for Isabel. On the one hand "divine commands" of the "heaven-begotten Christ" compel him "to befriend and champion Isabel, through all conceivable contingencies of Time and Chance" (*P*, V, v:106). But at the same time, Pierre is aware of "insidious inroads of self-interest" (*P*, V, v:106), whereby "he was assured that, in a transcendent degree, womanly beauty, and not womanly ugliness, invited him to champion the right" (*P*, V, vii:107).

Pierre's proposed pseudo-marriage to Isabel captures the perfect ambiguity of his altruistic and his sexual attraction to her. Consciously put forward as the only way for them both to "reach up alike to a glorious ideal . . . without jeopardizing the ever-sacred memory" of their father (*P*, XII, i:192), Pierre's proposal is as sexually explicit as Melville dared write, leading Pierre to "a terrible revelation":

> he imprinted repeated burning kisses upon her; pressed hard her hand; would not let go her sweet and awful passiveness.
> Then they changed; they coiled together, and entangledly stood mute. (*P*, XII, i:192)

Melville, however, wasn't primarily interested in writing a book about incest. In fact, *Pierre* is no more concerned with incest than *Moby-Dick* is concerned with sperm-whale stocks. Ultimately, the incest plot is merely the vehicle that allows Melville to explore the nature of human morality: the means by which a person makes judgments and life decisions, and the effects those decisions have on the person making them. Thus, the mental and moral process leading up to Pierre's "marriage" to Isabel is of far greater importance than the "wedding," which, if it does indeed take place, is not described in the book at all.

Brought up in an atmosphere of absolute morality, Pierre, not surprisingly, is absolutely confused by the "fall" of his father and the ambiguity of his own moral position. Stricken by the dissolution of all formerly held convictions, Pierre is "profoundly sensible that the fair structure of the world must, in some then unknown way, be entirely rebuilded again, from the lower-most cornerstone up" (*P*, V, i:87). All the teachings of his parents, the precepts of religion, the advantages of birth, wealth, and position are overturned and made nothing in Pierre's mind as he searches in his soul for that "indefinite but potential faith, which could rule in the interregnum of all hereditary beliefs, and circumstantial persuasions" (*P*, V, i:87).

Like the Ishmael of *Moby-Dick*'s "Epilogue," Pierre is abandoned at the very center of his world, lost in ignorance and self-doubt, an object of utter indifference to the silent forces surrounding him,[4] and *Pierre* explores the moral crisis that develops when "all hereditary beliefs, and circumstantial persuasions" are exposed as false and no new beliefs of comparable authority arise to take their place. This crisis of belief, with all its despair and anxiety is, of course, endemic to nineteenth-century British literature: we need think only of Carlyle, Tennyson, Browning, and Arnold. But to find the source of Melville's definition of the problem we need look no further than Concord, Massachusetts, no deeper than into the pale blue eyes of Ralph Waldo Emerson.

Pierre is Emerson's transcendental man, taken out of the study and put into the street by Melville. Whether he wants to or not, Pierre finds himself in an original relationship with his universe. Casting aside the dead hand of the past—"all the convenient lies and duty—subterfuges of the diving and ducking moralities of this earth" (*P*, V, vi:107)—Pierre "staggered back upon himself, and only found support in himself" (*P*, V, i:89). Finding in himself "a divine unidentifiableness, that owned no earthly kith or kin" (*P*, V, i:89), Pierre becomes, in his crisis, Emerson's self-reliant man.

As we might expect, self-reliance means something notably different to Melville than it does to Emerson.[5] Like Emerson's transcendental man, Pierre is led by his intuitive mystical attraction to Isabel into "trances and reveries" that carry him further and further away from "the assured element of consciously bidden and self-propelled thought" (*P*, IV, v:84) and deeper and deeper into the world of "irresistible intuitions" (*P*, V, i:85). In a passage that I think Emerson would have been proud to own, Melville lets us examine the assumptions underlying Pierre's thought and action:

> From without, no wonderful effect is wrought within ourselves, unless some interior, responding wonder meets it. That the starry vault shall surcharge the heart with all rapturous marvelings, is only because we ourselves are greater miracles, and superber trophies than all the stars in universal space. Wonder interlocks with wonder; and then the confounding feeling comes. No cause have we to fancy, that a horse, a dog, a fowl, ever stand transfixed

beneath yon skyey load of majesty. But our soul's [*sic*] arches underfit into its; and so, prevent the upper arch from falling on us with unsustainable inscrutableness. (*P*, III, ii:51)

This passage constitutes the nucleus of Melville's "solid purpose" in the novel. Pierre's transcendental assumptions of the correspondence between self and overarching majesty, between deeply felt intuition and divine Truth, do not in fact prove out, and Pierre is indeed crushed by the "unsustainable inscrutableness" of his world.

In a world deprived of hereditary values and traditional beliefs, Melville recognizes the appeal of "self-reliance." This entire novel is devoted to its possibilities, suggesting that he sees it as a last hope for establishing purpose and certainty in life. But there are two irreducible doubts in Melville's mind about any belief or course of action founded upon "irresistible intuitions" and "flashing revelations" of the self. First, as we have seen in his works from *Mardi* on, he doubts the integrity of the human personality itself. The "latent infiniteness and inexhaustibility" of the self, which appealed so strongly to Emerson, is precisely what most dismays the narrator. To "find out the heart of a man," as Melville's narrator attempts with Pierre, is "as descending a spiral stair in a shaft, without any end, and where that endlessness is only concealed by the spiralness of the stair, and the blackness of the shaft" (*P*, XXI, ii:288–89).

Ultimately for Melville, the self, or soul, exists without points of external reference, and for that reason its motions and promptings cannot be verified. The book is liberally sprinkled with the narrator's skeptical comments on the nature of the soul in which Emerson and Pierre place so much trust, but outstanding in its summary indictment is the narrator's image of mining into the pyramid, only to find the empty sarcophagus: "appallingly vacant as vast is the soul of a man!" (*P*, XXI, i:285). As a critique upon transcendentalism and as an ironic bildungsroman, *Pierre* chronicles the life of a young man whose "sublime intuitiveness... paints to him the sun-like glories of god-like truth and virtue... casting illustrative light upon the sapphire throne of God" (*P*, VI, i:111), but whose experience leads him to acknowledge, with the narrator and Melville, "the everlasting elusiveness of Truth; the universal lurking insincerity of even the greatest and purest written thoughts" (*P*, XXV, iii:339).[6]

Once "fairly afloat in himself," Pierre is constantly nagged by self-doubt. In an attempt to delineate the "rebellion and horrid anarchy and infidelity" in Pierre's soul (*P*, XIV, i:205), the narrator resorts to retelling a "singular story once told in the pulpit by a reverend man of God" (*P*, XIV, i:205). For our purposes the story is singular indeed; it bears an unmistakable resemblance to Emerson's own personal crisis and resignation from the ministry. The story tells of a priest who "in the act of publicly administering the bread at the Holy Sacrament of the Supper" is struck by "the possibility of the mere moonshine of the Christian Religion" (*P*, XIV, i:205). Unlike Emerson, the priest does not renounce his pulpit: he is held to his "firm Faith's rock" by "the imperishable monument of his Holy Catholic Church; the imperishable record of his Holy Bible; the imperishable intuition of the innate truth of Christianity" (*P*, XIV, i:205). Emerson's intuition, as we know, led him elsewhere. So does Pierre's, and the narrator's rhetorical question echoes throughout the narrative: "But Pierre—where could *he* find the Church, the monument, the Bible, which unequivocally said to him—'Go on; thou art in the Right; I endorse thee all over; go on'" (*P*, XIV, i:205).

This second critique on transcendental self-reliance is closely related to the first. Because Melville sees the soul as "appallingly vacant" in itself, he cannot but question the sources and implications of its promptings. The narrator is bluntly skeptical: "IN THEIR PRECISE TRACINGS-OUT and subtile causations, the strongest and fieriest emotions of life defy all analytical insight" (*P*, IV, i:67). Every event "is but the product of an infinite series of infinitely involved and untraceable foregoing occurrences" (*P*, IV, i:67). Applying this Humean logic to "every motion of the heart," the narrator thoughtfully concludes that the strongest human feelings of "enthusiasm" or "scorn" are "not wholly imputable to the immediate apparent cause, which is only one link in the chain; but to a long line of dependencies whose further part is lost in the mid-regions of the impalpable air" (*P*, IV, i:67).

As the novel works itself out, the narrator's views prove both authoritative and far-reaching in their implications. Thrown back upon himself, Pierre is incapable of making a "right" decision in any philosophical sense. Incapable of judging the causes behind his own feelings, he is incapable of judging the implications of his decisions and actions. Comparing Pierre's situation with that of the priest mentioned earlier, the narrator points out that "with the priest it was a matter, whether certain bodiless thoughts of his were true or not true; but with Pierre it was a question whether certain vital acts of his were right or wrong" (*P*, XIV, i:205). Guided by "enthusiastic Truth, and Earnestness, and Independence," Pierre perforce comes to see "all objects ... in a dubious, uncertain, and refracting light" (*P*, IX, i:165), and in the exploration of his moral Arctic, Pierre discovers only that "it is not for man to follow the trail of truth too far, since by so doing he entirely loses the directing compass of his mind; for arrived at the Pole, to whose barrenness only it points, there, the needle indifferently respects all points of the horizon alike" (*P*, IX, i:165).

The ironic disjunction between narrator and protagonist becomes overwhelming as the book proceeds. Even as he recounts Pierre's pursuit of "the sun-like glories of god-like truth and virtue," the narrator reminds us that "far as we blind moles can see, man's life seems but an acting upon mysterious hints" (*P*, X, i:176). What Emerson and Pierre assume to be a world of equational correspondence between self and divinity, intuition and truth, intent and virtue, the mind, matter and spirit, Melville's narrator finds to be a world of ineluctable mystery. The all-benevolent Nature that for Emerson and Pierre is "her own ever-sweet interpreter" (*P*, XXV, iv:342)—giving us language that we might see through the facts of the world to the spiritual world beyond—is for the narrator "the mere supplier of that cunning alphabet, whereby selecting and combining as he pleases, each man reads his own peculiar lesson according to his own peculiar mind and mood" (*P*, XXV, iv:342). For Emerson, the all-centering circumference of divinity abides in all things and speaks to humanity in all things. For *Pierre*'s narrator, "Silence is the general consecration of the universe. . . . Silence is the only voice of our God" (*P*, XIV, i:204).

The progression of Pierre's self-reliance and, as it turns out, his radical isolation, is dramatized most clearly when in desperation he seeks counsel from that surrogate father—also man of God, the Reverend Mr. Falsgrave. Much like the insufferable Mr. Collins of *Pride and Prejudice*, Reverend Falsgrave is "mild and meek; . . . an image of white-browed and white-handed, and napkined immaculateness" (*P*, V, iv:99), but his Christian faith is pompous, platitudinous, and superficial. Confronted by Pierre's direct and (as we know) pressing question—whether the legitimate child of a parent should "refuse his highest sympathy and perfect love for the other [the illegitimate child], especially if that other be deserted by all the rest of the world" (*P*, V, iv:101)—Mr. Falsgrave confesses embarrassment and pleads the complexity of moral issues that are "incapable of a definite answer, which shall be universally applicable" (*P*, V, iv:103). Thus rebuked by Mr. Falsgrave—friend, counselor, Christian, and man of God—Pierre reaches the conclusion he later enunciates after his second meeting with Falsgrave: he must seek counsel "direct from God himself, who . . . never delegates his holiest admonishings" (*P*, VIII, vii:164).

Pierre himself is painfully aware of his moral isolation from family, from friends, and, as he soon discovers, from God. His self-reliance and freedom are dearly bought at the cost of uncertainty and angst, long before there was a Sartre to rationalize his precarious situation for him. Like Stephen Crane's protagonists some forty years later, Pierre stands dumfounded and helpless, seeking assurance from a voiceless God, pleading with a God in whom he can no longer believe.

The image of Pierre's God is the Memnon Stone set amid the "deep forest silence" and emanating a "ponderous inscrutableness" (*P*, VII, iv:133–34). Although the stone is inscribed "S. yᵉ W.," which a white-haired old kinsman tells him stands for "Solomon the Wise" (*P*, VII, iv:133), Pierre thinks of the stone as the "Terror Stone" (*P*, VII, iv:134). In the throes of trying to decide upon the "right" thing to do, Pierre turns to this stone for a sign, sliding himself into the "horrible interspace" between stone and ground and calling upon the stone's "Mute Massiveness" to fall upon him (*P*, VII, v:134). Pierre's sophomoric outburst should not blind us to the importance of the scene in the book's development. Briefly, *Pierre* offers the proposition that if we can know neither the motivations nor the implications of our thoughts and acts, then morality is but a fiction. And if morality is a fiction, all human life becomes meaningless.[7] Although Pierre fights against these paralyzing propositions with every ounce of moral energy he possesses, the narrator leaves little doubt about the eventual outcome, for "Memnon was that dewey, royal boy . . . who . . . fought hand to hand with his overmatch, and met his boyish and most dolorous death beneath the walls of Troy" (*P*, VII, vi:135).

Rejected by man, abandoned by God, Pierre finds his "overmatch" in his own ambiguous nature. Once again the narrator defines Pierre's predicament and his decision. Lacking the "steady philosophic mind" that "reaches forth and draws to itself, in their collective entirety, the objects of its contemplations" (*P*, X, i:175), Pierre, the young enthusiast, commits himself to "four unitedly impossible designs"—all eager "to involve himself in such an inextricable twist of Fate, that the three dextrous maids themselves could hardly disentangle him, if once he tie the complicating knots about him and Isabel" (*P*, X, i:175). Seeking a perfect solution to an insoluble problem, Pierre wishes first, "to hold his father's fair fame inviolate from anything he should do in reference to protecting Isabel"; second, to extend to Isabel "a brother's utmost devotedness and love"; third, to avoid shaking his "mother's lasting peace by any useless exposure of unwelcome facts"; and finally, "to embrace Isabel before the world, and yield to her his constant consolation and companionship" (*P*, X, i:172–73).

Not surprisingly, Pierre is initially paralyzed by the weight of his impossible task. Indeed, in all of Melville's fiction after *Pierre* no theme is more dominant or compelling than that of the individual's paralyzed mind and will when confronting the unravellable knots of life's ambiguities. Bartleby, his lawyer-employer, Captain Delano, Captain Vere—all, with Pierre, are persuaded by *Hamlet*'s theme:

> 'The time is out of joint;—Oh cursed spite,
> That ever I was born to set it right!'
>
> (*P*, IX, ii:168)

Unlike his later counterparts, Pierre does not remain paralyzed, however. With Dante's admonition clearly before him—"All hope abandon, ye who enter here" (*P*, IX, ii:168), Pierre takes another lesson from Hamlet and from Ahab—"that all meditation is worthless, unless it prompt to action" (*P*, IX, iii:169).

Pierre does act in the instant of conviction, but his "most singular act of pious imposture," his decision "to assume before the world, that by secret rites, Pierre Glendinning was already become the husband of Isabel Banford" (*P*, X, i:173) is a lightning-bolt that scorches and destroys in its blinding imprecision. Indeed, the two halves of the novel make absolutely clear Melville's conviction that the self-reliant man is trapped in a hopeless moral dilemma. The first half of the novel, through Book XI, dramatizes the indecision and paralysis of the self-reliant man who has no means of understanding, let alone verifying, his own ambiguous impulses, feelings, thoughts, and motivations. But to free himself from the paralysis of indecision and contrary impulses, Pierre, Melville's modern Everyman, must act in ignorance—ignorance both of his own motivations and of the implications of his thoughts and actions. The skeptical conviction that had been growing in Melville's art since *Mardi* is given its most undiluted expression in *Pierre*: first and final causes alike are hidden from us; we must act out our life dramas in darkness and pain, tragic dramas that end only in death.

The depth and intensity of this skeptical, even despairing, conviction, at times overpower the art in *Pierre*, for in making the terms of Pierre's moral predicament clear, Melville makes Pierre wooden and unbelievable—to a large extent a mere counter in a roman à clef. Conversely, there is a true power in *Pierre*'s intense evocation of moral issues. If in broad terms the novel depicts the disjunction between humanity's aspirations and accomplishments, in more precise terms it reveals Melville's most reluctant, yet insistent, belief that modern man lives in a moral vacuum. And as *Pierre* puts it, when we are incapable of assessing accurately the motivations and implications of our acts, morality no longer exists; good and evil alike are but fortuitous results of decisions made in impenetrable darkness.

Pierre's imposture of marrying Isabel is, indeed, "pious," for Pierre's resolution is founded on his dedication to right the wrongs of the past and treat Isabel justly without hurting anyone but himself, a resolution "wonderful," as the narrator tells us, "in its unequalled renunciation of himself" (*P*, X, i:172). In the abstract, Pierre is a perfectly moral, altruistic man. But the immediate results of Pierre's good intentions are nothing if not an index of horror and death. His beloved mother is first maddened and then brought to an early grave by the aberration of her son-lover. His fiancée, Lucy, is momentarily maddened by grief, to the point of death, and recovers only to renounce herself in deference to Pierre's inexplicable will. Lucy's brother, enraged at the dishonor of his sister, joins forces with Pierre's cousin Glen, and together they taunt and threaten Pierre until he too is maddened and in a fit of rage and frustration extinguishes "his house in slaughtering the only unoutlawed human being by the name of Glendinning" (*P*, XXVI, v:360). Disowned by his family, cast out by society, a failure in life and letters, a criminal in law, Pierre, imprisoned, takes his own life, but not until Lucy has fallen dead at his feet from grief, and just before Isabel takes her own life.

The puppet-show melodrama of it all would be utterly insupportable as art were it not for the fine, strong threads of moral concern in the second half of the novel. *Pierre* is not mere melodrama, but melodrama with a "solid purpose"—that of defining our hopeless position in a world lacking moral direction and certainty. The failed metaphysical quests of Melville's first six novels, which end so definitively with the sinking of the *Pequod*, serve as foundation to the central moral inquiry of *Pierre* and the works that follow.

That shift in direction and purpose is made trenchantly clear in the narrator's comment on Pierre when he "crosses the Rubicon" and makes the decision that affects so many lives: "Pierre was not arguing Fixed Fate and Free Will, now; Fixed Fate and Free Will were arguing him, and Fixed Fate got the better in the debate" (*P*, XI, i:182). To the narrator, as well as to the Melville who had made his way through the wilderness of *Moby-Dick*, there are no "couriers in the air," no "high beneficences," no "sweet angels" to warn humanity away from the unseen perils of its acts and resolutions, and as the narrator observes, "the wisest man were rash, positively to assign the precise and incipient origination of his final thoughts and acts" (*P*, X, i:176).

Once having defined the ambiguous essence and implications of Pierre's moral decision, Melville moves the narrative along very rapidly. In fact, Books XI, XII, and XIII are the three shortest books in the novel by a considerable margin, once again suggesting that the weight of Melville's emphasis falls upon the moral equation rather than upon the surface narrative. Lucy, who so dominates the first half of the novel, is scarcely given a speaking part in what we would expect to be a dramatic confrontation with Pierre. He baldly states, "'Lucy, I am married'" (*P*, XI, ii:183)—and she swoons, not to reappear in the novel until Book XXIII, when she sends Pierre her "artless, angelical letter" (*P*, XXIII, iii:311). Even Mrs. Glendinning's response to Pierre's shocking news is underplayed, although abruptly clear as she bans him from home and family (cf. *P*, XI, iii:185).

The first implications of his rash idealism thus reveal themselves quickly to Pierre. His first lesson learned and the first he imparts to Isabel, his sister-bride, is that "the infinite entanglements of all social things, . . . forbid that one thread should fly the general fabric, on some new line of duty, without tearing itself and tearing others" (*P*, XI, i:191). The metaphor of Pierre as the castaway Ishmael is furthered by his burning of his father's portrait and of all other memorials of his once seemingly solid past.

We cannot ignore the implication that, for Melville, Pierre's fate is the fate of everyone forced to live out life in a world without "certain significance." When Pierre, Isabel, and Delly leave Saddle Meadows, they leave an Eden that in truth never was, founded as it was upon lies, hypocrisy, and the cosmetic power of wealth and convention. But the lessons Melville learned in *Mardi, Redburn,* and *Moby-Dick* cannot be unlearned, and for Pierre there are no golden isles, no "home," no end to the noble quest. There is only a frightening and disorienting nightmare world viewed as life's prison, the world so powerfully evoked in the New York City of the last half of the novel.

Melville takes pains to balance the two halves of the book quite neatly, giving some foreshadowing of the balance to be found in his short stories; the opening twelve books of the novel (dealing with the romantic idyll and leading to *Pierre's* resolution) are perfectly balanced against the last twelve books (describing the effects of that decision that lead to Pierre's downfall).[8] Book XIII, "They Depart the Meadows," and Book XIV, "The Journey and the Pamphlet," form the bridge between the two distinct "halves" of *Pierre*, and because Melville suggests a causal relationship between the idyllic opening and Pierre's moral resolution, and between that resolution and the outcome of the novel, it is only natural, not to say compelling, to look to Book XIV for an answer, or at least a hint of an answer, to Melville's larger purposes in the novel. What we find in Book XIV, of course, is what Pierre found upon entering the coach for New York City—the pamphlet by Plotinus Plinlimmon.

Although there is almost universal agreement among readers of the novel that the Plinlimmon pamphlet is crucial to the novel's significance, there is considerable disagreement about what precisely the pamphlet means. The problems in interpreting the pamphlet spring from the un-yielding, impenetrable ambiguity of the pamphlet itself, for, in the end, there is no resolution to the conflicting issues raised in the pamphlet, no interpretation of "Ei" that will put Pierre's Humpty-Dumpty world back together again.

The pamphlet itself, as the narrator describes it, is "a thin, tattered, dried-fish-like thing; printed with blurred ink upon mean, sleazy paper" (*P*, XIV, i:206). Actually, the papers Pierre finds crumpled in his hand on the most momentous occasion of his life are not a whole treatise at all, but merely the "opening pages" of some "ruinous old pamphlet" that in its entirety merely contained "a chapter or so of some very voluminous disquisition" (*P*, XIV, i:206). As the narrator wryly points out, "the con-clusion was gone" (*P*, XIV, i:206), and Plotinus Plinlimmon's first lecture on Chronometricals and Horologicals comes to "a most untidy termina-tion": "'Moreover: if—'" (*P*, XIV, iii:215). Surely Melville's intentions are clear: there are no "answers" to be found in the pamphlet. Surely we are firmly guided into agreement with the narrator's assessment of the pamphlet as a lecture that seems "more the excellently illustrated re-statement of a problem, than the solution of the problem itself" (*P*, XIV, ii:210).

If Melville shows all metaphysical searches at a dead blind wall in *Moby-Dick*, the implications of the utter wreck he foresaw in *Mardi* are made all too clear in *Pierre*. In 1852, Melville can neither see nor imagine a resolution to the self-confounding propositions of the Plinlimmon pam-phlet. The sophistical meanderings of Plotinus Plinlimmon, which begin with the contrary assertions that on the one hand "we mortals have only to do with things provisional" (*P*, XIV, iii:211) and that on the other "there is a certain most rare order of human souls, which if carefully carried in the body will almost always and everywhere give Heaven's own Truth" (*P*, XIV, iii:211) must, and do, inevitably argue the absurd. Thus Plinlimmon concludes that "the earthly wisdom of man be heavenly folly to God; so also, conversely, is the heavenly wisdom of God an earthly folly to man" (*P*, XIV, iii:212), yet argues that "it follows not from this, that God's truth is one thing and man's truth another; but—as above hinted, and as will be further elucidated in subsequent lectures—by their very contradictions they are made to correspond" (*P*, XIV, iii:212).

If we accept Plinlimmon's role as God's apologist and humanity's law-giver,[9] which is implicit in the pamphlet itself and in his position as leader of the "Apostles," we then recognize very quickly just how devastating is Melville's satire on this nouveau Calvin and how forlorn is his vision of human existence. Amid the tangled argument of the pamphlet, one idea stands out for Plinlimmon as the most horrible of thoughts: "that whatever other worlds God may be Lord of, he is not the Lord of this; for else this world would seem to give the lie to Him; so utterly repugnant seem its ways to the instinctively known ways of Heaven" (*P*, XIV, iii:213). This fearful, infidel idea, that lurks beneath the surface of everything Melville wrote up to *Pierre*, has the ring of granite truth in the marshy context of Plinlimmon's pamphlet, and by the end of the novel it echoes back to us as an absolute certainty. Yet in the pamphlet, Plinlimmon would waft away this weighty, irresistible conclusion as the airiest of straw arguments, which simply "can not be so" (*P*, XIV, iii:213).

The last word on the significance of the pamphlet belongs, appropriately, to the narrator. When he states categorically at the beginning of Book XIV that "Silence is the only Voice of our God" (*P*, XIV, i:204) he states at once the problem and the insolubility of that problem. When he describes "those imposter philosophers" who "pretend somehow to have got an answer" (*P*, XIV, ii:290) he describes Plotinus Plinlimmon: the absurdity of Plinlimmon and of those who follow him being patent—"for how can a man get a Voice out of Silence?" (*P*, XIV, ii:208).

It is this radical, relentless skepticism that lies at the heart of Book XIV, the center of *Pierre*, and it is this same undeviating skepticism that underlies the falling action of this novel and permeates everything Melville writes after *Pierre*. Pierre, Bartleby, his lawyer-employer, Captain Delano, Benito Cereno, the passengers of the *Fidèle*, Billy Budd and Captain Vere are all trapped in a mysterious world that refuses to yield up its secrets, are all forced into moral decisions without having any clear sense of their own motivations or the implications of their choices. The world of open seas and the hope for new horizons disappear with *Moby-Dick*, and Pierre and his skeptical offspring find themselves imprisoned in a shrunken world, more and more isolated from their fellow prisoners and more and more reduced to talking to themselves for want of anyone else to listen.

Book XVI, which depicts the arrival of Pierre, Isabel, and Delly in New York City, is probably one of the best written and most effective sections in the novel, providing the first glimpse of that city of dreadful night, in which Pierre lives out the brief remainder of his life, and defining the arena in which Melville's subsequent protagonists must find their way. Dark, disorienting, and threatening, the city at night at once embodies and reflects Pierre's traumatized soul. Although Pierre does not see immediately into his dreadful future, the extremity of his immediate circumstances unhinges what a short time before had seemed to him his "serene and symmetrical" soul. Now, all seems to him bitterness, sadness, and death.

However extreme Pierre's responses, the city does indeed live up to Pierre's worst fears, and Melville makes it clear that Pierre is not reacting to threats that don't exist: the novel is not a fictionalized clinical study of abnormal psychology. Rather it is a study in an inherently maddening world and humanity's tragic inability to adapt to it. In this light Pierre's search for his kinsman's house is seen as a bitter parody of Melville's earlier questing novels. Pierre knows where he wants to go, but he knows neither its precise location nor the way to it. The coach driver takes on the aspect of a perverse demon-pilot, leading him not to his destination but to the embodiment of his worst fears—the watch house. But nightmare is piled upon nightmare. When Pierre finds his cousin's home, he gains reluctant entry only to be turned away—unrecognized and branded as a "remarkable case of combined imposture and insanity" (*P*, XVI, ii:239). Then, returning to the police station, Pierre finds it a madhouse of "all things unseemly," with "frantic, diseased-looking men and women of all colors, and in all imaginable flaunting, immodest, grotesque, and shattered dresses,...leaping, yelling, and cursing around him" (*P*, XVI, iii:240). From there it is but a short step to Pierre's final prison home—the Church of the Apostles.

The meteoric fall of Pierre from the state of idyllic happiness in the first half of the novel to that ever-intensifying state of despair in the second half defines the absolute skepticism with which Melville viewed the possibilities of man's creating an "original relationship with his universe." But the novel is more than just an exercise in naive pessimism. Melville knew—and defined—precisely what nineteenth-century humanity had lost in the inevitable process of philosophical, scientific, and economic "advances." Above all for Melville, a God without voice, a society without purpose, and a world without *some* certain significance doom the individual to a life of isolation, pain, and gratuitous, ambiguous acts ending in meaningless death. More immediately for Melville the writer, such a God, such a society, and such a world reduce literature to being the plaything of idle minds and empty hearts. There is no longer a Truth to be preached to the face of Falsehood. There are no lambs waiting to be fed, no preacher, no text, no doctrine, no church. And thus in this rank, unweeded garden of a world, literature for Melville becomes, merely words, words, words. In this regard, the last half of the novel is "autobiographical," but more in a literary than in a restrictedly literal sense. In the last third of the novel, Melville writes an intricate epitaph on the death of all serious thought and expression and defiantly berates the world that cannot sustain our highest dreams.

The two chapters that Melville devotes to "Young America in Literature" (Book XVII) and "Pierre as a Juvenile Author, Reconsidered" (Book XVIII) are not the subtlest in their satiric condemnation of popular authors, popular taste, and profit-oriented publishers, and perhaps it is a critical kindness not to dwell too long on the likes of "Wonder & Wen," publishers, "Peter Pence," designer, and the literary parasites who frequently petitioned teen-aged Pierre "for the materials wherewith to frame his biography" (*P*, XVII, iii:254). But although Melville's satiric weapons are crude in Book XVIII, the targets of his scorn do not escape for all that. The most immediate and obvious bête noire for Melville is the tasteless commercialism of the publishing trade, by which a work of art is tranformed into a thinly disguised profit ledger bound in finest Russian leather. But at the heart of the publish-for-profit motive is a horror even greater for Melville—the undeniable truth that what sells best, what is most easily published and most highly regarded by critics, is that literature which most nearly conforms to prevailing standards of taste, morality, and religion.

Take but one step aside from that well-traveled road of conventional, accepted opinion and, says Melville, one becomes irretrievably lost to the world. Yet that crucial step sideways is precisely the move that Melville says every true artist must take. Pierre has a chance to become a true writer only when he becomes aware of "the utter unsatisfactoriness of all human fame" (*P*, XVII, iii:255). Only then can he begin what for Melville is viewed as the long arduous process of "digging in one's soul for the fine gold genius" amid "much dullness and common-place" (*P*, XVIII, i:258). On the question of how the artist digs beneath the rubbish to find the gold, Melville is typically cryptic, the narrator muttering "that the wiser a man is, the more misgivings he has on certain points" (*P*, XVIII, i:258), but he does leave us with two words: "Grandeur and Earnestness."

Although Melville thus apparently clings to the vestiges of his earlier concept of the artist as truth-teller, there is a paradox here, for throughout *Pierre* Melville argues that whatever truth there is, or "might be," remains inaccessible to humanity. Clearly there is no possible resolution to this painful paradox that defines Melville's conception of the artist. Although Melville is "quite conscious of much that is so anomalously hard and bitter" in the artist's lot (*P*, XXII, iii:303), like Pierre, "knowing his fatal condition does not one whit enable him to change or better his condition. Conclusive proof that he has no power over his condition. For in tremendous extremities human souls are like drowning men; well enough they know they are in peril; well enough they know the causes of that peril;—nevertheless, the sea is the sea, and these drowning men do drown" (*P*, XXII, iii:303).

In sum, the last third of *Pierre* is Melville's portrait of the artist as a drowning man. It is his letter to the world that he didn't expect the world to read—the world in which "Grandeur and Earnestness" have given way to conformity and piety. The extent and depth of his bleak vision is revealed in the concluding paragraph of Book XVIII, where Melville's narrator directs our gaze to an inevitable future "when the mass of humanity reduced to one level of dotage, authors shall be scarce as alchymists are to-day, and the printing-press be reckoned a small invention" (*P*, XVIII, ii:264). Yet the narrator's response to this grim new world on the horizon is one of defiance and unshaken self-confidence: "—yet even now, in the foretaste of this let us hug ourselves, oh, my Aurelian! that though the age of authors be passing, the hours of earnestness shall remain!" (*P*, XXVIII, ii:264). And Books XIX through XXVI dramatize Melville's heroic conviction that although defeat may sometimes be inevitable, it need never be dishonorable.

Pierre represents the last vestige of the heroic in Melville, and he cannot prosper amid the "legal crowd" and the "miscellaneous, bread-and-cheese adventurers, and ambiguously professional nondescripts" (*P*, XIX, i:267) who inhabit the Church of the Apostles. Avatar of the new order is Charlie Millthorpe—shallow, vain, garrulous, filled with "harmless presumption and innocent egotism" (*P*, XX, i:279), above all, ambitious "to be either an orator, or a poet; at any rate, a great genius of one sort or other" (*P*, XX, i:279). Next to the lighthearted and light-headed Charlie, Pierre is presented to us as the heavy-burdened, grim old warrior with "Life his campaign, and three fierce allies, Woe and Scorn and Want, his foes" (*P*, XIX, ii:270). At once a lawyer and a devotee of the "seedy-coated Apostles" (*P*, XX, ii:280), Charlie is borne up and self-propelled by his "sophomorean presumption and egotism" (*P*, XX, i:276) into a self-defined and self-willed success. In his aspiration, self-deluded or not, he falls little short of seeing himself as a popular philosopher-king, preaching "philosophy to the masses" (*P*, XX, ii:280).

Pierre, in contrast, retreats further and further into himself, further and further from the world that no longer wishes to hear "deeper secrets than the Apocalypse" (*P*, XIX, ii:273). In terms of the Chronometrical-Horological conceit that dominates the closing chapters of the novel, Charlie does and must perforce succeed because he is the living embodiment of Plinlimmon's "virtuous expediency"—telling people what they want to hear. Conversely, Pierre's commitment to pass beyond "the uttermost ideal of moral perfection in man" and to "gospelize the world anew" (*P*, XIX, ii:273) seals his fate. As the narrator grimly reminds us, "it is the glory of the bladder that nothing can sink it; it is the reproach of a box of treasure, that once overboard it must down" (*P*, XX, i:280).

Pierre's aspirations as an author are certainly high enough: "to deliver what he thought to be new, or at least miserably neglected Truth to the world" (*P*, XXI, i:283). In this he cannot possibly succeed; the "Truth" cannot be grasped by Pierre, nor by anyone else, and even if it were, the "world" would not want to hear it. Thus, Pierre's decline is an unbroken, precipitous decline into the depths of frustration, rage, and despair.

Melville adopts an indirect method of revealing Pierre's moral decline in the closing stages of the novel. As Pierre becomes more and more absorbed in his masterwork, he becomes more and more isolated, not only from the world, which he views as indifferent, or even malicious toward him, but also from the very ones who love him most and sympathize most with his efforts. Second, Melville employs the extended imagery of physical discomfort as the metaphor for the mental anguish of the earnest writer at war with his world, his materials, his very self. The overriding image of Pierre in the last third of the novel is that of a man alone, struggling with demons he cannot see or touch, bereft of all hope, numb to all comforts.

Melville virtually buries Pierre in an avalanche of misfortune, the heavy melodrama in the concluding chapters of the novel only bearable, let alone artistically defensible, if we view it as a symbolic representation of Pierre's inner torments and ultimate disintegration. Thus, the death of Pierre's mother, his loss of the family patrimony, and the threatened "loss" of Lucy to Glen Stanly (see Book XXI, "Tidings from the Meadows"), are more important rhetorically for what they reveal to us of Pierre's growing sense of guilt, self-doubt, and despair than they are significant narratively. By Book XXI *Pierre* has become virtually a one-character book, and we care little or not at all about what happens to anyone except Pierre.

Melville's purpose and methods in the latter portion of the novel are centered in the relationship between Pierre and Plotinus Plinlimmon in Book XXI. Here Melville abandons all pretense of depicting Plinlimmon as a living, breathing person and translates him into an allegorical figure of abstract properties. In this allegorical role Plinlimmon's value is clearly relative rather than intrinsic, for we care about him at all only insofar as he reveals something important to us about Pierre. And this he does. Standing as the image and embodiment of Pierre's God, Plinlimmon reveals to us not what it is to be such a God, but what it is to be such a man as Pierre—in such a world with a Plinlimmon for a God.

In the literal terms of the narrative Plotinus Plinlimmon is merely an eccentric, ineffectual "Grand Master of a certain mystic Society among the Apostles" (*P*, XXI, iii:290). In view of the pamphlet "Ei," we might guess that Melville's original intention must have been to satirize the faddish transcendentalist philosophy of the 1840s, but by the time Melville brings Pierre and Plotinus face to face in Book XXI, his purposes seem to have deepened. No longer merely the object of a limited, occasional satire, Plinlimmon appears as the only God Melville can conceive of in 1852, defines all that is maddening to the earnest searcher after moral truth. By calling Plinlimmon's disciples the *Apostles*, Melville compels us to identify Plinlimmon with the object of *the* Apostles' worship—God Himself. And when Melville writes of Plinlimmon—"In that eye, the gay immortal youth Apollo, seemed enshrined; while on that ivory-throned brow, old Saturn cross-legged sat" (*P*, XXI, iii:290)—we either take the rather blunt suggestion and accept Plinlimmon as the face of God or remain forever lost to Melville's purposes in the conclusion of the novel.

The attributes of Plinlimmon-as-God are sharply defined. Suffused in an aura of "cheerful content," Plinlimmon nevertheless has something "latently visible" in him that Melville finally defines as "non-Benevolence" —because "it was neither Malice nor Ill-will; but something passive" (*P*, XXI, iii:290). And to "crown all" there is "a certain floating atmosphere" that seems to "invest and go along with this man"—an atmosphere "only renderable in words by the term Inscrutableness" (*P*, XXI, iii:290). As early as *Mardi* Melville had defined God as inscrutable and non-benevolent, but in the early novels this inscrutable, indifferent God was a faceless, distant being whose mystery inspired wonder and awe, if not reverence. But in the avatar of Plotinus Plinlimmon, God is all too inescapably immediate to Pierre. This "hat-lifting, gracefully bowing, gently-smiling, and most miraculously self-possessed non-benevolent man" (*P*, XXI, iii:290) haunts Pierre like a personal Nemesis and curses all his highest efforts.

When Melville attacks the "sleazy works that went under his [Plinlimmon's] name" as being "nothing more than his verbal things, taken down at random, and bunglingly methodized by his young disciples" (*P*, XXI, iii:290), we might well take it as a thinly veiled attack upon Emersonian transcendentalism, or dogmatized Christianity, entrenched in its power through "hearsay" Biblical authority (one thinks back immediately to the Reverend Mr. Falsgrave). But when he takes direct aim at Plinlimmon, Melville is assaulting God Himself.

Pierre's confrontation with this Nemesis-God is truly one of the most effective passages in the novel. Of course there can be no "confrontation" in the usual sense, for as Melville has repeatedly reminded us, God is a transcendent being whose only voice is Silence.[10] Thus, Pierre declines Charley Millthorpe's proffered introduction to the great man. And thus, Pierre's efforts to procure another copy of "Chronometricals and Horologicals" come to naught: "Plotinus himself could not furnish it" (*P*, XXI, iii:292). Rather, Pierre's confrontation with Plinlimmon takes the dramatically passive form of Pierre looking at Plinlimmon looking at him.

Looking out the window of his chamber Pierre observes Plinlimmon's "steady observant blue-eyed countenance at one of the loftiest windows of the old gray tower" (*P*, XXI, iii:291) and is struck by that unnerving face of repose—"repose neither divine nor human, nor anything made up of either or both—but a repose separate and apart—a repose of a face by itself" (*P*, XXI, iii:291). At this juncture Melville lets the veil slip from his ultimate purpose, having the narrator remark that "one adequate look at that face conveyed to most philosophical observers a notion of something not before included in their scheme of the Universe" (*P*, XXI, iii:291). We don't have to wait long to get a notion of what that "something" is. In its immediate effect upon Pierre the face of repose is an inverted reminder of his own failures and imperfections. Thus it seems to say to him "Vain! vain! vain!"; "Fool! fool! fool!"; "Quit! quit! quit!" (*P*, XXI, iii:293). And, eventually, "the face at last wore a sort of malicious leer to him" (*P*, XXI, iii:293).

Pierre is not a madman in a sane world; he is Everyman in a maddening world. And the face of his God is the face of scorn and reproach. The face manifests itself and dominates Pierre when he is in "moods of peculiar depression and despair," when he is obsessed with "dark thoughts of his miserable condition," and when he is beset by "black doubts as to the integrity of his unprecedented course in life" (*P*, XXI, iii:292). But Melville doesn't stop with this statement of how God affects us. He goes on to provide a definition of what God is in Himself—a definition that prevails, either explicitly or implicitly, in everything Melville writes after *Pierre*.

For Melville, the essence and whole of God's being are contained in His transcendence of this world. That is the central theme of Plinlimmon's pamphlet and the salient feature of Plinlimmon himself.[11] Haunted by the self-contented reproach of Plinlimmon's gaze, Pierre is maddened by the impregnability of that reproach. Pierre can mentally interrogate the face "as to why it thrice said Vain! Fool! Quit! to him," but "here there was no response" (*P*, XXI, iii:293). And the narrator's gloss upon the situation provides us with the disillusioned Melville's unadorned, yet devastating conclusion about God: "that face did not respond to any thing" (*P*, XXI, iii:293). In fact, as the narrator goes on to say, God is defined precisely by His total separateness from this world: "Did I not say before that that face was something separate and apart; a face by itself? Now any thing which is thus a thing by itself never responds to any other thing. If to affirm, be to expand one's isolated self; and if to deny, be to contract one's isolated self; then to respond is a suspension of all isolation" (*P*, XXI, iii:293).

Although the death of God becomes a familiar enough theme in late-nineteenth-century Western literature, and although a recognition of His death has become a staple a priori assumption of most twentieth-century literature, nowhere before or after Melville do we find a more telling statement of the mid-nineteenth-century individual's sense of having been betrayed by God. For Melville, and for many of his contemporaries, the Word that had been in the beginning no longer was, nor ever would be. For Pierre, after his confrontation with Plinlimmon in Book XXI, there is no "way out" of his orphanage world, there is no quest, and there are—bitterest reality of all—no companions. Although he has Isabel, and eventually Lucy too, "Pierre, nevertheless, in his deepest, highest part, was utterly without sympathy from any thing divine, human, brute, or vegetable" (*P*, XXV, iii:338). Surrounded by "hundreds of thousands of human beings, Pierre was solitary as at the Pole" (*P*, XXV, iii:338).

Having worked his way unflinchingly to the inevitable implications of humanity's persistent search for "Truth," Melville in the closing pages of *Pierre* consciously or unconsciously reverts to two dominant images of the earlier quests. Pierre "solitary as at the Pole" takes us back to the white-blinded Laplanders of "The Whiteness of the Whale," for whom all distinctions are erased, all bearings obliterated, all directions alike. And in the very next paragraph Melville takes us back further to a yet more dominant image from *Mardi*. Taji, the demigod, who sets out in bold quest comes to life again in Pierre, and the suspended ending of that earlier novel is finally resolved: "His soul's ship foresaw the inevitable rocks, but resolved to sail on, and make a courageous wreck" (*P*, XXV, iii:339).

Book XXI marks the end to the major thematic concerns in *Pierre*, and we feel Melville's impatience as he rushes headlong, and sometimes care-lessly, to the disaster-laden conclusion of the novel. He tries to pull to-gether the now drifting elements of the Lucy-Isabel-Pierre melodrama, but the strain of the attempt is apparent. Lucy's prescient understanding of Pierre's motivations and behavior is scarcely believable to him, let alone to us (see *Pierre*, XXIII), and the behavior of Lucy, Isabel, and Pierre together at the Apostles frequently takes on the aspect of bad farce rather than tragedy.

At this point Melville's interests are so far removed from the marriage-incest-jealousy-love tangle of the surface narrative that he resorts to the grossest kind of contrivance to extricate himself from its coils. The visit of Isabel, Lucy, and Pierre to the art gallery, for example, is an embarrass-ingly manipulated scene—with Lucy "standing motionless" before a copy of "The Cenci" of Guido (*P*, XXVI, i:351)—which just happens to face "the stranger's head, by an unknown hand"—which just happens to have a family likeness to Pierre and Isabel. The scene itself does little more than stir our memories into a recollection of the almost forgotten origins of Pierre's plight; it certainly doesn't resolve any of the ambiguities surrounding Pierre's decision, and it does little more than stir our interest in Isabel's "true" identity or past. At this point in the novel, it is hard to disagree with Pierre's admonition to the electrified Isabel: "'Let us begone; and let us keep eternal silence'" (*P*, XXVI, i:352).

Melville's true concerns in the closing pages of the novel lie in the philosophical implications of what it means for us to live in a world without God. Thus, Book XXII ("The Flower-Curtain Lifted") and Book XXV, containing the scenes of "Pierre at His Book" and his dream vision of "Enceladus," are definitely more central to our understanding of the novel (and are infinitely better written) than the Lucy-Isabel-Pierre narrative passages.

Neither of these two important chapters offers any relief from the extreme pessimism implied in Book XXI. Certainly, these chapters suggest no possible redeeming grace for Pierre. His condition is compared unfavorably, in that notorious passage, to the "savage and untamable health" of the "Texan Camanche" (*P*, XXII, ii:302). The author-hero of his book, who is "directly plagiarized from his own [Pierre's] experiences" owns himself "a child of the Primeval Gloom" (*P*, XXII, iii:302) and rages that he hates the world and could "trample all lungs of mankind as grapes, and heel them out of their breath, to think of the woe and the cant,—to think of the Truth and the Lie!" (*P*, XXII, iii:303).

Pierre's despair and sense of futility do not spring only from his awareness of an unappreciating world. It is one thing for him to discover—and then accept—that "the wiser and the profounder he should grow, the more and the more he lessened the chances for bread" (*P*, XXII, iv:305). But it is far more devastating to discover "the everlasting elusiveness of Truth" and the "universal lurking insincerity of even the greatest and purest written thoughts" (*P*, XXV, iii:339).

The implications of this admission by Pierre are dramatized in his immediate and rapid descent into oblivion. Abandoned by God, shunned by society, his writing thus reduced to pointless scratchings upon paper, Pierre, like Lear, throws himself into the tempest. Melville instinctively returns to the metaphor of the sea and storm-lashed ships to dramatize Pierre's failure and, by implication, the failure of humanity's bold quest. As Pierre walks through the stormy streets of New York, "the innumerable shop-awnings flapped and beat like schooners' broad sails in a gale, and the shutters banged like lashed bulwarks; and the slates fell hurtling like displaced ship's blocks from aloft" (*P*, XXV, iii:340). Walking first down the emptied thoroughfares of the city, Pierre feels a "dark, triumphant joy; that while others had crawled in fear to their kennels, he alone defied the storm-admiral, whose most vindictive peltings of hail-stones,—

striking his iron-framed fiery furnace of a body,—melted into soft dew, and so, harmlessly trickled from off him" (*P*, XXV, iii:340).

Pierre has no Kent, no Fool, no Edgar, and finally nothing but "utter night-desolation" will content him (*P*, XXV, iii:341). Here, amid the "obscurest warehousing lanes" of New York, Pierre finds himself at that dark axis of reality that forms the pivot point of Melville's fiction. Melville's extended description of Pierre's descent into a "general and nameless torpor—some horrible foretaste of death itself" (*P*, XXV, iii:342) contains probably the best writing in the novel, and it is certainly as significant as the Enceladus dream that it introduces.

Pierre's dream of Enceladus is little more than a symbolic dream commentary on the elements of his own experience. Enceladus, son of Coelus and Terra, becomes in Book XXV, the summary image of Pierre's heaven-assaulting idealism and inevitable failure, intensifying rather than adding to our understanding of his essential plight. Pierre like Enceladus is "scarred and broken," "mutilated," and "vanquished" (*P*, XXV, iv:345), and he is "eternally defenceless" and "impotent" (*P*, XXV, iv:346). He is defiant in his hatred of a heaven that is invulnerable and unyielding, yet perversely creates in Titan-man an "ever-encroaching appetite for God" (*P*, XXV, iv:345). We have seen these radical "ambiguities" in Plinlimmon's abstract pamphlet, "Chronometrics and Horologicals," and we have seen them dramatized symbolically in Pierre's confrontation with the window-gazing Plinlimmon. What the myth of earthbound Enceladus does is fix permanently, with no chance of further revision, the terms of humanity's agony. For Pierre there is no "final comfort" in the fable—its aridity incapable of quenching "his painful thirst" (*P*, XXV, v:346).

Given Melville's conception of the human condition, he brings Pierre to his only possible end—total annihilation. However melodramatic and contrived Pierre's murder of Glen Stanly might be, we should not blind ourselves to the import of that murder. In killing his cousin, Pierre kills the last living member of the Glendinning line. With Pierre's and Isabel's suicides, the family line becomes extinct. With the death of Lucy there is not even "one who alone survives to tell the tale." There is only Isabel's dying statement: "'All's o'er, and ye know him not'" (*P*, XXVI, vii:362)[12]—a statement both absolute and comprehensive in its finality.

Most emphatically, *Pierre* realizes Melville's prophetic fears in *Mardi* that our bold quest for another, better world might, indeed, come to an utter wreck. Having laid bare Pierre's inability to find any certain moral significance in the events of this world, and his conviction that whatever God that might be is forever remote and unapproachable, Melville forces the novel to the further conclusion—that without such fixed points of reference individuals are forever imprisoned within themselves, as remote as God, as inscrutable to each other as nature. In the works that come after *Pierre*, in "The Piazza," "The Encantadas," "Benito Cereno," "Bartleby," *The Confidence-Man, Clarel*, and *Billy Budd*, Melville describes the hapless survivors of this world's wreck, forced to live out their empty lives in confusion, fright, and ignorance.

6

The Short Stories, *Israel Potter,*
The Confidence-Man: "Runaways,
Castaways, Solitaries,
Grave-Stones, Etc."

the special curse, as one may call it, of the Encantadas, that
which exalts them in desolation above Idumea and the Pole,
is, that to them change never comes; neither the change of
seasons nor of sorrows. Cut by the Equator, they know not autumn, and they know not spring; while already reduced to the
lees of fire, ruin itself can work little more upon them. The
showers refresh the deserts; but in these isles, rain never falls.
Like split Syrian gourds left withering in the sun, they are
cracked by an everlasting drought beneath a torrid sky. "Have
mercy on me," the wailing spirit of the Encantadas seems to
cry, "and send Lazarus that he may dip the tip of his finger in
water and cool my tongue, for I am tormented in this flame." [1]

*P*ierre, the long, crabbed postscript to the "Epilogue" of *Moby-Dick,*
is Melville's pained memorandum to himself that fixes once and for
all the terminus ad quem of humanity's bold quest: certain significance
does not lurk in all things and all things are, indeed, of little worth. After
Pierre, with the notable exception of "The Piazza," Melville does not
write a single piece of fiction that is even remotely like the quest novels
of his early career. That persistent, if uneven, sense of motion in the early
fiction, that movement always toward an unrealized but vividly imagined

goal, is replaced in the late fiction by unrelenting stasis and inertia. The most manifest and tangible human goal of the early fiction—to find and keep a friend, a comrade, a lover—in the late fiction becomes of all human dreams the most impossible. In the world of Melville's late fiction each individual is an island in an archipelago of other human islands, each cut off from the other by an impossible gulf.[2]

The shaking, even the shattering, of personal faith is, of course, a common theme in nineteenth-century literature, and in the largest cultural terms, one can say that the entire Western world in the nineteenth century saw theism gradually but surely give way to doubts, denials, and a host of secular, substitute "faiths." But Melville of all his contemporaries provides the clearest and the fullest paradigm of the movement from faith to hope to doubt to skepticism to unbelief, and Melville is unique in having possessed the courage to recount in precise detail the disintegration and ruin of our fondest beliefs.

The working out in *Moby-Dick* and *Pierre* of all the problems generated by the earlier fiction precipitated in Melville a crisis that was artistic as well as philosophical. Until 1852, Melville's fiction was built on the assumption that however disappointing the world of experience, there were other, better worlds to be discovered. The fiction after *Pierre* portrays the self as standing at "ground zero" in a "closed" world, devoid of possibilities for the searcher after truth. Faced with the loss of everything familiar to his mind and fertile for his art, Melville did a remarkable thing: he adopted a virtually new artistic stance and set about to capture the essence of his impoverished world.

Perhaps the most elemental shift in Melville's artistic perspectives after 1852 is to be noted in the likeness of the various works. The dialectic of mind and art we have noted in the early novels comes to rest after 1852 in a grim thesis that allows for no progression, no antithesis. The development of theme from work to work as found in the early fiction is virtually absent from the late works, and although "Benito Cereno," "Bartleby," and *Billy Budd* do pose "problems," the working out of these narratives precludes any conceivable solutions. In this sense there is no necessary or inherent "order" in the late works comparable to the developmental order of the novels *Typee* through *Pierre*, and *The Piazza Tales, The Confidence-Man,* and *Billy Budd* can, in a sense, be read in any order without harming our sense of the individual works or their combined effect. The theme of all the late works is the unrelieved isolation of the individual, and it is apt that each work stands, as it were, alone. But taken together the works embody Melville's conviction that isolation is the absolute as well as the principal condition of all of us, and, therefore, it is equally apt that each work stands as a replicative commentary on the others.

"The Piazza"

"Bartleby," "Benito Cereno," and *Billy Budd* are comparable to *Moby-Dick* in intellectual force and artistic impact, and I will turn to them shortly. But to glimpse the full dimensions of the alterations in Melville's art after 1852 I would first like to approach two "lesser" works: "The Piazza" and "The Encantadas." "The Piazza" was written specially for the book publication of five tales previously published in *Putnam's*, and since Melville saw fit to give its title to the complete volume, and clearly intended it as a preface or fictional gloss upon the other tales, I see no reason to ignore his intentions.[3] In sum, "The Piazza" is about vision—about how and why and to what ends we look for and see the things we do; in its full implications "The Piazza" encompasses all the failed visions of those characters who people the pages of *The Piazza Tales, The Confidence-Man*, and *Billy Budd*.

In its wearied recitation of old dreams, new nightmares, "The Piazza" stands as a perfect link between the hopeful aspiration of the early fiction and the bleak disenchantment of the later works. The narrator in "The Piazza" is an old, sick seafarer who has gone to ground by taking a house in the country. And although we are told little or nothing about the narrator's history before his retreat into the country, we infer a good deal from his observations on and responses to his new situation. The narrator's house is set within a "monastery of mountains" ("Piazza," 439), and this sense of enclosure prevails throughout the tale. Little matter what brought him inland; it is clear he will never return to the sea. Yet old habits and old urges die hard, and although his one-time horizon-to-horizon outlook has shrunk to a "circle of the stars cut by the circle of the mountains" ("Piazza," 437), nevertheless he must have his perspective, his inland quarterdeck—his piazza.

Much to the amusement of "all the neighborhood" ("Piazza," 440), the narrator decides upon a north-facing piazza, the ostensible reason being that a northerly piazza captures the view of "Greylock, with all his hills about him, like Charlemagne among his peers" ("Piazza," 438). But in a flourish of rhetorical antithesis reminiscent of his manner in *Moby-Dick*, Melville fixes the true significance of the narrator's choice by his reasoned rejection of the other perspectives open to him. East, south and west variously, but cumulatively, offer prospects of pastoral peace, even Edenic tranquillity. South, west, and east offer "very fine," "sweet," and "goodly" sights to be sure ("Piazza," 439), but the compass of the narrator's soul points to the magnetic truth of Greylock's north. The truth of this northern prospect lies in its similarity to the sea, by which the one-time wanderer can survey "the vastness and the lonesomeness . . . oceanic, and the silence and the sameness" of his world ("Piazza," 440). Another of Melville's unaccommodated men, the narrator "even in December" is not repelled and "with frosted beard" paces "the sleety deck, weathering Cape Horn" ("Piazza," 440).

There are many examples of stoical resignation in the other late tales —in "Bartleby," "Benito Cereno," "The Encantadas," and *Billy Budd*, but "The Piazza," as an "introduction" to Melville's late work, gives the reader an overarching, definitive statement of what we have given up and what we must resign ourselves to. Melville embodies in the person of the "Piazza" narrator one final Midsummer Night's Dream, one last "inland voyage to fairy-land" ("Piazza," 440); at the end of this voyage the narrator will launch his yawl "no more for fairy-land": henceforth he will forever "stick to the piazza" ("Piazza," 453).[4]

The narrator's journey up the mountain to Marianna's hut is the last romantic quest to be found in Melville's fiction. Old, sick, and world-weary, the narrator is no Taji ready to jump ship in mid-Pacific in search of golden isles, but on one "mad poet's afternoon" ("Piazza," 441), the old embers of dying dreams are stirred one last time by the glimpsed sight of "one spot of radiance, where all else was shade" ("Piazza," 442). In fancy, the narrator sees the radiance as "some haunted ring where fairies dance" ("Piazza," 442); in more mundane terms, he sees it as a mountain cottage, "magically fitted up and glazed" ("Piazza," 443), inhabited by "some glad mountain-girl" ("Piazza," 444).

What sets this old narrator apart from naive Tommo and dreamy Taji is that he knows his fancies are mere fancies. Although he reads *Midsummer Night's Dream* and calls Don Quixote the "sagest sage that ever lived" ("Piazza," 444) and invokes Edmund Spenser as his guide to fairyland, what finally sets him off on his journey is his immediate and absolute dissatisfaction with reality. All the dismay and disappointment of the narrator's closed-in life and the essential irony of the entire tale are captured by Melville in the memorable image of the Chinese creeper which, having climbed the post of the piazza, "had burst out in starry bloom," only to reveal beneath its leaves "millions of strange, cankerous worms" ("Piazza," 444). With this image of blighted hope fixed firmly in his mind the narrator sets out "with faith" ("Piazza," 444) on his voyage to fairyland.

The narrator's journey up the mountain proves to be an exercise in unrequited hope. Like Browning's Childe Roland, Melville's narrator traverses a landscape of abandoned efforts and thwarted hopes. At the very beginning of his tale the narrator characterizes his age as a time of "failing faith and feeble knees" ("Piazza," 438), and this sense of our world and faith being worn away relentlessly is captured in this mountain scene through the image of the "ceaseless whirling of a flintstone—ever wearing, but itself unworn"—a flintstone that churns out "skull-hollow" pots in the "step-like ledges of a cascade" ("Piazza," 445).

Haunted by visions of cankered flowers, wrecks, empty chapels, and hollowed skulls, the narrator continues his last necessary quest. His literal movement is up the mountain, but metaphorically his journey is backward through time. Passing beyond the old mill and a small clearing he comes upon a strange Eden, complete with "Eve's apples; seek-no-furthers" ("Piazza," 445). But the narrator refuses to take the clue, and Melville's readers are not allowed to. We push on with the narrator beyond convention to an elemental reality: "the way now lay where path was none, and none might go but by himself, and only go by daring" ("Piazza," 445–46). With the narrator we climb the mountain to yet another of Melville's Pisgah views—this time of a most unpromising land.

The fairyland of Marianna's cottage is defined, dominated rather, by its surroundings: "Near by—ferns, ferns, ferns; further—woods, woods, woods; beyond—mountains, mountains, mountains; then—sky, sky, sky. . . . Nature, and but nature, house and all . . ." ("Piazza," 447), and although this is not nature red in tooth and claw, it is an elemental nature, relentlessly indifferent to humanity and maddening in its indifference. The narrator's fond assumption that "Una and her lamb dwell here" ("Piazza," 447) is the last expression of hope in "The Piazza," and, it is worth noting, the final expression of hope to be found in all of Melville's fiction.

As "The Piazza" moves to its conclusion, the narrator's golden dream of Una and her lamb, with all their Spenserean connotations of Truth, Reason, Faith, and Salvation, becomes, through the alembic of Melville's irony, the most leaden vision of despair. Marianna, the orphan, who with her orphan brother inhabits "the sole house upon the mountain" ("Piazza," 448) is no Wordsworthian highland girl, "ripening in perfect innocence." She is, instead, nature's child maddened by the blank desolation of her life. "Knowing nothing, hearing nothing . . . never reading, seldom speaking, yet ever wakeful" ("Piazza," 451), her life is reduced to the lowest level of human existence: "weariness and wakefulness together" ("Piazza," 451). Living amid a "stillness . . . so still, deafness might have forgot itself" ("Piazza," 451), Marianna lives only with the shadows of her mind. Tortured upon a wheel of endless "thinking, thinking" ("Piazza," 452), Marianna's only hope for a cure is to "get to yonder house, and but look upon whoever the happy being is that lives there!" ("Piazza," 452).

Her wish, of course, provides the two-edged irony of this grim little tale's conclusion, an irony honed even finer by the narrator's response: "I . . . well could wish that I were that happy one of the happy house you dream you see; for then you would behold him now, and, as you say, this weariness might leave you" ("Piazza," 452–53). Ironically, there is a truth to be found in Marianna's forlorn experience—the truth that affirms that happiness is but a figment of mind, founded upon, and dependent upon, distance, ignorance, and a willingness to disbelieve one's own experience. And it is in this context that the narrator's response to Marianna is fraught with so much meaning. His self-denial confirms at once his own unhappiness and his recognition that all dreams of happiness are but shadowy fictions of tortured minds. Marianna's dream of his happy, sun-gilt house perfectly mirrors his dream of her fairy cottage, and the weary wakefulness of her empty life is a mirror of his own pained existence.

The narrator's conclusion is both abrupt and definitive: "—Enough. Launching my yawl no more for fairy-land, I stick to the piazza" ("Piazza," 453). This beginning to the story's penultimate paragraph yields what appears to be the narrator's contentment as he sits in his "box royal" looking out at his "theatre of San Carlo" ("Piazza," 453). But although there might be something of Keats in Melville's conception of this tale, there is nothing of that latter-day Keats—Wallace Stevens. For Melville, illusion is illusion, and fiction, supreme or otherwise, is fiction, and both are but veneers to the truth that "every night, when the curtain falls, . . . comes in with darkness" ("Piazza," 453). Thus, as the tale ends, the narrator is possessed by the same demon of wakeful weariness that possessed Marianna. Sleepless, the narrator paces his piazza deck "haunted by Marianna's face, and many as real a story" ("Piazza," 453).[5]

Throughout the rest of his writing career Melville dramatizes the finality of his conviction that the individual lives in utter isolation from all other individuals. Passivity, stasis, impotence, the illusion of beauty and the futility of dreams characterize not just "The Piazza" but virtually all of Melville's late fiction, and in their various ways "Benito Cereno," "Bartleby," and *Billy Budd* are perhaps best read as elaborations on the weary face behind the window and the sleepless pacing of the one-time searcher after truth who is appalled by the awful truth he has found.

"The Encantadas"

Companion to "The Piazza" in narrative voice, theme, and "philosophical" conclusion is "The Encantadas," Melville's collection of ten loosely linked sketches on the Galapagos Islands. As the title to "Sketch Tenth" indicates, these are tales of "Runaways, Castaways, Solitaries, Grave-Stones, Etc." ("En," 113), the compound effect of which is to evoke the tenor and texture of life in a world that is essentially uninhabitable. From first sketch to last Melville makes it inescapably clear, through allusion, metaphor, and overt comparison, that what he describes is not the biological, topographical, and geographical reality of the Enchanted Isles, but the metaphorical truth of humanity's fallen world. With or without Darwin, Melville in the Galapagos finds and formulates hints toward his theory of the creation and perpetuation of life on earth. In a canon not overly memorable for its optimism and reassuring vision, the sketches of "The Encantadas" represent, perhaps, Melville's deepest probing at the darkest axis of reality.

"Sketch First" is on "the isles at large," and sets the tone for the collection of sketches to follow. Most emphatically the epigraph to the first sketch effectively kills at birth any expectations or recollections in the reader's mind of the happy valleys and golden isles in Melville's early novels; the enchantment of these isles springs from Duessa not Una. They are "'Wandring Islands'" that "'to and fro ronne/in the wide waters'" drawing "*many a wandring wight/Into most deadly daunger and distressed plight*" ("En," 49).

The futility of searching for truth amid manifold fictions surfaces again and again in Melville's later writing, but nowhere is the negation of such a search put more elementally than in "The Encantadas." Here, through his narrator, Melville lets his darkest imaginings run unfettered among his remembered impressions of the stark Pacific archipelago. The islands are "five-and-twenty heaps of cinders," more desolate than "abandoned cemeteries of long ago" or the Dead Sea ("En," 49–50), more solitary than "the great forests of the north, the expanses of unnavigated waters, the Greenland ice-fields" ("En," 50). The isles look, in sum, "much as the world at large might, after a penal conflagration" ("En," 49).

In "The Encantadas," Melville sketches his vision of the world's end, but more than that, his vision haunts him and us as a not too distorted mirror of the world we live in. There is horror enough in the "emphatic uninhabitableness" of islands where "rain never falls" and "change never comes" ("En," 50), where "no voice, no low, no howl is heard" ("En," 51), and where vegetation consists of "tangled thickets of wiry bushes, without fruit and without a name" ("En," 51). This "Plutonian sight" leads the narrator irresistibly to the conclusion that "in no world but a fallen one could such lands exist" ("En," 51), and the nightmare of his experience intrudes itself, at the end of "Sketch First," into his waking world. At home in the Adirondack Mountains, the narrator recalls "as in a dream" his "far distant rovings in the baked heart of the charmed isles" and even in the midst of "social merriment and . . . revels held by candle-light" ("En," 54) he cannot resist the feeling that in his time he has "slept upon evilly enchanted ground" ("En," 54).[6]

The tortoises alluded to so ominously at the end of "Sketch First" become the subject proper of "Sketch Second." Again Melville is impressionistic rather than precise in depicting the islands' famous tortoises to his readers. The tortoises' great age makes a lasting impression on the narrator, for they are the "oldest inhabitants of this, or any other isle" ("En," 57), the breathing allegories of "dateless, indefinite endurance" ("En," 57). But a second trait of the tortoises makes an equally strong impression on the narrator—their determination. Lying awake in his bunk and listening to the "slow weary draggings of the three ponderous strangers" ("En," 57) across the decks above, the narrator muses on the tortoises' characteristic behavior of not moving aside "for any impediment" ("En," 58), and tells us of finding one of the tortoises "butted like a battering-ram against the immovable foot of the foremast, and still striving, tooth and nail, to force the impossible passage" ("En," 58).

This seemingly amusing little anecdote tells us more about Melville's view of human endeavours than about his view of Galapagos marine life. The narrator is uncertain whether he should term the tortoises' behavior a product of "stupidity" or of "resolution" ("En," 58). And this essential ambivalance in the narrator's mind is compounded as he muses. On the one hand, he sees them as "victims of a penal, or malignant, or perhaps a downright diabolical enchanter," but in the very next sentence he views them as self-determined heroes, ramming themselves "heroically against rocks, . . . nudging, wriggling, wedging, in order to displace them, and so hold on their inflexible path" ("En," 58). Finally, he concludes, "Their crowning curse is their drudging impulse to straightforwardness in a belittered world" ("En," 58). No divinity nor diabolism here—merely the irreducible fact that tortoises move in straight lines, whatever the consequences.

Melville is indeed attempting to survey the shaky "foundations of the world," for in the context of "The Encantadas," not just tortoises, but all living things, including human beings, are resolute, or stupid, or both, in their persistence amid the punishing impediments of this world. Toil is as hopeless as it is necessary. Straightforwardness is a curse in a bent, belittered world, and those who survive are both heroes and victims by virtue of this survival.

There is little comfort to be found in the first two sketches of "The Encantadas," for the microcosm of Melville's Galapagos is a flinty, intransigent world, mutely mocking the life that stubbornly clings to it. For Darwin the biologist, the Galapagos Islands recalled the dawn of time, prompting that great imaginative intuition of the *Origin of Species*. For Melville the artist, those same islands and that same imagined dawn prompt a wondrous horror at the harlot nature that for once refuses to paint herself and thus shows freely to the world the charnel house within.

The next eight sketches of "The Encantadas" present variations on this dominant theme of life being tenuously, if stubbornly, clung to in the midst of inhospitable and unrelenting nature. The third and fourth sketches are digressive and dilatory, presenting the reader with some general history, topography, and geography of the isles. But in this anti-Eden, this infinitely fallen world, this microcosm of a world created out of indifference, it is the human element that especially intrigues Melville. The fifth and sixth sketches offer the first cursory glimpses of pirates, explorers, and sailors who had touched upon the islands, but in the last four sketches, Melville deals in greater detail with the sometime inhabitants of the isles, and it is in these sketches that his writing takes on its greatest power and conviction.

The last four sketches of "The Encantadas" represent a descent into the lower reaches of hell, with Melville's narrator serving as our Virgilian guide.[7] The tales of the buccaneers of Barrington Isle, the Dog-King of Charles' Isle, the Chola widow of Norfolk Isle, and the hermit despot, Oberlus, of Hood's Isle present a memorable drama of ever-increasing human suffering and depravity. Together the sketches represent sardonic variations on the popular romantic theme of the noble savage, for all the tales depict the behavior of people who have been able to step aside from historical precedent and social convention and return to a state of nature. Melville's summary judgment is uncompromising and harsh: in the world of the Encantadas the strong steal, torture, murder and rape; the weak suffer and die. This is Melville's portrait of the state of nature, this abandoned Eden with no God and no Satan, with only humanity, naked and alone in a frightening world.

The first of Melville's "noble savages" depicted is the Creole Dog-King of "Sketch Seventh." The sketch in its larger purposes might be viewed as Melville's sardonic exposé of the failure of all political and social systems. By thus polarizing the terms of social and political order and dramatizing their inevitable failure Melville suggests quite emphatically that people in groups are essentially ungovernable. Founded upon coercive force and the fear it engenders, the Dog-King's absolute power defeats itself in its own exercise: the Dog-King decimates the population of his kingdom by hunting down and shooting his "rebellious" subjects ("En," 82); and, on the other hand, his attempt to increase power by recruiting malcontents from passing ships leads directly to discontent and ambition among his "aristocracy," culminating in a mutiny and the defeat and banishment of the Creole.

The defeat of the despotic Dog-King and the proclamation of a republic by the mutineers do not usher in a golden era of life, liberty, and the pursuit of happiness, however. Instead, the new order is described by Melville's narrator as a "permanent *Riotocracy* in which all sorts of desperadoes . . . in the name of liberty did just what they pleased" ("En," 84). In "Sketch Seventh," neither absolute monarchy nor republicanism holds any promise; in Melville's "state of nature," the self's radical isolation and consequent self-interest allow for no middle ground between the tyranny of an absolute sovereign and the anarchy of a democracy.

In all the post-*Pierre* fiction Melville tends to polarize his terms of reference with regard both to character and to theme. This polarizing, disjunctive logic was present in the early fiction as well, but in a critically different form. From *Typee* to *Pierre*, the disjunctive choices presented to Melville's protagonists took the form of complex, but mutually exclusive options. Tommo must choose between Typee or Happar—cannibal or happy savage; Taji must choose between Yillah or Hautia—dream maiden or witch; Ishmael must make a fine, perhaps moot, choice between a wisdom that is woe and a woe that is madness. But by the *Piazza Tales*, Melville's depiction of humanity's shattered beliefs and despair push him toward a disjunctive form of logic expressed as a negation of all options. Neither Marianna's mountain retreat nor the old sailor's piazza provides respite from life's weary wakefulness. Neither authority nor liberty gives direction to our rudderless drifting before life's indifferent winds. Neither absolute faith nor total faithlessness shields us from the hammering pain of living.

This disjunctive logic that annihilates all hope dominates Melville's greatest last works—"Bartleby," "Benito Cereno," and *Billy Budd*, but perhaps the clearest expression of the ethical void that underlies these great works is found in the humbler, more elemental "Encantadas." Although Melville dramatizes in Hunilla and Oberlus the antithesis of the absolutely good heart (faithful, loving, and kind) and the absolutely evil, degraded heart (vicious, hateful, and cruel), in the process of this dramatization he demonstrates the common experience of hopelessness and degradation in the best and worst of humanity.

It is easy to sympathize with Hunilla, the Chola widow. Betrayed and abandoned by the false promises of the French whaling captain and robbed of her husband and brother by a fickle sea that kills even as it offers life-giving sustenance, Hunilla is depicted as a saint by the narrator and his peculiarly sensitive and reverent shipmates. But her holiness and the reverence she inspires spring wholly from her ability to endure unrelenting pain, Norfolk Isle thus becoming "a spot made sacred by the strongest trials of humanity" ("En," 86).

Hunilla is indeed the quintessence of lost, orphaned humanity. Deprived of all human contact by the death of her husband and brother, waiting for a rescue ship that will never come, Hunilla becomes "entirely lost" in the labyrinth of time. Keeping faith while gods, "who never plighted it" ("En," 91), are faithless, "out of treachery invoking trust" ("En," 94), Hunilla is the living emblem of those who must endure, not live, life. Her life, like Marianna's, becomes merely one "long night of busy numbering, misery's mathematics, to weary her too-wakeful soul to sleep; yet sleep for that was none" ("En," 94–95).

We last see Hunilla "passing into Payta town, riding upon a small gray ass" ("En," 101). But the momentary sense of triumph invoked by this allusion to Christ's entry into Jerusalem gives way in the closing words of the sketch to the unrelieved pain of crucifixion: "and before her on the ass's shoulders, she eyed the jointed workings of the beast's armorial cross" ("En," 101). Suffering without salvation, miraculously sustained by a pointless, cruel faith, Hunilla is the "heart of earthly yearning, frozen by the frost which falleth from the sky" ("En," 101).

In "Sketch Ninth," the narrator takes pains to make clear that in recounting the life of Oberlus he is presenting us a picture of human life in its most degraded form. In nature, Oberlus is "warped and crooked" ("En," 103), and his appearance is that of a "victim of some malignant sorceress" ("En," 103). A self-confessed Caliban, he brings to the savage Hood's Isle "qualities more diabolical than are to be found among any of the surrounding cannibals" ("En," 102). But he is no monster in the common sense of the term. Rather, he might well be viewed as the product of the essential human condition as Melville defines it in "The Encantadas." He is Hunilla devoid of all mad hope, fashioning a modus vivendi out of sane despair. This self-wrenching solitude is not peculiar to Oberlus but, rather, is the essential condition of human existence in the Encantadas (i.e., the world). Oberlus' twisted misanthropy is presented not as extraneous but as intrinsic to the human condition, and in Oberlus we recognize, however reluctantly, the distorted but recognizable reflection of ourselves.

The tenth and final sketch, "Runaways, Castaways, Solitaries, Grave-Stones, Etc.," provides a summary view of human existence in such an inhospitable world. And here, as in "The Piazza," that existence is defined as solitary pain. The stopping place for "ships bound on dreary and protracted voyages" ("En," 113), the Enchanted Isles are emblematic of the larger world in which "an intolerable thirst is provoked, for which no running stream offers its kind relief" ("En," 114). In this demimonde of "vanishing humanity" ("En," 115) there is no society—only castaways, runaways, and solitaries. And there is no communication—only letters sealed and corked in bottles, holding out hope in the midst of despair while "long months and months, whole years glide by and no applicant appears" ("En," 116). In the end there are only gravestones. In a complex double simile, the narrator likens the Encantadas to "those old monastic institutions of Europe" and to "the great general monastery of earth" whose "inmates go not out of their own walls to be inurned, but are entombed there where they die" ("En," 116). And he concludes his sketches of the Encantadas, fittingly, with two epitaphs. Death is the inevitable end to all life, of course, but more than that, Melville suggests, that bleak end haunts the gaiety and gameness by which we, with Hunilla, "repulse a sane despair with a hope which is but mad" ("En," 93–94).

"Benito Cereno"

As paradigms for Melville's late fiction, "The Piazza" and "The Encantadas" define the implications of the failed quest. Failing to find the best of all possible worlds, Melville keeps his courage to the end and describes for us instead what Schopenhauer terms the worst of all *possible* worlds, a world so precariously perched on the verge of dissolution that the slightest tip of its axis would send it perishing into the void.

Such is the world of "Benito Cereno." In setting, character, and theme, "Benito Cereno" presents a gray, surreal world of stasis, non-events, uncertain meanings, and dead-end clues, pretty well signifying nothing throughout the main body of the tale, but erupting into sound and fury in its close. Essentially a tedious narrative with its self-negating suppositions and counter-suppositions by Captain Delano and its hints and counter-hints by the smugly ironic narrator, it generates our interest and maintains our attention only by leading us to expect that truth will out in the end.[8] Like readers of an Agatha Christie mystery we nervously await the denouement when some Melvillean Poirot will trace effect back to hidden cause, winnow out the chaff of irrelevancy, and return us to our safe, predictable world. The denouement in "Benito Cereno" falls far to the side of our expectations, however, and the haunting power of the tale's conclusion issues from our recognition, in contrast to Captain Delano's, that there is no unknotting the mystery of Don Benito Cereno and the *San Dominick*—and no safe, predictable world to go back to.[9]

The opening three paragraphs of "Benito Cereno" set the tone and tempo for the entire tale. The first paragraph takes us, with Amaso Delano, to the outermost edge of the world—to a "small, desert, uninhabited island toward the southern extremity of the long coast of Chile," and it fixes us there "at anchor" ("BC," 255). The second paragraph tersely introduces the dramatic center of the narrative, the confrontation of Captain Delano of the *Bachelor's Delight* and Don Benito Cereno of the *San Dominick*. But it is the third paragraph that gives tone to these images of isolation, stasis, and marginal existence: "everything was mute and calm; everything gray" ("BC," 255). The world of "Benito Cereno" is, indeed, a world of gray muteness, with a sea "fixed" like "waved lead that has cooled and set in the smelter's mould" ("BC," 255). Overhead is the "gray surtout" of the sky, while skimming over the leaden sea are "gray fowl, kith and kin with flights of troubled gray vapors among which they were mixed" ("BC," 255). The disembodied "gray" narrator adds the final word to this ominous opening: "shadows present, foreshadowing deeper shadows to come" ("BC," 255).

The narrative that follows this ominous opening is centered in Captain Delano's meeting and coming to terms with Benito Cereno of the *San Dominick*. Once again the narrator foreshadows coming events when he tells us that Captain Delano is "a person of a singularly undistrustful good-nature, not liable, except on extraordinary and repeated incentives, and hardly then, to indulge in personal alarms, any way involving the imputation of malign evil in man" ("BC," 256), and this observation leads the narrator to ask the question that will haunt the tale—"whether, in view of what humanity is capable, such a trait implies, along with a benevolent heart, more than ordinary quickness and accuracy of intellectual perception" ("BC," 256).

This quick, but sharp and emphatic, characterization of Captain Delano identifies him for us as a loyal son of the late eighteenth century—a "sentimentalist" believer in the benevolence of humanity, and as the narrative unfolds we find him similarly loyal to the corollary eighteenth-century belief in the regularity and predictability of a rational universe. "In the year 1799, Captain Amaso Delano, of Duxbury, in Massachusetts" ("BC," 255) is seen as the inheritor of a century's beliefs and, more particularly, of eighteenth-century America's belief in self-evident truths, the inalienable rights of man, and the sovereignty of the individual.

"Benito Cereno," like much of Melville's fiction early and late, is based upon a "problem," the problem in this case being whether or not the beliefs and assumptions of sentimentalism and rationalism, of the Declaration of Independence and the American Constitution, can prevail in the harbor of "a small, desert, uninhabited island toward the southern extremity of the long coast of Chile." In more immediate terms, the "problem" of this tale is whether or not these beliefs and assumptions will allow Captain Delano to understand and survive his own immediate experience.

Expressed in this schematic way, the problem of "Benito Cereno" would appear to be fairly straightforward and clear-cut, but Melville's working through the problem produces an intricacy of meaning that is anything but simple. From Captain Delano's first sighting of the vapor-shrouded hull of the *San Dominick* to the post-voyage trial of Babo and his conspirators, the tale, in all its aspects—its characters, its events, and its meanings—presents itself as ambiguous, partial, and inconclusive.

The *San Dominick* itself stands as a fit emblem of the tale's essential mystery. Wrapped in vapors and driven by a wind "extremely light and baffling," she reveals an uncertainty in her movements that makes it difficult for Delano "to decide whether she meant to come in or no—what she wanted, or what she was about" ("BC," 256–57). Mysterious in the dawn's uncertain light, the *San Dominick* is no less enigmatic to Captain Delano when he sees her close up. Then she appears like a "whitewashed monastery after a thunder-storm" ("BC," 257), a decrepit hull launched "from Ezekiel's Valley of Dry Bones" ("BC," 258). The *San Dominick* is a floating "relic of faded grandeur" ("BC," 258), the primary vestige of which is "the shield-like stern-piece, intricately carved with the arms of Castile and Leon, medallioned about by groups of mythological or symbolic devices; uppermost and central of which was a dark satyr in a mask, holding his foot on the prostrate neck of a writhing figure, likewise masked" ("BC," 258–59).

This heraldic device is the first and one of the most memorable of several emblematic devices that punctuate the tale. The stern-piece, the shrouded figurehead with the motto "sequid vuestro jefe," the Spanish sailor's intricate knot, the choric oakum pickers and axe polishers, the key around Don Benito's neck, and the empty scabbard at his side all contribute to our sense of the tale as a cryptograph waiting to be solved if we could just assign the proper value to one of the unknown ciphers. In this regard we are like Captain Delano, who is also trying to solve the puzzle of the *San Dominick* and its strange captain, crew, and cargo, and the key to the puzzle is Don Benito Cereno. Until he speaks, Captain Delano muddles his way through the events and appearances of the tale by conjecture and guess, the result being that both Delano and reader are forced to hold several hypothetical interpretations in their minds simultaneously, interpretations that necessarily contradict each other. For Captain Delano, the result of this mental juggling act is indecision, self-doubt, and anxiety, leading to a passivity and moral paralysis by which he can only respond to the world of the *San Dominick*, not initiate any significant action in it. For the reader intent on understanding what he or she reads, this mental juggling produces a keen sense of frustration and impatience to get to the bottom of things.

Throughout the main "action" of the narrative, Captain Delano and reader alike are frustrated in their efforts by the maddening reticence of Don Benito. He is, as Captain Delano sees him, the "involuntary victim of mental disorder" transformed "into a block, or rather a loaded cannon, which, until there is call for thunder, has nothing to say" ("BC," 265). Cold and distant in demeanor, laconic in reply to Captain Delano's questions, apparently indifferent to all that takes place, Don Benito holds out no assistance to Captain Delano or the reader intent on solving the riddle of the *San Dominick*. As the "key" to the riddle he is as puzzling as the riddle itself.

Thwarted repeatedly by Don Benito's defensive, unyielding posture, Captain Delano finds himself in a perfect quandary—a very uncomfortable position for a man who craves only a "pleasant sort of sunny sight" ("BC," 292). Faced with only two explanations for Don Benito's behavior—"innocent lunacy, or wicked imposture" ("BC," 279)—Captain Delano relentlessly, if circuitously, gropes his way through the maze of appearances to the former rationalization. The man unwilling to appear uncivil even to incivility itself just cannot for very long endure the thought that "under the aspect of infantile weakness, the most savage energies might be couched" ("BC," 280), cannot sustain his worst imaginings—that the *San Dominick*, once near his own ship, might "like a slumbering volcano, suddenly let loose energies now hid" ("BC," 286). The cornerstone to Captain Delano's rationalization is his unshakeable belief in the predictability and benevolence of the world and the self and the integrity of his own experience.

Captain Delano's reductive, simplistic response to his tangled world is captured most vividly in the "knot" scene.[10] As the narrator observes, Captain Delano's own mind passes "by a not uncongenial transition, . . . from its own entanglements to those of the hemp" ("BC," 296) being worked by the old Spanish sailor. But our expectations that Delano will unravel this "double-bowline-knot, treble-crown-knot, backhanded-well-knot, knot-in-and-out-knot, and jamming-knot" narrative ("BC," 296) are thwarted once again. The sailor's invitation to Delano to "undo it [the knot], cut it, quick" ("BC," 296) produces paralysis in Delano: "knot in hand, and knot in head, Captain Delano stood mute" ("BC," 296). In an effective anticlimax, one of the old Negroes takes the knot from Captain Delano's hand and "with some African word, equivalent to pshaw, . . . tossed the knot overboard" ("BC," 297).

Captain Delano simply cannot fathom his own experience. Paralyzed and mute, like the Chola widow, and like Marianna, he can merely endure it. Surely this is the low point in the narrative for a man of "a singularly undistrustful good nature" committed to sunny sights and civil sociability. Yet it is precisely at this point of low-ebbing spirits that Captain Delano's self-rationalization reveals its nature and power most clearly—as his ship's boat, the *Rover*, comes into view. All his doubts about Don Benito and the strange happenings aboard the *San Dominick* evaporate not because the *Rover* promises reinforcements, but because the boat prompts familiar associations that remove his mind from the strangeness of the *San Dominick* and return him to his erstwhile world of predictability, order, and well-being. Reminiscing on his childhood, Captain Amaso Delano cannot believe that "little Jack of the Beach, that used to go berrying with cousin Nat and the rest" is "to be murdered here at the ends of the earth, on board a haunted pirate-ship by a horrible Spaniard" ("BC," 297). Celebrating a rare marriage of egotism and naivety, Captain Delano exclaims to himself, "Who would murder Amaso Delano? His conscience is clean. There is some one above" ("BC," 298).

The impropriety and irony of Captain Delano's self-assurance is borne out by the following narrative. Repeatedly, his perceptions and assumptions work at cross purposes, his perceptions leading him to the brink of truth and his assumptions pulling him back.[11] The threat of his being murdered is "nonsensical," the intuition that Babo is threatening Don Benito's life with the razor is a "vagary," and the use of the Spanish flag as a lap cloth (or mort cloth) is turned to a feeble joke. His response to Don Benito's remarkable tale of storms and two months' calms is virtually Tertullianesque—turning doubt into belief, absurdity into fact. Captain Delano's will to believe, in fact, has no bounds. Although he continues to have doubts about Don Benito and the *San Dominick*, he represses those doubts on the assumption that nothing bad or untoward can happen to "little Jack of the Beach." Wonderfully oblivious to the trials and vicissitudes of life, ignoring all evidence of Babo's dogging his movements and precluding any private conversation with Don Benito, Captain Delano pilots the *San Dominick* to "safe" anchorage at the side of the *Bachelor's Delight*.

At this point in the narrative, precisely when the danger is greatest for Don Benito, Captain Delano, and the *Bachelor's Delight*, immediately preceding Don Benito's desperate leap into the *Rover* and Babo's murderous leap after him, Captain Delano is lifted to his highest point of ebullient optimism and self-assurance, seeing only "the benign aspect of nature" ("BC," 324). Standing on the decks of the *San Dominick*, the volcano ready to erupt, Captain Delano smiles "at the phantoms which had mocked him" and feels "something like a tinge of remorse, that, by harboring them even for a moment, he should, by implication, have betrayed an atheist doubt of the ever-watchful Providence above" ("BC," 324).

Captain Delano's sanguine reflections are, of course, acutely inappropriate to his true situation, as he himself discovers moments later. All his musings, conjectures, doubts, and self-assurances fuse, then explode in the tumultuous climactic action of the tale, which occurs "with such involutions of rapidity, that past, present, and future seemed one" ("BC," 327). With Don Benito pinned in the bottom of the boat and the crazed Babo thrusting at his "master's" heart with a dagger, Captain Delano finally has "a flash of revelation . . . , illuminating, in unanticipated clearness, his host's whole mysterious demeanor, with every enigmatic event of the day, as well as the entire past voyage of the *San Dominick*" ("BC," 328).

Although emphatic, this climactic revelation does not resolve the issues of the tale, however. The pursuit and capture of the *San Dominick* by the mate and crew of the *Bachelor's Delight* occupy but a few pages of the text, and these concluding "events" of the narrative are far less significant than the lengthy account of the Peruvian tribunal's inquiry into those events. In the records of this trial, and particularly in the deposition given by Don Benito concerning his fate as captain of the *San Dominick*, Melville dramatizes once again the individual's and society's attempt to rationalize and regulate a world that is palpably irrational and uncontrollable.

Melville's view of the law and the judicial system as merely conventional and merely regulatory would probably be endorsed by most modern theorists of jurisprudence, but Melville's concerns are more philosophical than legal, and in "Benito Cereno," as in *Billy Budd* later, he probes the assumptions, workings, and implications of that system without which society could not exist. The conventionality of both the law and the society it upholds is the dominant theme in the closing pages of "Benito Cereno." The stolid assumptions of the tribunal and the stilted conventions of the pseudo-legal rendering of Don Benito's deposition form a stark contrast to the implied horror of Don Benito's experience. As we carefully sift through the "partial translation" ("BC," 333) of Don Benito's statement, incomplete in every sense of the word, it becomes more and more apparent that the "truth" of Don Benito's experience aboard the *San Dominick* will never be known by anyone—except himself. It is certainly not known by the inquiring tribunal, which is satisfied without knowing. And it is certainly not known by Captain Delano who, clearly enough, would prefer not to know.

The narrator emphasizes the point that the tribunal found Don Benito's testimony in itself very dubious, holding to "the opinion that the deponent, not undisturbed in his mind by recent events, raved of some things which could never have happened" ("BC," 333). As a comment upon the singular experience of Don Benito, surely this says more about the law's inability to deal with unprecedented events than it says about the possibility of such unprecedented events taking place. And in fact, the tribunal retraces Captain Delano's own passage from confusion to skepticism to revelation, until finally it is forced to find that "things which could never have happened"—did.

The signal predicament of the tribunal in dealing with events it intrinsically cannot countenance cannot be passed over lightly, for it epitomizes the central problem of the tale—the problem of how both the individual and society come to terms with the unpredictable and the unprecedented. The Law, with its emphasis on precedents, is founded upon the rational principle that all people under certain circumstances will govern themselves in a certain, predictable fashion. Even law *breaking* is rationalized by the codification of "conceivable" crimes with specified appropriate punishments. The point of consternation for the tribunal, as it was for Captain Delano—and for Don Benito originally—centers in Babo. For both captains and for the judges of the *San Dominick* affair Babo is an enigma, a man without precedent—sui generis. The terrible acts he commits aboard the *San Dominick* are monstrous in the eyes of Don Benito, Captain Delano, and the court simply because they cannot fathom Babo's motivations. That is, they cannot dispossess themselves of their own assumptions and "precedents" of experience to see the world as Babo does.[12]

For the tribunal and Captain Delano, catharsis is straightforward. Once convinced of the nature of the crimes and the extent of Babo's guilt, the court sentences him to death and closes the case.[13] Once judgment has been passed, Captain Delano calmly resumes his innocence, for to him "the past is passed" and should be forgotten ("BC," 351).[14] That this innocence survives the grim events of "Benito Cereno" is perhaps the ultimate irony of the story, but for Don Benito, however, the shadow of Babo cannot be dispelled, and his pain yields only to silence and, ultimately, death.

However tantalizing and uncertain the narrative line of "Benito Cereno" might be much of the time, the philosophical implications of its conclusion are clear. As Don Benito tells Captain Delano in the end, "even the best man" may err "in judging the conduct of one with the recesses of whose condition he is not acquainted" ("BC," 351). And as the entire tale demonstrates so clearly, no one—not even the best man—can ever be acquainted with the recesses of another's condition. These two propositions in fact constitute the only solid standpoint from which we can view the tale. From this solid, although narrow, footing we see that in the world of "Benito Cereno" facts and acts have absolute value: they are unyielding and unquestionable. We also see that all values, judgments, and inquiries into motivations are of "little worth." What

Babo *does* transcends everyone's attempt to explain his motives and his character. The tribunal does not understand Babo; indeed, they are given no chance to do so. "Seeing all was over," Babo, like Iago, "uttered no sound, and could not be forced to. His aspect seemed to say, since I cannot do deeds, I will not speak words" ("BC," 352). Conversely, the hollow words of the tribunal's hollow ruling, as empty as Don Benito's artificially stiffened scabbard, give way to the solid enough fact of Babo's hanging.

This absolute disjunction between human acts and human understanding of those acts is characteristic of all Melville's writings after *Moby-Dick*. In "Benito Cereno" the absolute incongruity between what happens aboard the *San Dominick* and the survivors' attempts to rationalize and assimilate those events into their understanding promulgates Melville's view of solipsistic men playing blindman's buff in a world of random, accidental events. It is difficult to find a definitive term for the deep disillusionment of "Benito Cereno." Melville's dramatic depiction of the philosophical, moral, and social vacuum that displaces the human search for some certain significance in all things falls outside the familiar handbook definitions of relativism, nihilism, absurdism, and existentialism. Perhaps the closest I can come to expressing the singular philosophical base of "Benito Cereno" (and "Bartleby," *The Confidence-Man*, and *Billy Budd*) is to term it a radical skepticism (à la Sir Thomas Browne and Pierre Bayle), which, having explored and exposed all false and erroneous explanations of the human condition, discovers that there are no possible explanations left.

The death of expectation is indeed the central and pervasive theme in all Melville's late writings. The notion of regeneration in *Typee, Mardi, Redburn, White-Jacket*, and *Moby-Dick* does not survive in *Pierre* and *The Piazza Tales*. In "Benito Cereno" there are no heroes, and no villains, really; in this world of random encounters there are only random casualties and random survivors.

"Bartleby"

Although "Bartleby" was the first-written of the stories that became the *Piazza Tales*, I have delayed my discussion of it to this point because in many ways it stands as the last word on Melville's concerns and methods between the writing of *Pierre* and the publication of *The Confidence-Man*. "Bartleby" is Melville's reductio ad absurdum on the themes of human isolation and inconsequence in a world of random events and random encounters. Consonant in theme and tone with the stark dreariness of "The Piazza" and "The Encantadas," comparable to "Benito Cereno" in its sharp, dramatic focus, "Bartleby" unfolds with an absolute economy of expression that gives it an intensity unmatched by any of the other *Piazza Tales*. Along with *Billy Budd*, this halting account of an unaccountable scrivener by an unnamed narrator stands as Melville's most trenchant artistic expression of how little has survived the romantic quest's utter wreck.

Above all else, "Bartleby" is a tale of restriction. Its setting is claustrophobic and smothering, its characters few and partially developed, its "action" minimal and repetitive, its themes woven of ignorance, confinement, and death. At the center of this shrunken, and still shrinking, indeterminate world stand the lawyer and Bartleby, the detritus of humanity's struggle to order its world and its experience.[15] Without doubt, the reduced dimensions of the lawyer's and Bartleby's world account for the intensity of the tale, but if for a moment we break the hypnotic spell cast by the fixed center and fixed margins of this claustrophobic world and let our minds drift back to the open seas and open dreams of *Typee*, *Mardi*, and *Moby-Dick*, we gain perhaps the clearest and most emphatic perspective on Melville's altered vision. The writer who would have seized all experience and all knowledge has seen the sands of both sift through his ever-tightening grip until in "Bartleby" only the final few grains remain.

The comparison of "Bartleby" with Melville's earlier fiction is neither gratuitous nor rhetorical. One of the best ways to get at the constantly beckoning, constantly retreating "meaning" of "Bartleby" is to view it as the literary and philosophical antipodes to Melville's earlier quest fiction.[16] It is, as it were, Melville's rejoinder to the romantic suppositions of the earlier fiction, an autopsy performed on the death of the quest. The dynamic, if shifting, world of *Typee*, *Mardi*, and *Moby-Dick* is lost forever, and the world in "Bartleby" is essentially static and moot. The dynamism of doubt and longing that fueled the impatient quests of Tommo, Taji, Redburn, Ahab and Ishmael gives way to the bewilderment and spiritual entropy of the lawyer and Bartleby. In the full ripeness of its disillusionment, "Bartleby" presents a world in which truly "all things are of little worth."

Vacuity of meaning is the dominant and persistent theme of "Bartleby." At the outset of his narrative-life of Bartleby the lawyer confesses that "no materials exist, for a full and satisfactory biography of this man" ("B," 3), and adds that "Bartleby was one of those beings of whom nothing is ascertainable, except from the original sources, and, in his case, those are very small" ("B," 3). If anything, the lawyer's "authorial disclaimer" is an understatement, and the full extent of the narrator's ignorance is revealed in the last pages of the tale, where he confesses he is "wholly unable to gratify" the reader's and his own curiosity "as to who Bartleby was, and what manner of life he led" prior to the events just recounted ("B," 46).

The lawyer's narrative perforce, then, focusses on Bartleby's brief stay in the lawyer's office and the curious relationship that grows up between the two men—a relationship based upon ignorance, separation, and rejection. Indeed, the lawyer-Bartleby relationship, which is both center and circumference of the tale, epitomizes the disintegration of social ties within the microcosmic world of the lawyer's chambers, and the failure of the lawyer and Bartleby to form a viable bond epitomizes the ultimate failure of all humanity. If the post-*Pierre* fiction reveals a general shift in Melville's concerns from metaphysical to social questions, in "Bartleby" Melville makes it painfully clear that there is no longer anything at all to be explored or even questioned "out there," and the characters in this tale are thrown back upon themselves—uneasy cell-mates in a prison world.

Almost all readers agree that the physical setting of the lawyer's chambers dramatically defines the confined lives of those who work and "live" there. Located on the second floor of a building surrounded by other tall buildings, the chambers at one end look out upon "the white wall of the interior of a spacious sky-light shaft" ("B," 4–5) and at the other end command "an unobstructed view of a lofty brick wall, black by age and everlasting shade" ("B," 5). It is difficult for readers of Melville to resist the suggestiveness of white skylights and age-blackened walls, and a reader fresh from reading *Mardi* or *Moby-Dick* might eagerly, or resignedly, await the poetic flourishes on heavenly light, Tartarean blackness, the ambiguity of all things mortal, etc., etc. But in "Bartleby" there are not authorial flights on the whiteness or blackness of walls, there is no procession of dramatic personae to comment on or interpret the walls that define their world. In "Bartleby," these walls remain walls—blank, opaque limits that neither Bartleby, nor lawyer, nor we can go beyond.

Until the lawyer removes himself from the premises and Bartleby is taken to the Tombs, we are allowed scarcely a glimpse of the world outside the lawyer's chambers. This almost total containment of setting, character, and action within the confines of the lawyer's office suggests quite forcefully that it is the larger world writ small, a microcosm of a world that offers nothing but suffocating despair. And the external walls closing in the lawyer's chambers from without find their counterparts within—in the partition that separates the lawyer from Turkey, Nippers, and Ginger-Nut, and the double partitions that separate Bartleby from both the lawyer and his fellow copyists. The lawyer congratulates himself on the device by which "privacy and society were conjoined" ("B," 12), but as the history of Bartleby unfolds the lawyer's sanguine view of his perfect office arrangement turns to horror as he comes to realize the infirmity of the social bond and the terrible isolation of all humanity.

Social disintegration and the isolation of the individual are indeed the defining terms of life within the lawyer's chambered world, for in this cramped, closed world propinquity produces friction, not fellowship. In this regard the tale's minor characters of Turkey, Nippers, and Ginger-Nut typify the general social disorder and through them we are able to diagnose the specific failings in the relationship between the lawyer and Bartleby.

The foremost trait defining Turkey and Nippers is an inability to express themselves as whole men. In fact, Melville's careful Dickensian caricaturing of the two presents them to us as perfect half-men. The lawyer provides little explanation for the strange "split personalities" of his two clerks, and in fact it is the lack of explanation, and by implication the impossibility of one, that gives such persuasive force to their fractional natures. Finding themselves together by mere chance and circumstance, Turkey and Nippers do not communicate with each other at all. At odds and evens throughout the day, they only accommodate themselves to each other in a peripheral way, to whatever degree their warring temperaments allow.

When the lawyer congratulates himself on the fact that since Turkey's and Nippers's fits "relieved each other, like guards" he "never had to do with their eccentricities at one time" ("B," 10), we sense not his victory over circumstance but his capitulation to it. Unable to modify the recalcitrant behavior of his two clerks, the lawyer rationalizes his position by conjuring up a worse scenario. But because a worse scenario implies Turkey or Nippers or both not working at all, or ruining more copy than they complete, we see the lawyer as much a victim to his world as Turkey and Nippers are, the three together performing the most tenuously balanced social dance in which one false step would send all three into confusion.

It is within this context of tenuous existence in a closed world that we view the lawyer-narrator's character. Above all else, the lawyer is a conservative in the essential meaning of the word, holding tenaciously to what he has. Priding himself on his reputation as "an eminently *safe* man" ("B," 4), the lawyer describes his work as "a snug business among rich men's bonds, and mortgages, and title-deeds," performed "in the cool tranquillity of a snug retreat" ("B," 4), but more accurately, the lawyer is a man in retreat. In contrast to the adventurous, expansive narrator-protagonists of Melville's early quest fiction, the lawyer, like the narrator in "The Piazza" and like Captain Delano, pulls his world in about him and aspires to nothing greater than to live out his days in peaceful security. Thus he quietly gloats at having been named a "Master in Chancery"— a "not very arduous office, but very pleasantly remunerative" ("B," 4). Without hope or ambition, the lawyer lives like a "cornered," defeated man: he wishes to survive in whatever comfort is still possible.

Even these radically reduced wants of the lawyer are subject to diminution however. John Jacob Astor is dead and his patronage but a fond memory to the lawyer, and at the time of the telling of the tale the office of Master in Chancery has been abolished. Further, the irascible, however predictable, temperaments of Turkey and Nippers allow for almost anything but tranquillity and security in the lawyer's office world. Thus viewed in the broad perspective, "Bartleby" is the lawyer's narrative account not merely of his strange new scrivener, but of his already narrow world narrowing further. And to a large degree, the fates of Bartleby and the lawyer are so inseparable, their worlds so conjoined, that we view the two central characters of the tale as refractions of each other.[17] The medium of that refraction in the tale is time. The lawyer sees in Bartleby, with horrifying clarity I think, the irresistible future of his own dwindling soul. Reciprocally, as Bartleby completes his irreversible descent into oblivion, he recognizes in the lawyer the last vestige of meaningful human existence.

There is a palpable, although quiet, desperation in the lawyer's behavior even before Bartleby enters his office and his life. Dedicated to tranquillity, the lawyer must make a number of concessions to the disruptive personalities of Turkey and Nippers. He tries to overlook as much as possible Turkey's eccentricities, and when he does remonstrate with him he does it "very gently" ("B," 6). He even suggests that it might be well to "abridge his labors" ("B," 6–7), and he gives Turkey a "highly respectable-looking coat" ("B," 9). But Turkey remains immune to such appeals. The warm coat makes him "insolent" rather than grateful, and the offer of semiretirement provokes in him a defense of old age with the telling conclusion, "sir, we *both* are getting old" ("B," 7).

Faced with Turkey's recalcitrance, the lawyer is characteristically passive and compromising, and he is similarly passive and accommodating with the dyspeptic and recalcitrant Nippers. Thus, one must strongly resist the reductive, if convenient, view of the lawyer as a Wall Street entrepreneur-capitalist, exploiting his poorly paid underlings and revelling in his own financial well-being. Certainly there is considerable social criticism in the tale, and the squinting poverty of the copyists laboring over "rich men's bonds, and mortgages, and title-deeds" ("B," 4) constitutes one of the tale's more memorable images and themes, but Melville's concerns go far beyond the rudimentary terms of "class struggle" as seen by social historians and political scientists cum literary critics. His concerns in "Bartleby" are not with working conditions and wages, nor, ultimately, is the tale about "employer-employee" relationships. Rather, "Bartleby" is an inquiry into the nature of human relationships on the most elemental level. In this regard it is not so much a critique of Wall Street society, or capitalist society, or even American society, as it is a critique of society per se, and with the arrival of Bartleby in the office, the tale becomes Melville's withering critique of the absolute failure of society.

Bartleby's entry into the narrative, his acceptance of a position in the lawyer's chambers, is fraught with great promise. Bartleby is the first, and so far as we know the only, applicant for the additional position of copyist, but the lawyer views him as the answer to a prayer and hires him immediately, for "pallidly neat, pitiably respectable, incurably forlorn," Bartleby impresses the lawyer as someone who "might operate beneficially upon the flighty temper of Turkey, and the fiery one of Nippers" ("B," 11). This typically understated observation by the lawyer-narrator suggests just how quietly desperate he is to order his fragmented, unstable world, for however pallid, pitiable, and forlorn Bartleby might appear, he represents to the lawyer his last chance to make his world whole.

Clearly, Bartleby is not just another copyist to the lawyer. The lawyer places Bartleby's desk on *his* side of the ground glass folding doors that separate the lawyer from Turkey and Nippers and then places a high green folding screen between himself and Bartleby, which, he observes, "might entirely isolate Bartleby from my sight, though not remove him from my voice" ("B," 12). The lawyer's elaborate arrangement allows him, he says, "to have this quiet man within easy call, in case any trifling thing was to be done" ("B," 11), but beneath this subdued, self-effacing statement we recognize the lawyer's employment of Bartleby as his intermediary with the world. In spite of the lawyer's disposition to view Bartleby as intermediary and "savior," it is worth stressing that the lawyer's spontaneous and complete faith in Bartleby is totally misplaced. As the continuing narrative shows, the lawyer's world is completely beyond redemption and Bartleby, after all, is but a savior manqué.

Although in the beginning Bartleby does "an extraordinary quantity of writing" ("B," 12), the lawyer senses the desperation of his cheerless industry and soon abandons his conceit of Bartleby as a meliorating force in the office, finding in him, instead, the source of his greatest discomfort and unrest. The initial source of the lawyer's discomfort, not to mention astonishment, is Bartleby's blank refusal to aid the lawyer in verifying the copying of a law document, a refusal expressed in the soon to become habitual phrase: "I would prefer not to" ("B," 13). More importantly, the lawyer quickly discovers that Bartleby's refusal is not the product of a whim or an erratic swing of temperament akin to Turkey's or Nippers's shifts in mood. On the contrary, the lawyer recognizes that Bartleby's entire identity is bound up in the numbing phrase, "I would prefer not to."

Bartleby's characteristic response to almost all questions, admonitions, and commands is the same: he either replies "I would prefer not to" (on at least twenty-one occasions by rough count) or he remains totally silent. The phrase and the silence are intimately connected of course and comment upon each other. Bartleby's reiterated preferences "not to"— not to read copy, not to go to the Post Office, not to fetch Nippers, not to explain himself or his past—are negative expressions of Bartleby's negated self, so marginal as expression at all that the lawyer's repeated attempts to get beyond them to their cause generates in Bartleby only silence.[18] There is thus (as a number of critics have pointed out in various contexts) a close kinship between Bartleby and Marianna, Hunilla, and Don Benito. Like them, Bartleby appears beaten by life, but also like them he resists our best efforts to get to the bottom of the pain—not to cure it but to understand it. The lawyer does, indeed, try. Far from being the exploitive capitalist-employer of melodrama, the lawyer first acquiesces to Bartleby's refusals, and then goes further, protecting Bartleby from the self-righteous indignation of Turkey and Nippers.

The lawyer provides himself with a rationale for his apparent "weakness" in dealing with a pale young scrivener permanently exempt from being "dispatched on the most trivial errand of any sort" ("B," 20). With a naive, counting-house Christianity common and popular enough in the nineteenth century, the lawyer confesses to purchasing a "delicious self-approval" ("B," 17). But this confession of smug self-righteousness rings false, belied initially by the lawyer's genuine and persistent concern for Bartleby's well-being and ultimately by his profound sense of defeat at Bartleby's death. Either the lawyer feels uncomfortable telling his true motivations to his readers and seeks to disguise them in the conventional garb of an "acceptable" faith, or he is self-deceiving, averting his gaze from self-truths that it would be too painful to confront directly. In fact, both factors operate strongly in the lawyer's character. As the lawyer becomes more and more intricately and intimately involved in Bartleby's life, the shock of recognizing his own fate in Bartleby's is so immediate and frightening that the lawyer prefers to be considered smug, petty, and self-righteous rather than be recognized for what he is: alone and terrified.

Initially, the lawyer responds to Bartleby's passive resistance with a matching, quiet acquiescence—a characteristic response to opposition perfected through years of dealing with Turkey and Nippers. But almost simultaneously the lawyer confesses to another impulse: "to encounter him in new opposition—to elicit some angry spark from him answerable to my own" ("B," 17). This impulse is not to be confused with Nippers's peevish desire to "kick him out of the office" ("B," 15) or Turkey's threat to "step behind his screen, and black his eyes for him" ("B," 18); their aggression springs from a simple desire to rid themselves of a problem they can neither understand nor resolve. The lawyer's motivation is much more complex. His desire to elicit in Bartleby an angry spark answerable to his own suggests an identification with his new clerk that he cannot ignore, and his confession that he "burned to be rebelled against again" ("B," 19) betrays his pained awareness that his own sense of identity and place is intricately bound with Bartleby's.

The issue is not that the lawyer's self-esteem is dependent upon Bartleby's "giving in" to his wishes. The issue, rather, is that because Bartleby cannot be made to conform to the lawyer's wishes or to the conventions of behavior in chambers—the world as the lawyer knows it—he represents an absolute challenge to those wishes and that world. Further, the mild ease with which Bartleby rejects his world and everyone in it reveals how few and how slender are the threads that hold it together. This is the challenge the lawyer must meet: his very being depends upon his meeting it successfully.

In effect, Bartleby becomes the "secret sharer" of the lawyer's own self-doubts, a wraith, projecting at once the image of futility in the lawyer's chambered world and the image of emptiness beyond. The lawyer's entire narrative is freighted with his shocked recognition that Bartleby is very much like himself, with his fear that he might become exactly like Bartleby, but the lawyer's doubts about Bartleby and about himself are brought to sharp focus in the chance Sunday encounter of the two men in the lawyer's chambers. On his way "to Trinity church, to hear a celebrated preacher," the lawyer walks round to his chambers "for a while" ("B," 21)—only to find his entrance blocked by "the apparition of Bartleby, . . . saying quietly that he was sorry, but he was deeply engaged just then, and—preferred not admitting me at present" ("B," 21). The lawyer leaves his own premises, returning after a few minutes to find the office accessible, but Bartleby gone. Horrified at his recognition that Bartleby has been "keeping bachelor's hall all by himself" ("B," 22), shocked most of all by the horrible solitude of Bartleby's life, the lawyer knows whereof he speaks. He too is a bachelor, he too is a Wall Street brooder of a Sunday, and he too has gravitated to his offices—"deserted as Petra" ("B," 22–23)

Our identification of the lawyer with Bartleby is not left to mere inference, however. Confessing to a "feeling of overpowering stinging melancholy" ("B," 23), the lawyer recognizes "the bond of a common humanity" that draws him "irresistibly to gloom" ("B," 23). In Bartleby the lawyer sees the forlornest of humanity, "alone, absolutely alone in the universe . . . , a bit of wreck in the mid-Atlantic," ("B," 29), and he sees himself: the traumatic disclosure of Bartleby's secret life has brought to the lawyer an equally traumatic disclosure of his own empty life. On his way to church, the lawyer has learned too well the lesson for the day: "Both I and Bartleby were sons of Adam" ("B," 23).[19]

The lawyer tries to dismiss his melancholy thoughts as "chimeras, doubtless, of a sick and silly brain" ("B," 23), but prudence cannot stifle his "presentiments of strange discoveries" hovering round him, nor can it blot out his prophetic image of "the scrivener's pale form . . . laid out, among uncaring strangers, in its shivering winding-sheet" ("B," 23). The etched clarity of the lawyer's insight into Bartleby's life and prefigured death, coupled with the no less sharply felt sense of his common humanity with Bartleby, produces in the lawyer urgent, but strongly conflicting emotions. His original feelings are those of "pure melancholy and sincerest pity" ("B," 124), but as he ponders more deeply the "forlornness" of Bartleby he finds "that same melancholy merge into fear, that pity into repulsion" ("B," 24). Persuaded by that Sunday morning insight into Bartleby's life that his scrivener was "the victim of innate and incurable disorder" ("B," 25), he vows to make one last attempt to understand Bartleby by putting "certain calm questions to him the next morning, touching his history, etc." ("B," 25) and, failing in that, to turn him out with "a twenty dollar bill over and above whatever I might owe him" ("B," 25).

Bartleby prefers not to answer the lawyer's questions about his birth, history, etc., and yet the lawyer does anything but turn out this "forlornest of mankind" ("B," 26). It is not mere melancholy that prompts the lawyer's inaction, nor simple pity; rather, the precarious balance in the lawyer of melancholy and fear, pity and repulsion create in him a suspension of purpose and the subsequent anxiety he feels to the end of the narrative. Bartleby thus exerts a "wondrous ascendancy" ("B," 32) over the lawyer that the lawyer vainly struggles against. The struggle is unequal from the start, for Bartleby is a living lesson that the lawyer can't unlearn, a living embodiment of the awful truth that life is an activity without purpose, sustained only by a constant and willing suspension of disbelief. It is a complete inversion and failure of will that Bartleby expresses in the form of his negative preferences, and it is the lawyer's recognition of the possibility, or perhaps one should say the inevitability, of a like failure that drives him to get rid of Bartleby.

The lawyer's struggle to rid himself of Bartleby is a struggle to survive in the face of overwhelming evidence that survival is pointless, and perhaps the permeating irony of the lawyer's situation is that, for him, survival, life itself, is reduced to a Bartleby-like negative preference—a preference not to die. There is nothing in the lawyer of Tommo's or Taji's naive optimism and very little if any of the desperado hope of Redburn or Ishmael. The lawyer has no goals, no dreams, no hopes, no anticipation of havens ahead, and few recollections of havens astern. As Bartleby appears to him, so does he appear to us: "alone, absolutely alone in the universe. A bit of wreck in mid Atlantic."

When the lawyer concludes that Bartleby will not leave him, he decides that he must leave Bartleby. And this he does, tearing himself "from him whom I had so longed to be rid of" ("B," 38). The lawyer can leave Bartleby, but he can't escape him. Haunted by the recollection of Bartleby, and both fearing and expecting his reappearance, the lawyer keeps "the door locked" in his new quarters and starts "at every footfall in the passages" ("B," 38). But rather than follow the lawyer to his new quarters, Bartleby succeeds in drawing the lawyer back to him. As the story presses to its inevitable conclusion it becomes more and more clear that Bartleby represents all that the lawyer does not want to know about himself. He is at once the lawyer's past, which cannot be willed nor wished away, and the lawyer's future, which is both dreaded and inescapable.

The past catches up to the lawyer in the form of the new occupant of his old office, who comes seeking the lawyer's aid in removing Bartleby from the premises. The lawyer immediately, if reluctantly, resumes responsibility for Bartleby, but once again his efforts to sound Bartleby are futile. Even the lawyer's offer to take Bartleby home with him ("B," 41)—the ultimate gesture of one person to another in need—is killed by Bartleby's reply: "No; at present I would prefer not to make any change at all" ("B," 41).[20] Bartleby will not and cannot be saved, and the lawyer, horrified at his closeness to the absolute emptiness of his fellow man, literally runs for his life.

The lawyer is never able to free himself from Bartleby, and when Bartleby is taken to the Tombs at the request of the landlord, the lawyer is called upon "to appear at that place, and make a suitable statement of the facts" ("B," 42). In this last interview between the lawyer and Bartleby, which constitutes a notable anticlimax to the story, the lawyer has two motivations, although the two are closely related. On the one hand he still wishes to help Bartleby if he can, giving the "grub-man" some silver, to get Bartleby the best dinner available. But the lawyer is also seeking to ease his sense of guilt. "It was not I that brought you here, Bartleby," he says ("B," 43)—as much to himself as to his former scrivener, who stands "all alone in the quietest of the yards, his face towards a high wall, while all around, from the narrow slits of the jail windows, . . . [were] peering out upon him the eyes of murderers and thieves" ("B," 43). All is for naught, however. The lawyer's last efforts, however pure or impure in motivation, have no effect on Bartleby. Bartleby prefers not to speak, and he prefers not to dine. In the end, "he slowly moved to the other side of the inclosure, and took up a position fronting the dead-wall" ("B," 44).

Don Benito's words to Amaso Delano at the end of "Benito Cereno" seem strikingly appropriate: "So far may even the best man err, in judging the conduct of one with the recesses of whose condition he is not acquainted." By placing Bartleby so far out of human reach, Melville suggests that touching the recesses of his condition, and thereby getting to "know" him, involves more risk than anyone should, or should want to, take. But the tale does not end with the lawyer's inconclusive first visit to the Tombs, and he is not allowed to remain in the sanctuary of his dubious ignorance.

Returning for a second visit, the lawyer finds Bartleby dead— "strangely huddled at the base of the wall, his knees drawn up, and lying on his side, his head touching the cold stones" ("B," 45). Bartleby's fetal position, his head touching the stone wall of his prison, and, in broader perspective, the image of his huddled corpse amid what the lawyer calls "the heart of the eternal pyramids" ("B," 45) remarkably enough prompt little comment from the usually voluble lawyer. Rather, he confesses to an elemental human response: "Something prompted me to touch him" ("B," 46). And he does touch Bartleby—with stunning effect: "I felt his hand, when a tingling shiver ran up my arm and down my spine to my feet" ("B," 46).

The dramatic force of that electric touch is inestimable.[21] It annihilates rather than resolves the lawyer's earlier doubts, confusions, queries, and rationalizations. No questions now of Bartleby's being useful, desirable, efficient, annoying, frustrating, maddening; the partitions are gone, and Bartleby stands as an all too true mirror of the lawyer's sole self. The lawyer and we recognize in Bartleby and ourselves the true unaccommodated man—without wealth, power, friends, breath—without all.

The lawyer ends his direct narrative of Bartleby at this point and concludes his tale with the "little item of rumor" that Bartleby had at one time been "a subordinate clerk in the Dead Letter Office at Washington" ("B," 46). This closing passage has been exhaustively discussed by critics of the tale, and the essential relevance of the dead letter office to Bartleby's isolated life is probably clear enough, but a few particulars bear emphasizing. First, the rumor of Bartleby's dead letter occupation is not a flat report under the heading of "previous employment," but rather is given shape, dimension, and color by the lawyer-narrator.[22] It is he who sees something in the rumor that will put finis to his life of Bartleby. In typical understatement the lawyer first confides that "this vague report has not been without a certain suggestive interest to me" ("B," 46), but two sentences later the guise of detached, quiet curiosity is thrown away: "When I think over this rumor, hardly can I express the emotions which seize me" ("B," 46). And no wonder!—for the image of dead letters quickly expands in the lawyer's mind to become a metaphor of life itself: "Dead letters! does it not sound like dead men?" ("B," 46). Of course "dead letters" do not *sound* like "dead men" at all, but having made the identification, the lawyer pours forth a litany of life's wasted dreams and horrible isolation. Charity, pardon, hope, and good tidings, the cardinal points of Christian faith, make no headway against the grave, and in the end the lawyer sees these letters, these men, more clearly than he might have wished: "On errands of life, these letters speed to death" ("B," 47).

Melville's preoccupation with death from *Typee* onward is patent, but in "Bartleby" we find more than just a variation on a persistent theme. In the early romances death is depicted as a simple threat to existence, as a curtailment of human experience, as the vaguely, if intensely, feared unknown. In "Bartleby," death is depicted not as a curtailment or threat or bar to life so much as an extension and intensification of it. In "Bartleby," life itself is infinitely deadening, and the isolation and futility of Bartleby's existence is so overwhelming that death itself becomes the most imperceptible of transitions. As the lawyer says to the grub-man, Bartleby in death merely "lives without dining" ("B," 46). The lawyer's final words in the tale—"Ah, Bartleby! Ah, humanity!" ("B," 47)—testify to the lawyer's recognition that he and Bartleby and all humanity share a common fate.[23]

Israel Potter and *The Confidence-Man*

None of Melville's other fiction written in the 1850s is comparable in depth or intensity to "Bartleby," "Benito Cereno," "The Encantadas," or "The Piazza." The remaining *Piazza Tales*—"The Lightning-Rod Man" and "The Bell-Tower" are slight indeed, "The Lightning-Rod Man" being the most narrowly topical kind of tale, "The Bell-Tower" being a simplistically heavy allegory that falls by its own weight.

Although confined to two characters and less than a dozen pages, "The Lightning-Rod Man" lacks essential coherence, as Melville plays cat's paw with the notions of skepticism and faith, terror and security—all within the confined, and quite tedious, context of the disputed efficacy of lightning rods as a safeguard against annihilation. By tale's end the reader is left with precious little to choose between the twisted misanthropy of the salesman who proudly avows, "of all things, I avoid tall men" ("L-R M," 220) and the Pollyanna certitude of the narrator who counters, "In thunder as in sunshine, I stand at ease in the hands of my God" ("L-R M," 221). The confrontation between narrator and salesman is irreducible and irredeemable, and perhaps the most that can be said for the brief tale is that it resonates quietly the larger and more disturbing confrontations of the greater *Piazza Tales*.[24]

"The Bell Tower" represents Melville's one attempt to write a pure allegory. The tale centers relentlessly on Bannadonna, the mechanician, in his attempt to outdo, outwit, and transcend nature and the limitations it places on man. Its stark economy of narrative and characterization reminds one of Hawthorne's tales in general, and in theme, characters, and conclusion it seems virtually a reprise of "The Birthmark" in particular. Yet Melville's tale fails where Hawthorne's does not. We are told little, and nothing of substance, about Bannadonna's motivations, and without that bearing the tale lumbers along—an allegory without direction and without destination. Compared to Aylmer's attempt to remove Georgiana's birthmark and the weighted significance of his "success," Bannadonna's killing of the workman in the foundry is an act of consequence but no significance; Bannadonna's death at the hand of his robot does not generate awe or horror in the reader, but merely indifference. The tale's last paragraph, with the cliché "and so pride went before the fall" ("B-T," 373), is a very dull gloss indeed for a tale and a character that scarcely get off the ground to begin with.

In view of Melville's nagging financial difficulties in the 1850s it is difficult not to conjecture at least, if not conclude, that Melville undertook much of his magazine publication as a job—"done for money,—being forced to it, as other men are to sawing wood" (Leyda, *The Melville Log*, 1:316; Melville's comments, of course, referred to his writing of *Redburn* and *White-Jacket*). The metaphor of sawing wood is quite applicable, I think, to the manner in which Melville seemed to apply himself to most of the highly schematic, one-chord pieces that appeared in *Harper's* and *Putnam's* monthlies from 1853 to 1856. To pursue the metaphor, some of these pieces—such as "The 'Gees," "The Happy Failure," and "Cock-a-Doodle-Doo!"—are so lightweight as to be considered literary kindling, whereas even the "better" pieces—such as "Poor Man's Pudding and Rich Man's Crumbs," "The Paradise of Bachelors and the Tartarus of Maids," and "I and My Chimney"—seem sawn to a length on the themes of success and failure, wealth and poverty, privilege and deprivation.[25]

Lacking the force of artistic statement found in "Bartleby" and "Benito Cereno," they are the broken pieces of a Romantic conception of a universe that can never again be made whole. The spirit of quest is dead, or worse than dead as we find it in the painfully parodic and ironic search for the singing cock in "Cock-a-Doodle-Doo!" Heroism is defunct and irrelevant in the world of "The Happy Failure," "The Fiddler," and "Jimmy Rose," where imagination, exceptional gifts, and flowered success lead quickly to failure, obscurity, and death. Finally, and perhaps most importantly, Melville in these lesser pieces reiterates again and again that the camaraderie of humanity and the fellowship of souls is no more.

In these tales each individual is an island, and what we call society is an unstable and therefore potentially explosive coming together of mutually repellant individuals—individuals of isolated sensibilities, understandings, and needs, incapable of communicating with each other. In "Poor Man's Pudding and Rich Man's Crumbs" not only are rich and poor supremely ignorant of each other, but the narrator can and does do nothing to mediate between the two solitudes. In like manner, but more dramatically, "The Paradise of Bachelors and Tartarus of Maids" projects a world of absolute sterility in which both plenty and want are equally suffocating, equally self-consuming. Melville leaves himself and us little reason to hope for a bettering of such a world: his characters in these tales seem gripped by circumstances strong as Fate. The model for survival in such a grim world is perhaps the narrator in "I and My Chimney," who is not heroic, but merely stubborn—fighting a rear-guard action against inevitability.

Israel Potter, probably the most barefaced of Melville's "commercial" writing ventures, provides a rather predictable and perfunctory continuation of the themes of social isolation, failure, and ignominious death that are central to the *Piazza Tales*. Because the book does have some fine passages, I don't wish to be too denigrating; however, neither do I think it necessary to belabor its details at this point in my argument. One can only wonder at the judgment of *Putnam's* editors in seeing the novel as an appropriate "Fourth of July Story" (the novel's subtitle). Far from the jingoistic sentiments of self-praise usually associated with Fourth of July orations, sermons, and celebrations, *Israel Potter* is sometimes quietly bitter, sometimes blackly comic in its indictment of a world that cannot or will not recognize and reward heroism.[26]

There are chauvinistic sentiments in the novel, expressed mainly by Israel Potter himself, but the apostrophes to self-reliance, independence, loyalty, and patriotism take on a distinctly ironic, if not sardonic, cast when set against the actual history of Israel, who—fittingly named— endures hardship, humiliation, and homelessness in his search for his promised land—a free and independent America. The climax of the novel, of course, is the scene depicting the famous sea battle between the *Serapis* and the *Bon Homme Richard*, and nowhere are the book's ironic purposes more clear-cut. The action-narrative, which probably contains the finest writing in the novel, concludes not with a paean to victory and American courage but with the disarming question: "Is civilization a thing distinct or is it an advanced stage of barbarism?" (*IP*, 19:130).[27]

The battle is won. Even the war is won eventually. But for Israel there is no victory. If there is a personal victor in the novel it is not Israel and not John Paul Jones, who, wild enough for war but too wild for peace, unceremoniously disappears from the narrative in mid-Atlantic when Israel is taken captive in a sea fight. By implication the one who profits most from the intrepid exploits of Israel and John Paul is Benjamin Franklin—"Jack of all trades, master of each and mastered by none—the type and genius of his land" (*IP*, 8:48).

Melville neither needs nor chooses to recount Franklin's postwar political successes to a mid-nineteenth-century audience, but Franklin's often-recounted fame and fortune in the post-Revolutionary years stand in sharp contrast to the poverty and ignominy experienced by Israel in the last forty-five years of his life. The humorous, if not comic, first meeting between Israel and Franklin (in Chapter 7) defines the gulf between them in the same terms of social and economic distinction found in "Rich Man's Pudding and Poor Man's Crumbs." Franklin is generous and free—with advice, and Israel is admonished to be generous and free with his body, his soul, and his life.

In its ironic conclusion *Israel Potter* is, in fact, more subversive than "patriotic." Israel's final reward for loyal service to his country and its leaders is fifty years in exile—an "Israel in Egypt" (the title of Chapter 23). In London, the "city of Dis" in Chapter 25, Israel lives out his life "like some amazed runaway steer or trespassing Pequod Indian" (*IP*, 25:164), in obscurity and desperate poverty. Even at this low ebb of fortune, however, Israel maintains his dream of America and tells his "now motherless child" of the "far Canaan beyond the sea" (*IP*, 25:166). But in 1854, no such fond fancies can survive the world of experience for long. Israel and his son make the journey to America, landing in Boston on the 4th of July, 1826, and in a revealing, if none too subtle, bit of irony the old Israel narrowly escapes "being run over by a patriotic triumphal car in the procession, flying a broidered banner, inscribed with gilt letters:

BUNKER HILL
1775
GLORY TO THE HEROES THAT FOUGHT
(*IP*, 26:167)

There is no hero's welcome for Israel, no family, no friends, no homestead, no pension, "his scars" proving to be "his only medals" (*IP*, 26:169).

As discussed previously, after *Pierre*, Melville's fictional worlds seem held together by a thread. The characteristic pattern of *The Piazza Tales* and the other fiction of the 1850s is founded in the depiction of this tenuous world *as* it breaks up, the conclusion of each work impressing upon the reader a sense of complete vacuity. In *The Confidence-Man*, the thread is already broken on page one, and the entire novel depicts a vacant world that has already dissolved. The novel is a disjunctive narrative of disjunctive human events—events without purpose, direction, achievement, or promise. Not different in kind, *The Confidence-Man* serves as a summation to the fiction of the 1850s—Melville's extended inventory of the bits and pieces of wrecked humanity adrift in a chartless world.[28]

It is little wonder that recent critics have found this tantalizing, "Humpty-Dumpty" novel irresistible, but attempts to put the novel "together" again have failed, for it is a novel that in its essence negates normal critical assumptions about coherence and continuity of character and narrative. The narrative in *The Confidence-Man* is unarguably uncertain and "incomplete"—a collocation of broken threads and loose ends, and this discontinuity is largely a result of Melville's conception of the chameleon confidence-man, who is many things to many people and no certain thing to anyone.

Although the discontinuity of thought and action and the incoherence of human experience figured large thematically in the earlier novels, they always operated in conflict with Melville's narrative attempt to close the circle and make our experience and world whole. By contrast, in *The Confidence-Man*, discontinuity of narrative and incoherence of character become the cardinal principles of Melville's art. Early in the novel he confesses how consistency of character in fiction either presents a partial view or is "very untrue to reality" (*C-M*, 14:69–70),[29] adding that "no writer has produced such inconsistent characters as nature herself has" (*C-M*, 14:70) and concluding that "experience is the only guide here" (*C-M*, 14:70). The search for an integrated self in a putatively coherent universe, which forms the heart of *Typee, Omoo, Mardi, Redburn, White-Jacket*, and *Moby-Dick*, and which is still discernible in the ironic shadows of *Pierre* and the *Piazza Tales*, is abandoned altogether in *The Confidence-Man*. The countless wonders of the universe that beckoned Melville's early wanderers in the form of voyages on the mysterious, irresistible sea are reduced in *The Confidence-Man* to the Babel of fast talk and tall tales on the deck of the bank-bound riverboat that touches nervously at many ports yet has no discernible destination. The confidence-man in his various avatars and his victims reciprocate the anxiety and desperation of ambivalent feelings toward uncertain goals in a world utterly ambiguous.

Because the one predictable and consistent feature of the novel is the pattern of psychology and assumption underlying the confidence-man's tricks and the victims' susceptibility to them, the essential basis of "confidence" in a few crucial episodes of the novel defines the pattern and establishes the central principle for the other episodes in the book. Early in *The Confidence-Man*, Melville establishes the *Fidèle* as a microcosm ship of fools, "always full of strangers" and continually adding to or replacing them "with strangers still more strange" (*C-M*, 2:8). The essence of that "Anacharsis Cloots congress of all kinds of that multiform pilgrim species, man" (*C-M*, 2:9) becomes all too clear in the course of the novel. From the tangled and incomplete histories of Black Guinea, John Ringman, Pitch, and Moredock, from the shifting shapes and ploys of the confidence-man, emerges the cardinal definition of human experience as endlessly variable, endlessly conditional and unpredictable—stated most succinctly by the merchant in Chapter 13: "the common occurences of life . . . never, in the nature of things, steadily look one way and tell one story, as flags in the trade-wind" (*C-M*, 13:66). The mutability and uncertainty of events that constituted the "problem to be solved" in the early novels, in *The Confidence-Man* become the absolute "givens" of nature. The merchant's definition of this, nature's ineluctable reality, leads irresistibly to the conclusion that "if the conviction of a Providence, for instance, were in any way made dependent upon such variabilities as everyday events, the degree of that conviction would, in thinking minds, be subject to fluctuations akin to those of the stock-exchange during a long and uncertain war" (*C-M*, 13:66).

The world of the *Fidèle*, in short, is the world of Plinlimmon's "Ei" carried to its logical extreme. In *The Confidence-Man*, humanity lives in a conditional world whose motto is "If—." Deprived of all access to certainty, the inhabitants of this world are susceptible to all appearances of conviction in others; susceptible to all appearances of conviction, they are given to ever-changing loyalties, and—like the coquettes in Pope's "Rape of the Lock"—"old impertinence expel by new."

The rootless, totally ambiguous nature of human experience is depicted dramatically and emphatically from the very beginning of the novel.[30] In Chapter 1, the confidence-man sets up shop as a deaf-mute shill for "charity"—right next to the placard advertising an award for his arrest. At the same time a shipboard barber announces his availability with a placard bearing the likeness of a razor and the words "No Trust"

(*C-M*, 1:5). The contradiction between the confidence-man's "Charity thinketh no evil" and the barber's "No Trust" is absolute, and the effect on the crowd of these contrary appeals manifests the confusion and volatility of the human mind lacking all conviction. Forced to guess the intentions of the cream-suited deaf mute with his admonitions to "charity," the crowd can reach no agreement. To one he is an "odd fish," to another a "poor fellow"; to others he is a "green prophet from Utah," or a "Humbug" or an "escaped convict, worn out with dodging" (*C-M*, 2:7). In this scene so clearly redolent of "The Doubloon" in *Moby-Dick*, Melville depicts humanity itself as the ultimate hieroglyph—engendering curiosity and fervor of response, but revealing no certain significance to its mystery.

Further, Melville hints in Chapter 1 at the violent implications of the instability of human belief when he shows how the uncertain significance of the deaf-mute causes "some stares to change into jeers, and some jeers into pushes, and some pushes into punches" (*C-M*, 1:6). Throughout the narrative the uncertainty of perception, the fallibility of memory, and the variability of judgment charge the novel with an explosive quality. The endless disputes, wrangling, and tug of wills between the confidence-man and his victims push relentlessly toward a flash point where irreconcilable words can, and do, give way to physical violence.

Ambiguity of situation and character, ambivalence of mind, and incipient violence all make their presence felt in Chapter 3, which serves as a model for the chapters to follow. The chapter, "In Which a Variety of Characters Appear," centers around the character of Black Guinea, the crippled Negro who solicits charity by "throwing back his head and opening his mouth ... so that people may pitch pennies into it" (*C-M*, 3:11). As in Chapter 1, where the deaf-mute's appeal is countered by the barber's, Black Guinea's momentary success is challenged by the one-legged man who challenges Black Guinea's honesty and worthiness by croaking out "something about his deformity being a sham, got up for financial purposes" (*C-M*, 3:12).

Claim and counterclaim once again are absolute and mutually exclusive, and all attempts by the crowd to ascertain the truth of the situation are fraught with confusion, ambiguity, and indecision.[31] In a series of light-quick changes, the fickle crowd shifts its sympathy from Black Guinea to his accuser, back again to Black Guinea, and back once more to the one-legged man, manifesting all too clearly the narrator's ironic comment that "the right or the wrong might not have overmuch to do with whatever wayward mood superior intelligence might yield to" (*C-M*, 3:12).

As the chapter progresses it becomes clear that the foundations of all belief are set in sand. When the Episcopal clergyman, all "innocence, tenderness, and good sense triumvirate in his air" (*C-M*, 3:13) asks for references (i.e., authority) to substantiate Black Guinea's crippled condition and claim upon charity, the answer he gets is laden with compounded ironies. First, Black Guinea cites as his "references" the various avatars of the confidence-man as he appears in the novel. The fact that Black Guinea *is* the confidence-man and thus cannot be found elsewhere is but one element of the irony that eats away at the possibility of ever ascertaining truth in the novel. Even assuming that one of Black Guinea's references could be found, the validity of his recommendation would rest solely upon our acceptance of Black Guinea's initial recommendation. Thus we are forced to agree with the one-legged man when he calls the clergyman's search "a wild goose chase!" (*C-M*, 3:14).

Writ small in the drama of Black Guinea is the book's primary statement that phenomena, however ambiguous, uncertain, or even misleading, are, and can only be, self-evidencing. There is no appeal, and nothing or no one to appeal to, beyond the thing as it appears. The crowd's attempts to get at the truth of Black Guinea's condition are doomed to failure from the beginning. No mediation is possible between the one-legged man's absolute skepticism and the Methodist minister's admonition to "put as charitable a construction as one can upon the poor fellow" (*C-M*, 3:14). To the one-legged man "Charity is one thing, and truth is another" (*C-M*, 3:14); to the Methodist minister the one-legged man is a "Canada thistle" (*C-M*, 3:14). Ultimately, the irreconcilability of the two positions can lead to but one conclusion: violence. The Methodist minister picks up the one-legged man and shakes him by the coat collar "till his timber-toe clattered on the deck like a nine-pin" (*C-M*, 3:15).

Once again, however, just as in the opening scene of the novel, Melville compounds irony with irony in the closing pages of Chapter 3. The minister's driving off of the one-legged man does not resolve the issue of Black Guinea's identity, nor does it turn the crowd immediately in his favor. The crowd that cheers the minister's drubbing of the one-legged man is much less certain about Black Guinea's genuineness. Beset by claim and counterclaim, vacillating between contrary impulses of charity and doubt, the crowd is ultimately a creature of volatile perversity. Challenged by the one-legged man's skepticism, the crowd doggedly defends Black Guinea's claims, but once the "Canada thistle" is driven off, the crowd pulls back in their sympathy, demanding further "proof." In the end there is no resolution to the ambiguity of Black Guinea's claims. Although the country merchant gives Black Guinea money, the crowd at the end of Chapter 3 is as indecisive and undecided as it was at the beginning. The chapter ends not with a conclusion but with a distraction:

the steward summons to the captain's office all persons who have not purchased tickets.

These two opening scenes in the novel clearly establish the pattern of the novel's central concerns. Human rationality dissolves in a world of unyielding ambiguity, leaving everyone prey to the unstable, contrary forces of impulse, instinct, and emotion. Further, the predicament is circular and inescapable; lacking certainty in perception, all of us thus lack certainty of judgment and will and must act out of "confidence," which in the novel's ambiguous terms is defined contradictorily and simultaneously as necessary faith and gullibility.[32] Finally, under these terms of reference, life is shown to be little more than a comedy of vicissitudes—formless, and pointless, with no proper beginning and no certain end.

The novel's various episodes repeat this essential pattern of ambiguity, uncertainty, and confusion again and again, but if there is a locus classicus among the novel's numerous variations on the theme of "confidence" it rests in the confrontation between Pitch, the skeptical Missourian, and those two memorable confidence men—the man from the Philosophical Intelligence Office (PIO) and the Cosmopolitan. This double-barreled confrontation between the misanthropic bachelor and the smug promoters of faith occupies the very center of the novel and radiates its implications throughout the book.

Once again, the terms of conflict between the characters are absolute. Pitch, the skeptical and misanthropic bachelor from Missouri, declares bluntly that "all boys are rascals, and so are all men" (*C-M*, 22:126), while the PIO man no less assuredly declares that they "present as pure a moral spectacle as the purest angel could wish" (*C-M*, 22:119). The nominal topic of debate between the two men is the "philosophy of boys," but at stake really is the entire question of human society—its origins, its history, and its future.

Pitch's misanthropy is founded in his immediate experience with boys: "fifteen years' experience; five and thirty boys" (*C-M*, 22:117). Because each boy has revealed some viciousness wholly "peculiar to that one peculiar boy" (*C-M*, 22:117), Pitch has discharged them all, one by one, and concluded that "all are rascals." And, he continues: Because "'the child is father of the man,' hence, as all boys are rascals, so are all men" (*C-M*, 22:119). His bad experience with bad boys reinforced by his bad experience with the herb-doctor (in Chapter 21), Pitch in his misanthropy and skepticism would seem to be proof against the airy optimism of the PIO man. Pitch, the immovable object, finds more than his match, however, in the irresistible force of the PIO man's arguments. Arguing by a series of analogies, the PIO man stands developmental theory on its head in an effort to persuade Pitch that, treated with patience and confidence, a boy with "no noble quality" may be nurtured into a virtuous man. He makes little headway with his illustrations of rag-paper cartoons filling out into portraits, lily buds maturing into full blooms, and caterpillars transforming into butterflies, and for the better part of the chapter it seems apparent that the PIO man and Pitch will remain at loggerheads, one more instance of the book's many examples of irreconcilable contrariety. Yet, surprisingly, the PIO man eventually prevails: Pitch orders a boy from him, paying not only the $3.00 fee, but also volunteering the passage money for the boy.

Pitch's sudden, unpredictable conversion to the PIO man's faith is unexpected, and in view of Pitch's radical skepticism (not to say cynicism), his willingness to take a chance on yet another boy must be viewed as the confidence-man's greatest triumph. Pitch's change of heart is *so* sudden that at first there seems to be little or no discernible reason for it, but just as quickly all our curiosity is roused to understand what kind of argument could possibly appeal to skeptical, misanthropic Pitch, for surely the reader's inference at this point in the novel is that an argument that moves Pitch can move anyone.

Like Chaucer's Pardoner, the PIO man's "theme is always oon, and evere was," and eventually that one theme prevails against Pitch's manifold doubts. Simply enough the PIO man preaches the doctrine of hope—living in the expectation that things inevitably, eventually will get better. Although his individual analogies might fail against the skepticism of Pitch, eventually their cumulative weight "sounds a kind of reasonable, as it were," and Pitch admits that upon the whole the PIO man's "conversation has been such as might almost lead one less distrustful . . . to repose a certain conditional confidence in you" (*C-M*, 22:127). The appeal of hope—even to the most skeptical of men—is simple enough: it is based on the elemental assumption, both psychological and philosophical, that there has to be more to life than what we have already experienced. In essence, this assumption is instinct with, if not identical to, the will to live itself; thus its appeal in a real sense is absolute: to reject hope, or to lose hope, is to die.

The PIO man is correct in his assertion that "do what they will, society, like our office, at bottom has a Christian confidence in boys [i. e., the future]" (*C-M*, 22:126), for this, of course, is a generic, if perhaps circular, argument based on society's need to believe in its own perpetuation.[33] But the PIO man turns this argument into a particular appeal when he plies Pitch with the argument, "If hitherto, sir, you have struck upon a peculiarly bad vein of boys, so much the more hope now of your hitting a good one" (*C-M*, 22:127). This proposition, founded more upon mysticism than upon statistical probability can prevail only if Pitch accepts the primary proposition that individuals and society necessarily improve with time.

Although Pitch characterizes his acquiescence to the PIO man's appeals as a kind of "conditional confidence," there is nothing conditional about the $3.00 he gives the PIO man. Throughout *The Confidence-Man* the payment of money is the touchstone of unconditional confidence, the conjectures, doubts, opinions, and evidence of dispute becoming nil once money changes hands, for at that point commitment is made. Melville makes it quite clear that such commitment entails a leap of faith—from doubt to confidence—and as the PIO man observes, "without it, commerce between man and man, as between country and country, would, like a watch, run down and stop" (*C-M*, 22:128).

Chapter 22 thus presents a very strong case for the psychological and social necessity of "confidence," but as we quickly discover in Chapter 23, it makes no case at all for the certainty or continued viability of particular acts of confidence. No sooner does the PIO man leave with Pitch's money than the Missourian reawakens to all his original doubts—"like one beginning to rouse himself from a dose of chloroform treacherously given" (*C-M*, 23:129). His original doubts about the nature of humanity are intensified by his newly wakened awareness of the "mystery of human subjectivity in general" (*C-M*, 23:129), by which he, the philosopher, "had unwittingly been betrayed into being an unphilosophical dupe" (*C-M*, 23:129). Feeling self-betrayed by "his too indulgent, too artless and companionable nature," he resolves to be "a little splenetic in his intercourse henceforth" (*C-M*, 23:130).

Thus, Pitch completes the cycle of psychology that underlies all human intercourse in *The Confidence-Man*. Pitch, like the other victims in the novel, moves from doubt, to hope, to faith, to disillusionment, and back to doubt—turned about and confused by the "vicissitudes of light and shade" (*C-M*, 22:129) to which humanity is subject. And when he meets the Cosmopolitan in Chapter 24, Pitch is more resolutely misanthropic than ever.

Amid the novel's seemingly infinite permutations of shifting opinion and belief—dramatically encapsulated in Pitch's confrontations with the Herb-doctor, the PIO man, and the Cosmopolitan—there seems to be no cardinal belief or truth left intact. Indeed, the Cosmopolitan's plea to Pitch in Chapter 24 is not that he ought to think better of his fellow men (the PIO man's argument), but that he should give over expecting too much of his fellow man and join in Life's "pic-nic *en costume*" (*C-M*,

24:133), should give up the "notion of being lone and lofty" (*C-M*, 24:135) and tipple a little. The observation that "one cannot enjoy life with gusto unless he renounce the too-sober view of life" (*C-M*, 24:134) and the implicit admonition that therefore the best way to get on in life is to accommodate oneself to the general opinions and behavior of society and avoid fruitless criticism are probably as old as society itself. More explicitly, the Cosmopolitan reiterates the Horological philosophy of the Plinlimmon pamphlet in *Pierre*, and his argument is as seductive as it is specious. The Cosmopolitan is what modern psychology would define as a well-adjusted man. He is "a cosmopolitan, a catholic man, who, being such, ties himself to no narrow tailor or teacher, but federates, in heart as in costume, something of the various gallantries of men under various suns" (*C-M*, 24:132). Yet this self-styled catholicity is, from another perspective, from Pitch's perspective in particular, the absolute abandonment of self and any concept of truth.

In establishing and exploring this conflict between the Cosmopolitan's blanket relativism (philosophical, psychological, and anthropological) and Pitch's skepticism (founded upon a disappointed absolutism), Melville seems more committed to "the excellently illustrated restatement of a problem, than the solution of the problem itself" (as *Pierre*'s narrator comments upon Plinlimmon's pamphlet). Indeed, in the novel's terms there is no "solution" to the contrary claims made by Pitch and the Cosmopolitan because there is no ground upon which the two could ever meet to settle their differences. Virtually by definition, the Cosmopolitan's apology for uncritical amiability denies the virtue of truth-seeking, let alone truth-finding, and leads to the admonition that at life's "pic-nic *en costume*" one must "take a part, assume a character, stand ready in a sensible way to play the fool" (*C-M*, 24:133). Conversely, Pitch, who rates "truth, though cold water, above untruth, though Tokay" (*C-M*, 24:134), by his decision to stick to his "earthen jug" (*C-M*, 24:134) forever cuts himself off from society, cuts himself off, that is, from the Cosmopolitan and everything he represents.

The implications of Chapter 24 are ineluctable: happiness and wisdom are mutually exclusive within the human context, each difficult to attain in itself and impossible to maintain with the other. Thus the Cosmopolitan and Pitch talk across an impassable gulf—their parallel arguments on human imperfection destined never to meet. In the end the metaphysical questions of what "truth" is, and how one attains it, degenerate, or modulate, into the practical question of how we should govern our lives when given the exclusive choices of happiness *or* wisdom as goals.

Even this practical question resists solution, however, and the Cosmopolitan and Pitch end the chapter as they began it—at loggerheads. The Cosmopolitan's genial philosophy can make no headway against Pitch's Timonism, and in this chapter, as opposed to Chapter 22, Pitch turns the tables on the confidence-man, resolutely maintaining that the Cosmopolitan is in fact a "Diogenes in disguise" (*C-M*, 24:138). Thus the chapter ends—the Cosmopolitan-philanthropist moving away "less lightsome that he had come, leaving the discomfitted misanthrope to the solitude he held so sapient" (*C-M*, 24:138).

These three central chapters of *The Confidence-Man* make absolutely clear the psychological, philosophical, and social implications of life in a world without certainty. In such a world, with no fixed center, no stable reference point, all opinions and beliefs are, theoretically, equal. The preeminence of one opinion over another has nothing to do with propriety or rectitude or justice or truth, and everything to do with will, cleverness, persuasion, and appearance. Language becomes the tool not of communication, but of persuasion, and when language fails, when two opinions of equal strength are opposed, the resulting impasse inevitably leads the opposing parties to violence or isolation. In such a world there is no meaningful social contract, no significant self, no purposeful origin, process, or end to life at all. This all-negating vision pervades the novel and, in effect, puts a period to Melville's fiction of the 1850s.

In the closing chapters of the novel Melville makes it clear that this world without purpose is, in the most sardonic sense, a world without end. In view of Melville's central themes and concepts of characterization in *The Confidence-Man*, it is not surprising that the ending to the novel presents some critical problems. The question of whether the novel is "truly" finished can probably never be answered to everyone's satisfaction, but it advances our understanding of Melville and *The Confidence-Man* if we ask why this novel is difficult to bring to a proper "ending" and how the closing pages of the novel as published satisfy the aesthetic demands of the novel as a whole.[34]

The very concept of an ending implies an encompassing concept of form—itself a complex notion of shape, order, and aesthetic purpose. But as we have seen, the novel in theme and character denies any such ordering concept and threatens at virtually every step to disintegrate into chaos. In this sense at least there can scarcely be a conclusion more fitting to the novel than the one we have—with the Cosmopolitan leading the frightened old man away into the darkness. In a world depicted as filled with endless deceits and countless masquerades, surely the novel's closing line—"Something further may follow of this Masquerade" (*C-M*, 45:251)—is at once the mildest sort of litotes and the most bitter sort of hopeless glimpse into the future.[35] The closing chapter is, thus, a most apt conclusion to the novel. At the close of April Fool's day the Cosmopolitan and the unnamed old man play out the unending human drama beneath the decks of the *Fidèle*—in the boat's sleeping quarters—and as the last light wanes into darkness they recapitulate the terms of humanity's hard existence in an ambiguous, dark, and uncaring world.

7

Clarel and *Billy Budd*: No Other Worlds but This

Debate, which in confusion merges—
Din and clamor, discord's height:
Countering surges—paeans—dirges—
Mocks and laughter light.
  But rolled in long ground-swell persistent,
A tone, an undertone assails,
And overpowers all near and distant;
Earnest and sternest, it prevails.
  Then terror, horror—wind and rain—
Accents of undetermined fear,
And voices as in shipwreck drear:
A sea, a sea of spirits in pain!
  The suppliant cries decrease—
The voices in their ferment cease:
One wave rolls over all and whelms to peace.[1]

The dialogue that Melville holds with himself on the themes of quest and negation seems to reach a dead end, if not a resolution, in the conditional, April Fool worlds of *Pierre, The Piazza Tales*, and *The Confidence-Man*, and if Melville's career had ended with *The Confidence-Man* there would be a certain, if fearful, symmetry to his canon. Melville did not retreat into silence in 1856, however, for in the 1860s and 70s he wrote a substantial amount of poetry, including the massive *Clarel*, and in the last year of his life he fought toward the completion of *Billy Budd*.

Battle Pieces, John Marr and Other Sailors, Timoleon, Etc., and the miscellaneous poems shed little light on the central themes of quest and negation in Melville's works, for these relatively short pieces are essentially lyrical and occasional. As Melville observes in his headnote to *Battle Pieces*, "Yielding instinctively, one after another, to feelings not inspired from any one source exclusively, and unmindful, without purposing to be, of consistency, I see, in most of these verses, to have but placed a harp in a window, and noted the contrasted airs which wayward winds have played upon the strings."[2] That confession is itself perhaps sufficient commentary on Melville's sense of lost direction in the 1860s, but *Clarel* is certainly relevant to my exploration of negated quests in Melville's post-*Pierre* works. In length, multiplicity of character and incident, and in tone *Clarel* is essentially a novel in verse, and although the scope of this book precludes an extended analysis of this most labyrinthine poetic statement, I would like to suggest at least that its central theme of the failed quest puts it in a direct line of progression from *The Confidence-Man* to *Billy Budd*.[3]

If one defines "quest" in the loosest sense as the search for something, then *Clarel* definitely is a quest—as most commentators on the poem have agreed. But Clarel's search is qualitatively, categorically different from those of Tommo, Taji, Ahab, and Ishmael. The quests of Melville's early protagonists in intent were essentially progressive, ameliorative, and synthetic. Melville's early questers sought out new, better, other worlds to conquer and assimilate. In stark contrast, Clarel's search is an inverted, or regressive quest. Clarel's starting point is that of impasse, the patent failure of the human spirit to rise above the dust, and his "quest" in the poem is a journey backward through spiritual time in an effort to discover the dubious origins of hope and expectation.[4] Clarel's question, and the question of the poem, is "What ever led man to think there were better, newer worlds to conquer?" Founded upon the perceived failure of the Western world's spiritual quest, dramatized by Melville in *The Piazza Tales* and *The Confidence-Man*, *Clarel* pushes the implications of negation virtually to the breaking point.

Every aspect of *Clarel* is grounded in Clarel's, and by implication humanity's, inability to explain or comprehend spiritual longings. Clarel, the New World Everyman, begins his journey on the Vigil of Epiphany (*Clarel*, I, i:7–10), and the poem traces his circuitous path back to the origins of Christianity—Bethlehem and the birth of Christ. Clearly he finds no answer in Bethlehem, but neither are there answers in the endless dialogues among the poem's major characters, which include Clarel, Celio, Vine, Rolfe, and Derwent. The poem's manifold "readings" of life, death, faith, and disbelief take us back to the doubloon chapter of *Moby-Dick*, but more emphatically they are of a piece with the conditional world of "If—" found in *Pierre* and in *The Confidence-Man*. The poem ends not with "Easter" (*Clarel*, IV, xxxiii) and any promise of resurrection, but with Clarel's vision of the "Via Crucis":

> In varied forms of fate they wend—
> Or man or animal, 'tis one:
> Cross-bearers all, alike they tend
> And follow, slowly follow on.
> (*Clarel*, IV, xxxiv:41–44)

The "Epilogue" to *Clarel* is in the most literal sense an afterthought. Written in iambic pentameter, it seems infinitely removed from the tortured octasyllabic verse of the poem's body. Like the "Epilogue" to *Moby-Dick*, the "Epilogue" to *Clarel* is built upon subjunctive propositions and "if's," and the ambiguity that Vincent Kenny sees in *Clarel*'s conclusion[5] is more accurately seen as excruciating irony against the backdrop of death, darkness, and dryness that dominates the poem throughout.

The body of the poem provides dramatic evidence that "The running battle of the star and clod/Shall run for ever—if there be no God" (*Clarel*, "Epilogue," IV, xxxv:16–17). The Faith invoked in the "Epilogue," which "Inscribes even on her shards of broken urns/The sign 'o the cross—*the spirit above the dust*!" (*Clarel*, "Epilogue," IV, xxxv:10–11), shrinks to nothing against the image of life as cross-bearing pain in "Via Crucis" and against the pervasive, suffocating images in the poem of dust, stones, and aridity—the detritus of ruined Christianity and Western culture. In a poem structurally defined by the deaths of Clarel's companions and loved ones, culminating in the death and burial of Ruth and Agar, the conjecture in the "Epilogue" that Clarel *may* emerge "from the last whelming sea/And prove that death but routs life to victory" (*Clarel*, "Epilogue," IV, xxxv:33–34) is stunning in its misdirection.

There are echoes aplenty of Melville's fiction in *Clarel*. Virtually all the major characters are wandering Ishmaels, death haunts the pages and concludes every book of the poem, and, most significantly, Clarel as protagonist, like Ishmael of *Moby-Dick*, remains forever on the periphery of events—looking out upon a world that does not allow him to look in. His attempt to get at the origins of faith, hope, and aspiration proves, in the end, to be a quest of infinite regress. The world for him remains forever opaque, forever mysterious—remains, as Rolfe says, "This star of tragedies, this orb of sins" (*Clarel*, I, xxxi:183). And man remains, like Nehemiah, "a stone in vacant tomb,/Stone none molest, for it is naught" (*Clarel*, I, xxii:116–17).

Consistent in theme, tone, and perspective with the dark fiction of the 1850s, *Clarel* points directly to Melville's last work, *Billy Budd*. In the most legitimate sense *Billy Budd* serves as an eloquent afterword to

Melville's fictional canon. In the "Notes & Commentary" to their edition of the novel, Hayford and Sealts note the "number of passages in *Billy Budd* so closely resembling passages in Melville's earlier works as to raise the question whether he was deliberately borrowing from them or had read them so recently that he unconsciously echoed even their phrasing."[6] In either event the numerous "borrowings" place *Billy Budd* in direct line of descent from *Redburn, White-Jacket*, and *Moby-Dick*. The death of innocence, the futile search for justice and wholeness in a recalcitrantly disjunctive world, the failure of the self's best efforts to understand his fellow creatures, and, above all, humanity's inability to attain and maintain a solid moral vision by which to govern decisions and acts—all these run a direct line from *Typee* to *Billy Budd*. In the attractions and conflicts that arise between Billy, Claggart, and Vere we see for the last time, and perhaps most sharply drawn, Melville's ability to give equal expression to the human desire for camaraderie, love, and overarching order, and the human experience of enmity, antipathy, and confusion. In the persona-narrator of *Billy Budd*, Melville creates a definitive, mature voice which, with the unflinching honesty of a death-bed statement, sets down one last time a pained record of our failure to grasp the significance of this phantom life.

In spite of the narrative "incompleteness" of *Billy Budd*, we are as irresistibly drawn to this, Melville's last work, as Ahab was to the mystery of the white whale. Our compulsion to explain for ourselves what no one seems able to explain to us is a direct and irresistible consequence of *Billy Budd*'s essential nature—an utter ineffability of meaning that eludes us even as it beckons, and continually seduces us in our defeat.[7]

Given the ill-defined state of Melville's manuscript of *Billy Budd*, and given the further confusion of the manuscript's publication by Weaver and Freeman, we should perhaps not be surprised by the divergence of critical estimates up to 1962. But the publication of Hayford and Sealts' "definitive" text of *Billy Budd* in 1962, although in itself an admirable piece of careful and imaginative scholarship, has done little to realign and order critical stances taken toward the novel. The editors' bold forecast in their "Introduction"—"Now that a reliable text of the novel has been provided, we believe the way is cleared for definitive criticism" (p. 27)—has proved to be at least premature and perhaps misdirected altogether.

It is clear that the inordinate critical difficulties of *Billy Budd* do not lie in the external events of the tale. The sequence of events from Billy's impressment to the killing of Claggart, with the subsequent trial and execution of Billy, is simple to the point of being skeletal—capable of being put into a single sentence. These external, irreducible events of the novel are universally accessible and constitute the "outside" narrative of *Billy Budd*. But thanks to Hayford and Sealts we know that Melville conceived of *Billy Budd* as "an inside narrative," and that "inside" *Billy Budd* is not so easily grasped.

We expect at least two things from "an inside narrative." First, the phrase implies that the value of the tale does not lie in the external events per se, but in the motivations, causes, and implications of those events. Second, we assume that an "inside narrative" will reveal to us the heart of the matter—that it will present an insider's view of things, people, and events as they actually were, not merely as they appeared. This second assumption coupled with the first has in practice led to the innumerable efforts of twentieth-century readers to plumb the depths of *Billy Budd*, to solve its riddling values, to provide a "definitive criticism" of the text. That critical goal has proved painfully self-defeating, however, for although we have had a good deal of imaginative, perceptive, and genuinely helpful criticism of *Billy Budd*, the confirmed contrariety of that critical opinion suggests that we have been trying to "solve" a text that by its very nature does not allow solution.

Most criticism of *Billy Budd* has taken a wrong turn into the maze by concentrating its focus on Billy and Captain Vere. The critic who succumbs to what might be called the fallacy of projection, who identifies with Billy or Vere or—alternately—both, is turned round and round by the tale's essential moral ambiguity.[8] Billy is both innocent and guilty; Vere is both dreamily philosophical and expedient. There is a heavenly law, a natural law, and a codified law of the Mutiny Act. From such a slippery critical stance there has been been little agreement about the "definitive" values of the text.

There is, however, one line of development in the novel that is clear, if not necessarily straight or unbroken. There is the narrator. And although the narrator of *Billy Budd* is unquestionably the most elusive and difficult of Melville's narrators to deal with, he stands at the true center of the novel and provides at least a firm stance from which we can survey the sea-changes of *Billy Budd*'s world. Like Coleridge's figure of "long gray beard and glittering eye," and like the aged Melville, who forty or fifty years after his own seafaring days is compelled to tell one more tale of "the inner life of one particular ship and the career of an individual sailor" (*BB*, 3:54),[9] the persona-narrator of *Billy Budd* is an ancient mariner whose tale derives its primary significance from that persona's limited perspectives.[10]

It is clear by the narrator's selection of one ship and one sailor's career as the subject of his tale that they held uncommon significance for him. And it is clear from his focus upon the inner life of that ship and that sailor that his concern is with the meaning of the events and people he describes.[11] It is this narrative voice that promises us a clear insight into the events aboard the *Bellipotent* during the brief time that Billy Budd serves as one of her crew. What that voice delivers is disturbingly different.

The narrator has little difficulty in setting forth the facts of the narrative. Indeed, he has something of the historian's gift for noting and recollecting details of time, place, and circumstance, generating, as does any good historian, a reassuring sense of the factualness of his narrative. His account of Billy's impressment, complete with quotations from the impressing lieutenant and the details of Billy's kit being transferred from chest to bag (*BB*, 1:48), has the ring of firsthand observation. The authenticity of the narrator's knowledge of the events aboard the *Bellipotent* persists generally throughout the narrative, to the extent that at times he *appears* to be virtually omniscient. Nor do we question the recollective powers of a narrator who on the opening page of the novel can recall with photographic clarity the appearance of another "Handsome Sailor" whom he had observed "half a century ago" (*BB*, 1:43). The narrator who can recall after fifty years that it was "a hot noon in July," and who can see in his mind's eye the sailor's "gay silk handkerchief thrown loose about the neck" and recall the "big hoops of gold" in the sailor's ears and the "Highland bonnet with a tartan band" upon his "shapely head" (*BB*, 1:43) is a narrator whom we feel we trust to provide us with the truth, the whole truth, and nothing but the truth.

The narrator is not a mere chronicler with a photographic memory, however. He shares the historian's deeper concerns with relationships among events and people and thus sets his particular history of the *Bellipotent* and Billy within the larger historical context of the French Revolution and, more specifically, the Nore Mutiny (*BB*, 3:54). In this sense, the often discussed "digression" on Lord Nelson in Chapters 4 and 5 from the narrator-historian's point of view is not so much digression as necessary historical context to the immediate events of the narrative. To the narrator-historian, it is precisely because of the Spithead "commotion" in April of 1797 and the Nore Mutiny in May of 1797 that the events aboard the *Bellipotent* in the summer of 1797 can and do take place.

The narrator of *Billy Budd* is not merely a historical determinist, however. Billy, Claggart, and Captain Vere are not presented as mere historical make-weights to the grand drama of Lord Nelson and the British Fleet's darkest moment before victory's dawn. The narrator takes some pains to individualize Billy within the general category of Handsome Sailors and to define Claggart's special malignancy outside the bounds of his generally detested position as master-at-arms. More significantly, the nar-

rator avoids altogether the easy definition of Captain Vere as a naval commander governed by rigid and unequivocal rules of conduct, presenting
him instead as a complex personality faced with a complex task under
complex circumstances. In sum, the narrator presents his three central
figures working out their individual destinies in conflict with each other
in a large historical context of time and place that influences but does
not determine their fates.

By this formulation we can infer why the narrator is compelled to get
to the bottom of these events of long ago, and similarly we can understand why critics have been equally compelled to solve the problems of
the novel. The inner life of the *Bellipotent* provides a clear microcosm
of our floating world, and the career of Billy Budd epitomizes the life of
a man thrust into the world unceremoniously and just as unceremoniously thrust out again.

There is no doubt that the narrator attempts to present a whole and
rational narrative, but wholeness and rationality are beyond his best efforts and he, and we, are left with a tale that is maddeningly suggestive,
irresolvably incomplete. As the narrator admits near the end of the narrative, "Truth uncompromisingly told will always have its ragged edges;
hence the conclusion of such a narration is apt to be less finished than
an architectural finial" (*BB*, 28:128). In attempting to tell his tale of uncompromising truth, Melville's narrator focusses almost exclusively on
its three principle characters—Billy, Claggart, and Captain Vere, and although this narrow focus provides the illusion of clarity, in fact, the more
we attempt to get at the inner lives of the three main actors, the less we
really understand of them.

Both to the narrator and to his shipmates Billy Budd is the "Handsome
Sailor." The Handsome Sailor as defined by the narrator in the opening
pages is a "superior figure," the repository of all "strength and beauty"
(*BB*, 1:44). More than that, however, the narrator avows that in the
Handsome Sailor "the moral nature was seldom out of keeping with the
physical make" (*BB*, 1:44). As a type, then, the Handsome Sailor is a
paragon of beauty, strength, and goodness, a rather apparent fusion of
classical ideal and Christian virtue, and "such a cynosure . . . was welkin-
eyed Billy Budd" (*BB*, 1:44).

Billy's superiority is immediately manifest to everyone in the tale.
When Lieutenant Ratcliffe boards the *Rights-of-Man* in search of crew
for the *Bellipotent*, he pounces "plump upon Billy at first sight . . . even
before the merchantman's crew was formally mustered" and "him only
he elected" (*BB*, 1:45). Billy, lugging his chest of belongings, appears to
the lieutenant as "Apollo with his portmanteau" (*BB*, 1:48), and indeed
it is as hero demigod that Billy appears to the crew of the *Bellipotent*, to
the narrator, and to us.

Billy is the archetypal innocent, "such perhaps as Adam presumably might have been ere the urbane Serpent wriggled himself into his company" (*BB*, 2:52). Yet it is immediately and manifestly clear that the *Bellipotent* is no pre-lapsarian world and that it does not lack its resident Satan. If Billy signifies all that is naturally innocent and admirable in man, Claggart signifies in the narrator's eyes a natural depravity and madness of the most dangerous sort—a "lunacy... not continuous, but occasional, evoked by some special object" (*BB*, 11:76). The special object of Claggart's madness is, of course, Billy, and on the most elemental plane of the novel's action the conflict between Claggart and Billy springs from the former's "envy and antipathy" toward Billy's beauty and innocence (*BB*, 12:77).

Claggart's kinship with Milton's Satan is clearly self-evident in his "disdain of innocence" (*BB*, 12:78), and yet, again like Milton's Satan, "in an aesthetic way he saw the charm of it, the courageous free-and-easy temper of it, and fain would have shared it, but he despaired of it" (*BB*, 12:78). The narrator makes several crucial points of comparison between Claggart and Billy that suggest their uncanny kinship in spite of what proves to be a mortal antipathy, and that striking likeness amid contrariety underlies many of the problems the narrator has in weighing the conflict between the two men and reaching a stable conclusion. Like Billy, Claggart seems to have unceremoniously dropped into the navy and the *Bellipotent*'s world with no known background or antecedents, as much being known "of the master-at-arms' career before entering the service as an astronomer knows about a comet's travels prior to its first observable appearance in the sky" (*BB*, 8:67). The image of Claggart as a brilliant but "falling" heavenly body prefigures and then reinforces his Satanic image in Chapter 12, but more importantly there is both likeness and antithesis in Claggart as comet and Billy as Aldebaran or bright star: Claggart, with all his restless uncertain ambition cannot help but strike out in envy and antipathy at the certainty and repose of Billy's moral innocence.

There are other striking similarities between Billy and Claggart. Billy appears to be a product of "a presumable by-blow, and, evidently, no ignoble one" (*BB*, 2:52) and Claggart looks "like a man of high quality, social and moral, who for reasons of his own was keeping incog" (*BB*, 8:64). Billy has ears "small and shapely," and Claggart's hand is "too small and shapely to have been accustomed to hard toil" (*BB*, 8:64). If Billy's face might have served as a model for a Greek sculptor (*BB*, 2:51), Claggart's face "was a notable one, the features all except the chin cleanly cut as those on a Greek medallion" (*BB*, 8:64). Billy's prowess and superiority as a sailor are echoed in the narrator's account of Claggart's rise in the naval hierarchy, whereby his "superior capacity," coupled with "an

ingratiating deference to superiors, together with a peculiar ferreting genius" (*BB*, 8:67), abruptly advance him to the rank of master-at-arms.

The numerous similarities between Billy and Claggart give emphasis
to the narrator's striking observation that "one person excepted, the master-at-arms was perhaps the only man in the ship intellectually capable of
adequately appreciating the moral phenomenon presented in Billy Budd"
(*BB*, 12:78). Both Billy and Claggart are superior beings aboard the *Bellipotent*; both are handsome, intelligent, noble, and gifted in their work.
But for all that, Billy is an innocent and Claggart is corrupt. In the end,
the large number of similarities between Billy and Claggart merely accen-
tuates this essential moral difference, and the reduction of manifold likeness to essential difference concentrates the terms of the narrator's tale
into something like a parable or a morality play. In these terms Billy is
not so much innocent as Innocence itself; Claggart is not merely corrupt,
but Corruption.

The narrator's reduction of Billy's and Claggart's characters to moral
absolutes mirrors his compulsion to get a firm grip on the inner life of
the *Bellipotent*, to explain to himself, and to us, the certain significance
of it all. The concept of a struggle between natural goodness and innate
depravity is perhaps the most irresistible toy of the mind, and the narrator of *Billy Budd*, not unlike Melville's earlier narrators, sets himself no
less a task than discovering, then explaining, the full implications of that
struggle.

There are abundant signs from the very beginning of the narrative that
the narrator finds his materials resistant to the order and coherence he
tries to impose upon them. That the events of his narrative do not yield
their meaning easily or whole is manifested again and again in sentences
that are convoluted, over-modified, abstract, circumlocutious, elliptical,
and just plain awkward.[12] The narrator has little or no trouble in describing persons, appearances, or events clearly, but when he interprets
events and makes judgments on the tale's central themes and characters,
his ability to express himself falters badly, and in such a consistent and
habitual fashion that one can only take it as a reflection of his own imperfect understanding, and, thus, failed purpose.

The *Nore* mutiny and the Spithead commotion are central to the
events of *Billy Budd*, and the narrator devotes three early chapters to
the discussion of them and Lord Nelson. Many of the narrator's observations on them are tortured, obfuscated, and indeterminate. Whether the
narrator, an ex-seaman, was at the *Nore* mutiny or not, he clearly has
irresolute convictions about the meaning of it all, and that irresolution
carries through his discussion of the mutinies and into his narration of
the events aboard the *Bellipotent*. Alhough in retrospect the narrator

wishes to conclude that "the Nore Mutiny may be regarded as analogous to the distempering irruption of contagious fever in a frame constitutionally sound" (*BB*, 3:55), his own summation suggests a certain fevered ambivalence about "the spirit animating the men" (*BB*, 3:55).

The narrator never does clarify, let alone define, the spirit animating the men, and in view of the narrator's own persistent ambivalence toward the rights of men and the rights of authority and empire it is difficult to see how he could. To put it bluntly, the narrator's irresolvable ambivalence on these matters lies at the heart of *Billy Budd*; the "inner life of one particular ship and career of an individual sailor" (*BB*, 3:54) concentrate the terms of his own dilemma, compelling him, like Ishmael before him, to probe at the meanings of his tale even as he tells it. Time and again the meaning of the narrative eludes the grasp of its teller. If the larger stage of the *Nore* and Spithead mutinies is more than the narrator can grasp in toto, the concentrated, intense drama aboard the *Bellipotent* does not resolve the narrator's uncertainties so much as it magnifies his inability to get at the truth of the matter, to explain the essence of human conflict.

The narrator's problem is clear, if not simple. To understand the origins of human conflict, to get to the bottom of French Revolutions, wars, mutinies and murders, the narrator must understand Claggart. He must understand what it is in humanity that balks at beauty, chafes at innocence, and attacks moral purity. Although the narrator sees clearly enough that there is a natural antagonism between Claggart and Billy, his efforts to explain the origins of Claggart's animus toward Billy are fraught with uncertainty and frustration. At the outset, he admits that he will not be able to explain Claggart to himself or to his readers, because, he affirms, "what can more partake of the mysterious than an antipathy spontaneous and profound such as is evoked in certain exceptional mortals by the mere aspect of some other mortal" (*BB*, 11:74). The narrator is quite explicit: "For the adequate comprehending of Claggart by a normal nature these hints are insufficient. To pass from a normal nature to him one must cross 'the deadly space between'" (*BB*, 11:74).

To cross this deadly space the narrator must, as he says, resort to "indirection" (*BB*, 11:74), appealing to Plato's circular definition of the concept of "'Natural Depravity: a depravity according to nature'" (*BB*, 11:75) and holding forth on a self-defeating theory of a "protectively secret" madness that at its most active "is to the average mind not distinguishable from sanity" (*BB*, 11:76). In the end, the narrator's appeals to concepts of natural depravity and secret madness are but desperate gestures toward explaining the inexplicable. If Claggart is "something such an one" (*BB*, 11:76) as described by Plato and by the narrator's theories, in the end his is a "hidden nature" (*BB*, 11:76), and the narrator closes Chapter 11 with the catch-all, catch-nothing comment that "the resumed narrative must be left to vindicate, as it may, its own credibility" (*BB*, 11:77).

The narrative that follows is credible enough; what it lacks is a comprehending intelligence and a moral framework by which we can judge the all-too-believable events. Yet a certain moral framework and a comprehensive judgment is precisely what the narrator constantly seeks and attempts to salvage from his narrative. Thus it is that the narrator's ultimate fascination is with Captain Vere, who must first judge Claggart's accusation against Billy and then must judge Billy's killing of Claggart. In sum, the narrator is a secret-sharer of Captain Vere's stateroom and soul, searching through Vere's judgments and actions for a clue to his own truest self. And, in the end, Captain Vere's failure to resolve the ambiguity of events and moral law produces in the narrator a hopeless conviction that truth will always have its "ragged edges."

Captain Vere is introduced into the narrative in Chapter 6, immediately after the narrator's discussion of Lord Nelson and the *Nore* mutiny. This discussion leads directly to the narrator's implicit comparison between the two commanders, and rather than being digressive, it is, instead, absolutely central to our understanding of Vere's nature, central to our understanding of the entire narrative. Nelson, "'the greatest sailor since our world began'" (*BB*, 4:58), can lift up the mutineers of the *Nore* and inspire them to a "heroic magnificence in arms" that "stands unmatched in human annals" (*BB*, 3:56). He is the essential hero who vitalizes into acts "exaltations of sentiment" (*BB*, 4:58), who stands outside the boundaries of "personal prudence" (*BB*, 4:58) and outside the "*might-have-been*" thinking of the "Benthamites of war" (*BB*, 4:57). Nelson, sui generis, was and forever will be known simply as "the Great Sailor" (*BB*, 4:57).

In sharp and immediate contrast (Chapter 6 begins with a "But"), Captain Vere is a man "who whatever his sterling qualities was without any brilliant ones" (*BB*, 6:61). Although Vere is not deficient in the qualities that go to make up a naval commander and a leader of men, by the touchstone of the heroic Lord Nelson he is clearly inferior. Although the narrator tells us that Captain Vere "had seen much service, been in various engagements, always acquitting himself as an officer mindful of the welfare of his men, but never tolerating an infraction of discipline; thoroughly versed in the science of his profession, and intrepid to the verge of temerity, though never injudiciously so" (*BB*, 6:60), the fullness of his recommendation points to what Vere lacks and Lord Nelson possesses— personal vision and inspiration and the ability to vitalize into act "exaltations of sentiment." Not a hero, not "the Great Sailor," Vere is, for all that, a man—who must face whatever problems life thrusts upon him.

Whereas Lord Nelson is expansive to the point of recklessness, everything about Vere is cautious, self-containing, and restrictive. Vere is reserved in his thoughts and actions, more attracted to reading and "everything intellectual" than to "social converse" (*BB*, 7:62). His reading of "history, biography, and unconventional writers like Montaigne, who philosophize upon realities" (*BB*, 7:62) serves not as a means to understanding his contemporary world, however, but as a "dike against those invading waters of novel opinion social, political, and otherwise, which carried away as in a torrent no few minds in those days, minds by nature not inferior to his own" (*BB*, 7:62). In one sense Vere might be considered merely a conservative, holding on to "some positive convictions which he forefelt would abide in him essentially unmodified so long as his intelligent part remained unimpaired" (*BB*, 7:62). In another, truer sense, Vere is a man wholly alienated from his world, playing out his given role to its given end. When Vere stands "alone on the weather side of the quarter-deck, one hand holding by the rigging," he does not see great victories, glory, and "fame incorruptible" (*BB*, 4:57); he "absently gaze[s] off at the blank sea" (*BB*, 6:61).

In the matter of untoward and unwanted affairs like the *Nore* mutiny, Vere takes a defensive stance behind his dike of settled convictions and abstracts himself from a known reality until it comes flooding in upon him. Like Captain Delano of "Benito Cereno," "Starry Vere" trusts appearances in situations where appearances are at best ambiguous and at the worst totally deceiving. In the developing drama, Billy in his innocence simply *cannot* see Claggart's enmity, and Captain Vere, wrapped about by his settled convictions, simply *will* not recognize that enmity until it is too late. In an immediate sense Captain Vere's commitment to an eighteenth-century rational view of a world ordered by "lasting institutions" and his eighteenth-century sentimental belief that those institutions underlie "the peace of the world and the true welfare of mankind" (*BB*, 7:63) render him little more than a sophisticated innocent, as incapable of seeing Claggart whole and as vulnerable to him as Billy is. In the end Captain Vere is singularly ill-suited for the task that fate thrusts upon him—to sit in judgment on people and events that by their nature remain utterly mysterious to him.

Vere's response to Claggart's accusation against Billy dramatically defines his passionate desire for order and his unwillingness to recognize irrational, ulterior motives in man. Vere represses his instinctive, "vaguely repellant distaste" (*BB*, 18:91) for Claggart and resumes his "wonted official manner" in listening to his master-at-arms' complaint.

Vere has his misgivings, for Claggart's vague accusations and allusions to the *Nore* mutiny "looked under the circumstances something like an attempt to alarm him" (*BB*, 18:93), but misgivings or not, Vere falls victim to Claggart's sleights of mind and word and asks the fatal rational question: "'You say that there is at least one dangerous man aboard. Name him'" (*BB*, 18:94).

Vere is not taken in completely by Claggart's naming of Billy, for Vere has no illusions about Claggart's loyalty, and for the moment he stands convinced that Billy is a "King's Bargain" (*BB*, 18:95). But Vere is a man who lives by settled convictions, not by imperfect intuitions and doubts, and in the end he asks for certain proof: "'Do you come to me, Master-at-arms, with so foggy a tale? As to Budd, cite me an act or spoken word of his confirmatory of what you in general charge against him'" (*BB*, 18:95).

Vere's assumption that some certain significance lurks in all things proves his undoing—and the undoing of Claggart and Billy as well. Even at this early point in the debate over Billy's loyalty Captain Vere sees the issue in absolute terms. With the *Nore* and Spithead mutinies behind him and the French Revolution all round him, Vere sees himself as a bastion against disorder—prepared, even willing, to deal with any threat summarily. Thus he warns Claggart, "'Heed what you speak. Just now, and in a case like this, there is a yardarm-end for the false witness'" (*BB*, 18:95). In the restricted, if not actually reductive, mind of Captain Vere, the judgment has already been made that either Claggart or Billy must die.

The narrator makes it clear that Vere's rational assumptions and settled convictions do not allow him to get to the bottom of Claggart or his purposes. Although Vere is described as having an exceptional moral quality that makes him "in earnest encounter with a fellow man, a veritable touchstone of that man's essential nature, yet now as to Claggart and what was really going on in him his feeling partook less of intuitional conviction than of strong suspicion clogged by strange dubieties" (*BB*, 19:96). Even in this state of confusion and doubt, however, Vere remains consistent in his assumption that a disordered and ambiguous world can be reduced to order: "if Claggart was a false witness—that closed the affair. And therefore, before trying the accusation, he would first practically test the accuser" (*BB*, 18:96). He calls Billy to his cabin to confront Claggart.

Far from being the "quiet, undemonstrative" test that Vere envisioned (*BB*, 18:96), the confrontation between Claggart and Billy is one of primitive, uncontrollable energy and violence, far beyond Vere's ability to comprehend, let alone control. In this climactic scene of the novel Vere is reduced to the role of impotent bystander, vainly attempting to apply theories of rationality, order, and legal convention to a situation and to individuals totally outside his world of "lasting institutions." In accusing Billy, Claggart is not a plaintiff in a legal action, but a "serpent" or a "torpedo fish," with the "alien eyes of certain uncatalogued creatures of the deep" (*BB*, 19:98). Billy, in response, is not a defendant citing rules of evidence and legal precedent; he stands "like one impaled and gagged," struck by the "horror of the accuser's eyes" into a "convulsed tongue-tie" (*BB*, 19:98), ending his paralysis with a blow "quick as the flame from a discharged cannon at night" (*BB*, 19:99).[13] In the most profound sense, Vere's world of language, of law, of reason, argument, and judgment is annihilated by that blow that leaves Claggart dead upon his cabin floor.

Up to the point of Claggart's death the underlying dominant theme of the narrator's tale is the unpredictable ineffability of human nature. From the point of Claggart's death to the end of the tale, the narrator's central theme is the utter ambiguity and inexplicability of ineluctable event. Thematic echoes from *Moby-Dick, Pierre,* "Benito Cereno," "Bartleby," and *The Confidence-Man* reverberate throughout the last half of *Billy Budd* as Captain Vere, his drumhead court, and Billy play out their roles according to a logic and rationale that they, the narrator, and we, know have but the most tenuous ties to what actually has taken place. Once more, and for the last time, Melville dramatizes the universal tragedy of finite man, living in a world which outruns comprehension.

The narrator's fascination, and even identification, with Captain Vere become even more intense in the last half of the novel, for it is Captain Vere who assumes the responsibility for adjudicating the killing of Claggart and reestablishing "the peace of the world and the true welfare of mankind" (*BB*, 7:63). In the most practical sense Vere does ultimately succeed in restoring order to the *Bellipotent*. The Mutiny Act and "forms, measured forms" (*BB*, 27:128) do carry the day, and although there are murmurings among the crew there is no rebellion; after Billy's hanging and burial at sea, "toned by music and religious rites subserving the discipline and purposes of war, the men in their wonted orderly manner dispersed to the places allotted them when not at the guns" (*BB*, 27:128). As for grasping and weighing Claggart's character and motivations—without which no judgment of Billy can be meaningful—Vere remains to the end abysmally blind. As for judging Billy's own character and motivations, Vere is hopelessly incapable of integrating his fatherly view of the young Handsome Sailor and his commander's view of a seaman who has struck and killed a ship's officer. After Billy's blow to Claggart, Vere's first words are both judgmental and absolute: "'Fated boy'" (*BB*, 19:99). Vere's response to crisis is, thus, as unthinking and spontaneous, and as irrevocable, as Billy's blow to Claggart. In Vere's measuring mind Claggart cannot be brought back to life to answer for his actions, and Billy cannot avoid his doom.

In reconstructing the scene of Claggart's death and Vere's stricken response, the narrator asks himself the crucial question: "Was he [Vere] absorbed in taking in all the bearings of the event and what was best not only now at once to be done, but also in the sequel?" (*BB*, 19:99). The question is legitimate rather than rhetorical from the narrator's point of view, and it alerts the reader to all of the inherent ambiguities of Vere's situation and Billy's. What are persistent and penetrating ambiguities to the narrator and reader, however, prove to be merely transient and theoretical to Captain Vere. Although Vere casts Claggart in the role of Ananias and sees Billy as an avenging "angel of God," (*BB*, 19:100–1), nevertheless "the father in him, manifested towards Billy thus far in the scene, was replaced by the military disciplinarian" (*BB*, 19:100), and the military disciplinarian's judgment is immediate and absolute: "'the angel must hang!'" (*BB*, 19:101).

Vere never wavers for a moment from his initial judgment, and Billy does, indeed, hang. But Vere's resolute decision illuminates rather than resolves the ambiguity of his own character, Billy's situation, and the narrator's understanding of his tale. In Chapter 20, the narrator tells us of the ship's surgeon's "disquietude and misgiving" at Vere's behavior (*BB*, 20:101), raising the question in the surgeon's mind as to whether Vere is "unhinged" (*BB*, 20:102). The narrator himself is less than helpful in the next chapter. On the question of sanity and insanity, the narrator poses the manifestly unanswerable question, "who in the rainbow can draw the line where the violet tint ends and the orange tint begins?" (*BB*, 21:102). On the specific question of "whether Captain Vere, as the surgeon professionally and privately surmised, was really the sudden victim of any degree of aberration," the narrator resorts once again (as he did on the question of Claggart's "hidden nature") to the question-begging, question-evading proposition that "every one must determine for himself by such light as this narrative may afford" (*BB*, 21:102).

It is, in fact, the salient feature of this "inside" narrative that little or no light is thrown upon the innermost workings of its main characters. Claggart's is a hidden nature, Billy's is all-inarticulate surface, and Vere's to the end is self-possessing and secretive. The narrator can and does ponder and probe at the "jugglery of circumstances preceding and attending the event on board the *Bellipotent*" (*BB*, 21:103), and he juggles in his own mind the irony of how "innocence and guilt personified in Claggart and Budd in effect changed places" (*BB*, 21:103) and how a "legal view" and an indisputable deed "navally regarded" and a concept of "essential right and wrong" make it "so much the worse for the responsibility of a loyal sea commander" (*BB*, 21:103). In the end, however, these gestures toward truth remain but gestures, and once again, as in *Moby-Dick*, in *Pierre* and *The Confidence-Man*, we are left to drown in a sea of endless, self-confounding possibilities.

The drumhead court that tries and sentences Billy to hang dramatizes the way in which society functions in a world that is at once necessary and incomprehensible, the *Bellipotent* as microcosm being compressed yet further into this court as it seeks to understand and regulate its world. The compound ironies of the trial demonstrate clearly just how little understanding enters into the regulation of our world. The outward facts of Claggart's accusation and Billy's fatal response are quickly recounted by Vere and agreed to by Billy and readily accepted by the tribunal. Beyond those undisputed facts, however, little is clear, and nothing is straightforward. Billy avers that he is "true to the King" (*BB*, 21:106) and Vere believes him. Billy pleads "self-defense" in striking Claggart, and again Vere responds, "I believe you, my man" (*BB*, 21:106).

Notwithstanding Billy's protestations of "innocence" and Captain Vere's repeated acceptance of it, Billy is ultimately convicted and sentenced to hang, for Billy's fate is hinged to the question, posed by the officer of marines, of why Claggart should "have so lied, so maliciously lied" (*BB*, 21:107). The drumhead court's deliberations in general, and this question about Claggart's motivations in particular, echo the efforts of the tribunal in "Benito Cereno" to get at the truth of what took place aboard the *San Dominick*. But if that earlier tale paints a dark picture of society's failure to grasp the whole truth of an individual's actions and motives, *Billy Budd* paints a picture thrice black. In "Benito Cereno," the court's questions are blunted by Babo's wilful silence. In *Billy Budd*, when the officer of marines asks why Claggart should have "so maliciously lied" (*BB*, 21:107), Billy is struck dumb; Claggart himself lies a corpse who, as Vere says, "will not rise to our summons" (*BB*, 21:107); and Vere, both court convener and lone witness, bluntly declares the question "hardly material" (*BB*, 21:107). In *Billy Budd*, none of the principal actors in the drama can understand or explain exactly what happened or why—and neither, of course, can the narrator.

In *Billy Budd*, innocence and evil, life and death, judgment and punishment all dwell in the darkness of mystery, and perhaps it is the absolute darkness of that mystery that explains, if not justifies, Vere's retreat to his sanctuary of "settled convictions" and "forms, measured forms." Vere sees and admits that "there is a mystery" to Claggart and his inexplicable enmity toward Billy, but, he goes on to say, it is a "mystery of iniquity" suitable only for "psychologic theologians to discuss" (*BB*,

21:108), and he reduces the boundaries of the court's inquiry to "the prisoner's deed" (*BB*, 21:108). It is this cardinal interpretation of the court's jurisdiction and the limits of its inquiry that underlies Vere's address to the court at the end of Chapter 21 and precipitates the death sentence eventually handed out to Billy.

Vere's quasi-legal moral stance is adopted not to understand, which he admits he cannot do, but to respond responsibly to the "tongue-tie" of Claggart and Billy. To "accept" the inexplicability of Claggart's motivations and Billy's response can lead only to passivity and a paralytic contemplation of the dilemma. This Vere sees, and he sees it most clearly in the dubious, irresolute determinations of the drumhead court itself. Thus, he strives "against scruples that may tend to enervate decision" (*BB*, 21:110) and takes upon himself the task and the responsibility of galvanizing that court into an action that he sees from the first as absolutely necessary.

Once again Melville explores, as he does in every piece of fiction since *Moby-Dick*, the ambiguities and difficulties inherent in our attempt to act decisively in a world we cannot understand. In the midst of the scruples, internal conflicts, and anxieties that he recognizes in his court officers, and which he clearly feels within himself as well, Vere is nothing if not decisive. And his argument is deadly simple. The court is set "a case practical, and under martial law practically to be dealt with" (*BB*, 21:110). The question "How can we adjudge to summary and shameful death a fellow creature innocent before God, and whom we feel to be so?" (*BB*, 21:110) is neither answered, nor refuted by Vere. It is ruled out of court. The court's allegiance is not to God nor to Nature, but to the king and to martial law. And whatever the court's or Vere's scruples, whatever their doubts, their internal conflicts, their anxieties, their vowed "responsibility is in this: That however pitilessly that law may operate in any instances, we nevertheless adhere to it and administer it" (*BB*, 21:111).

Vere's arguments, based on allegiance to king, country, the need for military discipline in a troubled fleet, and the martial law that encompasses and codifies that allegiance, might well sound casuistic to a nineteenth-century reader, let alone to one of our age. Yet, the narrator undermines, or at least tempers, any quick judgment we might make with a statement from "a writer whom few know" about how "forty years after a battle it is easy for a noncombatant to reason about how it ought to have been fought" and how it is "another thing personally and under fire to have to direct the fighting while involved in the obscuring smoke of it" (*BB*, 21:114).

The moral and legal confusion over Claggart's guilt and Billy's innocence, the ethical dualism, not to say absolute ambiguity, of Vere's address to the court leave more than the court officers in a "harassed frame of mind" (*BB*, 21:113). The narrator, in trying to sort out and evaluate these events of long ago, resorts to the historian's tactic of comparison when he draws a parallel between the *Bellipotent* trial and the *Somers* mutiny trial of 1842 (*BB*, 21:113), but in the end the comparison tells us more about the narrator's state of mind than about either trial. The execution of a midshipman and two sailors in "a time of peace and within not many days' sail of home" (*BB*, 21:114), although a cause célèbre to Melville and his contemporaries, is to the narrator simply "history, and here cited without comment" (*BB*, 21:114).

In the very process of admitting his inability to explain either the *Somers* trial or the *Bellipotent* affair, the narrator clings to their one point of similarity: "the urgency felt, well-warranted or otherwise, was much the same" (*BB*, 21:114). This urgency to act amid confusing and ambiguous circumstances, Melville's ultimate paradigm for the human condition, produces the one clear feature of Billy's trial and the one eminently clear statement made by the narrator in the entire chapter: "in brief, Billy Budd was formally convicted and sentenced to be hung at the yardarm in the early morning watch, it being now night" (*BB*, 21:114).

If in Billy Melville recapitulates the tragedy of innocence that gives poignancy to the struggles of Tommo, Taji, Redburn, and White-Jacket, in Vere he gives final statement to the tragedy of will seen earlier in Ahab and Pierre, by which we necessarily take action in a sea of doubt and uncertainty. It is perhaps the culminating irony of that tragic vision that although action taken in uncertainty invariably produces unforeseen and undesired results, that action nevertheless dissolves uncertainty and becomes, as the narrator of *Billy Budd* would say, "history . . . cited without comment." Vere's manifest compulsion to try, condemn, and hang Billy can be explained only as an expression of his compulsion to restore predictability and order ("forms, measured forms") to his world—a world so rife in uncertain opinion that it threatens on the one hand to explode in anarchic revolution and on the other to become locked in a permanent paralysis of contrary wills.

Vere's commitment to the laws of this world rather than to the rules of "the Last Assizes" (*BB*, 21:111) makes it difficult not to judge him by the terms of Plotinus Plinlimmon's pamphlet in *Pierre*. But in creating Vere's character Melville goes beneath the surface to the heart of Plinlimmon's speculations on chronometrics and horologicals. Plinlimmon's pamphlet ends upon an "If—," yet it is just such a conditional state of mind and being that Vere abhors and struggles against. His decision that Billy must be hanged derives not from "expedience" in any political or self-serving sense, then, but from his pained determination to assert *something* of certain significance in a world of "ifs." [14]

It is precisely that—the significance of Vere's judgment—that eludes the narrator's sharpest inquiry. Once again, with the most profound implications, the narrator simply cannot get at the inside of his own narrative. From the first the narrator has described Vere as a very private, inward-looking man, but after the trial these inherent characteristics deepen yet further—making Vere totally inaccessible to the narrator. The blunt pronouncement of Billy's sentence at the close of Chapter 21 produces, in the following chapter, not illumination but darkness, not interpretation but conjecture. It is Vere who volunteers to communicate "the finding of the court to the prisoner" (*BB*, 22:114), and this meeting between the innocent but condemned Billy and the sympathetic but unyielding Vere gives promise of being the climactic scene of the novel. Yet our expectations are raised only to be dashed, for the narrator tells us in the second paragraph of Chapter 22 that "beyond the communication of the sentence, what took place at this interview was never known" (*BB*, 22:114).[15]

In recognition that this private meeting is all-important to his narrative, the narrator ventures "some conjectures" about his two protagonists. But "conjectures" are admissions of defeat to one who would tell an "inside" narrative, and this defeat is painfully clear to us—and the narrator himself—in the third paragraph of Chapter 22. Setting out with the supposition that "it would have been in consonance with the spirit of Captain Vere should he on this occasion have concealed nothing from the condemned one," the narrator continues with another conjecture— that "it is not improbable that such a confession would have been received in much the same spirit that prompted it" (*BB*, 22:115). Finally, the narrator tacks his way aimlessly through numerous "might have's" and "may have been's" only to come to rest—in mute calm (*BB*, 22: 115). The teller of this inside narrative frankly admits that "*there is no telling* the sacrament, seldom if in any case revealed to the gadding world, wherever under circumstances at all akin to those here attempted to be set forth two of great Nature's nobler order embrace" (*BB*, 22:115; my emphasis).

The similitude between the narrator's position at the close of *Billy Budd* and that of Ishmael at the close of *Moby-Dick* is all but complete. Both have tried to come to terms with the most compelling and haunting experience in their lives and both, after the most valiant efforts to get at the inside of "truth," find themselves on the perimeter of things, the opacities of event and of human nature itself standing as unyielding bars to their inquiries. Ahab, Moby Dick, the *Pequod* all lie fathoms below the surface of Ishmael's surviving vision, and the narrator of *Billy Budd* is forced to conclude his conjectures with the summary, but cryptic comment that "there is privacy at the time, inviolable to the survivor; and holy oblivion, the sequel to each diviner magnanimity, providentially covers all at last" (*BB*, 22:115). Neither the narrator nor we can ever know what was said between Billy and Captain Vere.

From this critical point to the conclusion of the novel the narrator deals with consequences of Claggart's death and Billy's trial, and the narrator's voice and the narrative itself take on a clarity and tone of assurance so notably lacking in the first twenty-two chapters. Billy's killing of Claggart and the court's condemnation of Billy, however uncertain, ambiguous, and ineffable in themselves, precipitate a sequence of events that have the inexorability of Fate and the irreducible density of fact. Vere addresses the crew in "clear terms and concise" avoiding any preachments on discipline, and the burial of Claggart's body is dealt with in a sentence, the narrator not wishing to "clog the sequel with lateral matters" (*BB*, 23:116). The last eight chapters of *Billy Budd* become, in short, "history to be cited with little comment" indeed.

This anticlimax to the narrative is predicated, clearly enough, on the narrator's failure to understand properly or wholly Claggart's evil, Billy's innocence, or Vere's judgment, and without that understanding, Billy's hanging becomes merely an extended non sequitur—an effect with no sufficient cause. In the hours of waiting before the hanging, Billy lies "as in a trance" (*BB*, 24:119), and in fact his suspension from reality is so great that his own imminent death has the quality of a child's dream or game. Billy proves to be wholly immune to the chaplain's efforts "to bring home to him the thought of salvation and a Savior" which, as the narrator puts it, "was like a gift placed in the palm of an outreached hand upon which the fingers do not close" (*BB*, 24:121).

Efforts to find some certain significance in the hanging scene and its aftermath are as futile as the chaplain's efforts to explain salvation to Billy, for the narrator gives us little of substance with which to build a persuasive explanation of anything. The assembled crew "spoke but in whisper, and few spoke at all" (*BB*, 25:123). The crew, "without volition, as it were" respond in "resonant sympathetic echo: 'God Bless Captain Vere'" (*BB*, 25:123). And Vere, "either through stoic self-control or a sort of momentary paralysis induced by emotional shock, stood erectly rigid as a musket in the ship-armour's rack" (*BB*, 25:123–24). The entire hanging scene is dominated by a conventionality and passivity that merely reach their highest expression in the mute and wondrously motionless form of Billy hanging from the main yard-end.

Although this scene has provoked, understandably enough, countless determined and ingenious analyses, it is perilous to ignore the narrator's own comments on the scene. For him, the scene is wrapped in silence—"silence at the moment of execution and for a moment or two continuing thereafter, a silence but emphasized by the regular wash of the sea against the hull" (*BB*, 27:125). And when that silence is broken it is by "a sound not easily to be verbally rendered" (*BB*, 27:126), a sound that "being inarticulate,... was dubious in significance" (*BB*, 27:126). Surely the narrator is telling us that in a world that murders innocence, the only reasonable human response is an inarticulate murmur, and just as surely the narrator reveals to us that although he can tell us what that "murmurous indistinctness" (*BB*, 27:126) sounds like, he can add nothing to it. There is, indeed, no one who can explain or explain away the hanging of Billy Budd. In Chapter 26, the purser and the ship's surgeon engage in a debate about the "phenomenal" absence of spasmodic movement in Billy's hanging body (*BB*, 26:124–25), but in the end the discussion can have but one conclusion: "'it was phenomenal ... in the sense that it was an appearance the cause of which is not immediately to be assigned'" (*BB*, 26:125).

In Chapter 29, the narrator presents the account of Claggart's death and Billy's hanging as published in "a naval chronicle of the time" (*BB*, 29:130), an account hopelessly innaccurate in detail and pathetically self-serving in its chauvinistic rationalizations. If the official account of the *Bellipotent* incident is founded upon self-serving rumor and misinformation, the response of the "bluejackets" is founded upon ignorance and superstition. Although their veneration of Billy and their primitive attachment to "any tangible object associated with some striking incident of the service" make them revere a chip from the hanging spar as "a piece of the cross," in the end they remain "ignorant ... of the secret facts of the tragedy" (*BB*, 30:131). Their mixed feelings toward Billy are a perfect reproduction of Captain Vere's perfect ambivalence: "not thinking but that the penalty was somehow unavoidably inflicted from the naval point of view, for all that, they instinctively felt that Billy was a sort of man as incapable of mutiny as of wilful murder" (*BB*, 30:131).

To the very end, neither ship's officers, nor ship's crew, nor ship's captain can explain the wholly mysterious "inner life of one particular ship and the career of an individual sailor" (*BB*, 3:54). When Vere dies with the words "'Billy Budd, Billy Budd'" on his lips they are "words inexplicable to his attendant" (*BB*, 28:129). And they remain inexplicable to the narrator and to us as well. Although the narrator can tell us that "these were not the accents of remorse" (*BB*, 28:129), he cannot and does not tell us what they were.

It is one thing for us to accept at face value the narrator's confession that "truth uncompromisingly told will always have its ragged edges," but it is another to recognize that in trying to set the historical record straight the narrator demonstrates all too clearly that "truth" is nothing but ragged edges. In the end, both the actors and the events aboard the *Bellipotent* prove to be all impenetrable surface to the inquiring gaze of the narrator, and his narrative recapitulates the failure of vision central to all the post-*Moby-Dick* fiction. The narrator's persistent inquiry in the face of this inevitable failure makes him, like the tortoises of "The Encantadas," both victim and hero in a recalcitrant world, and that paradoxical role, says Melville finally, is the role of all humanity. To the extent that we share in the narrator's essential humanity we will be forever compelled by *Billy Budd*, forever thwarted in our attempts to get at its heart; *Billy Budd*, like all great art, succeeds not because it makes us better, or wiser, but because it makes us all more aware of what it means to be human.

Epilogue

The trillionth part has not yet been said; and all that has been
said, but multiplies the avenues to what remains to be said.
—"Hawthorne and His Mosses"

In bringing this study to a conclusion, I must face the inevitable, yet
self-confounding task, defined so well by Melville, of trying to say
something finite about an infinite subject. In this book I have not tried to
tell, or re-tell, the history of nineteenth-century America, nor have I tried
much to rehearse the external events of Melville's life. There are, no
doubt, others who might wish to explore further some of these multiply-
ing avenues of inquiry. Rather, I have attempted to seize upon Melville's
living, creative mind and imagination in the best record we have of
them—his works.

Of all his literary contemporaries Melville had the keenest vision of
Western civilization's rapidly expanding, rapidly changing world experience, and he possessed the most critical awareness of his culture's shrinking capacity for comprehending, let alone assimilating, that experience.
And that vision, that awareness form the foundation to all Melville's art.
The radical, inquiring skepticism of his mind forced him to explore and
weigh the assumptions of romantic idealism, democratic optimism, na-
tional enthusiasm, and Christian assurance, but that same skepticism prevented his acceptance of any, let alone all, of these, the tribal idols of
mid-nineteenth-century America.

In his first six novels, from *Typee* through *Moby-Dick*, Melville relentlessly pursues every possible variation on the theme of humanity's quest

for completion and certainty in worlds that are both infinite and infinitely mutable. The dynamics of these fictions, culminating in *Moby-Dick*, focus upon the ground where experience and understanding meet—in the body and mind of the self, and as Melville, novel by novel, charts both the necessity of the quest and the impossibility of its completion, he draws ever-constricting definitions of the individual's capacity for wholeness, until in *Moby-Dick* and *Pierre* the self is defined expressly by its tragic alienation from the world, from all humanity and, finally, from any certain sense of its own identity.

The definitive statement of humanity's tragic plight, expressed dramatically in Ahab, Ishmael, and Pierre, serves as the terminus ad quem of the early fiction and becomes the terminus a quo of the fiction to follow. In *The Piazza Tales*, *The Confidence-Man*, and *Billy Budd*, Melville again explores variations on a theme—and again with tenacity and honesty. But in the late fiction the theme is that of disillusionment, disorientation, and, for at least some of his characters, despair. The vestiges of questing that are to be found in "The Piazza," *Clarel*, and *Billy Budd* are merely nostalgic and recollective, and in essence the subject of both story, poem, and novel is the death of idealism and "faith." The truest touchstone to the tonality of the post-*Moby-Dick* fiction is "The Encantadas," which, in its bleak, sardonic depiction of creation and humanity, defines Melville's keenest sense of life without aspiration, without purposive will, without belief, without "certain significance."

Although Melville, of all people, realized the difficulty of saying something finite on an infinite subject, in *Billy Budd* he regenerated all the old energies to create one last summary statement on humanity's fate. The questions raised in *Billy Budd* are the questions Melville had explored throughout a lifetime of artistic endeavor—questions of innocence and evil, justice and necessity, fate and free will, painful ignorance and tragic understanding. There are, of course, no answers to these questions in *Billy Budd*; that we should think there might be indicates the raw appeal and power of the novel. Perhaps the most remarkable feature of this remarkable book is that amid the darkness of its final implications we can still catch glimpses of the bright flashes of youth, of dreams, of "earnestness and grandeur." *Billy Budd* is a most fitting conclusion to Melville's art, for it is a testament to humanity's indomitable courage in prevailing to the end, in spite of, or rather because of, all the unanswerable questions that must be dived for, again and again, in the depths of humanity itself. In that final paradox we recognize Melville's heroic vision and his tragic vision—and the compelling essence of his art.

Notes

INTRODUCTION

1. A definitive apologia for biographical-historical-textual criticism is found in Hershel Parker, *Flawed Texts and Verbal Icons: Literary Authority in American Fiction* (Evanston: Northwestern University Press, 1984). I simply do not share Parker's absolute faith in biographical-historical "facts"—which in my view are as "flawed," partial, and subject to question and ambiguity as the flawed literary texts he rightfully abhors.

2. *Symbolism and American Literature* (Chicago: University of Chicago Press, 1953), p. 163.

3. *Symbolism and American Literature*, p. 163.

4. See Jane Mushabac, *Melville's Humor: A Critical Study* (Hamden, Conn.: Anchor, 1981), pp. 60–61: "Ideas in Melville come from and lead to questions. They are not stable entities but animated embodiments of what interests him, the experience of having a mind."

5. See Warwick Wadlington, *The Confidence Game in American Literature* (Princeton: Princeton University Press, 1975), p. 48: "If one word could sum up the enacted narrative posture, and also permit a generalization about Melville's works, it would be 'Nevertheless.' The attitude mediates between spirited affiliation and disabused intellect; between impossibility and necessity."

6. See T. Walter Herbert, Jr., *"Moby-Dick" and Calvinism: A World Dismantled* (New Brunswick, N.J.: Rutgers University Press, 1977), p. 2: "He [Melville] was not merely unable to choose among the various schemes of truth that his reading and experience made available; his doubts ran so deep as to divide the personal center in which religious ideas were deliberated. He experienced the contradictions between incompatible theories as an acute personal conflict, but instead of retreating before this painful circumstance, he was inspired to undertake a zealous meditative quest."

7. Again, I find myself admiring T. Walter Herbert, Jr.'s insight (*"Moby-Dick" and Calvinism*, pp. 36–37): "Melville's quest portrays the heroism of a man without a standard of final belief, who casts himself unreservedly into the search for it. The basic criterion of his quest remains insistently theocentric: he seeks a unified vision of ultimate reality that can gather all experience into an intelligible and coherent totality."

CHAPTER ONE

1. *The First and Second Discourses*, trans. Roger D. Masters and Judith R. Masters, (New York: St. Martin's Press, 1964), pp. 92–93.

2. Jay Leyda, *The Melville Log: A Documentary Life of Herman Melville, 1819–1891*, 2 vols. (New York: Harcourt, Brace, 1951), I:244.

3. Leyda, *Log*, I:246.

4. Ibid., I:216.

5. Ibid., I:210. Readers concerned with a more complete picture of contemporary reviews of Melville's works should consult Hugh W. Hetherington's *Melville's Reviewers, British and American, 1846–1891* (Chapel Hill: University of North Carolina Press, 1961).

6. Leyda, *Log*, I:212.

7. For a trenchant analysis of shifting and not-so-shifting attitudes toward *Typee*, see Milton R. Stern's introductory essay in *Critical Essays on Herman Melville's "Typee,"* ed. Milton R. Stern (Boston: G. K. Hall, 1982).

8. The tendency of modern critics to view *Typee* dualistically probably has its clearest source in Charles R. Anderson's *Melville in the South Seas* (New York: Columbia University Press, 1939). Anderson's summarily concludes that *Typee* contains Melville's indictment of civilization as it is epitomized in Christianity and exaltation of the primitive life as it is romantically idealized in the Typee savages (e.g., see pp. 121, 177, 240–41, 276–77, 336). Variations on this major theme have been played by almost every post-Anderson Melville critic. To cite one of the polar variations on the dualism in *Typee*, Loren Baritz, in *City on a Hill: A History of Ideas and Myths in America* (New York: John Wiley and Sons, 1964), p. 277, argues a *real* primitivism in *Typee*, and Rowland A. Sherrill, *The Prophetic Melville: Experience, Transcendence, and Tragedy* (Athens: University of Georgia Press, 1979) argues that "in the closing distance between the romanticist Tommo and the retrospective Tommo, . . . Melville negates the idea of paradisal innocence as a refuge from the world of experience by undercutting Tommo's romantic assumptions and by establishing an anthropology which includes the fact of the Fall" (p. 23). Closer to my reading of the novel is A. N. Kaul, who in *The American Vision: Actual and Ideal Society in Nineteenth-Century Fiction* (New Haven: Yale University Press, 1963), presents a view of Melville in absolute suspension between "actual" and "ideal" (see pp. 225–27, 234–35, passim).

9. Joseph Flibbert, *Melville and the Art of Burlesque* (Amsterdam: Rodopi N. V., 1974), p. 17, discusses the "assertion and counter-assertion, of balanced affirmation and rejection," that makes "suspect the once-common belief that Melville's first two novels affirm the preeminence of 'natural man' over institutional-

ized society." I agree with Flibbert's keen insight, even though he reaches an opposite conclusion to mine—to wit, that Melville, rather than embracing both cultures, mocks them both through burlesque and parody.

10. Herman Melville, *Typee: A Peep at Polynesian Life*, ed. Harrison Hayford, Hershel Parker, and G. Thomas Tanselle (Evanston and Chicago: Northwestern University Press and the Newberry Library, 1968). Future references citing chapter and page numbers will be included in my text, with *Typee* abbreviated as *T*.

11. "The Garden," *The Poems and Letters of Andrew Marvell*, 3d ed., ed. H. M. Margoliouth, rev. Pierre Leguis and E. E. Duncan-Jones (Oxford: Clarendon Press, 1971), I:52.

12. See John D. Seelye, *Melville: The Ironic Diagram* (Evanston: Northwestern University Press, 1970), passim. Seelye's observations on the two linear movements critical in Melville's works have been very helpful to my own thinking, although he places a different, but related, value upon them.

13. See Milton R. Stern, *The Fine Hammered Steel of Herman Melville* (Urbana: University of Illinois Press, 1957), p. 49: "Tommo's plight sounds the first note in Melville's thematic call to integration and completion. Body needs consciousness (Tommo can strike a Lucifer match, but Kory-Kory must struggle to produce a flame), and consciousness needs body (Kory-Kory must carry the injured Tommo) lest man become an invalid in the undeniable world of physical nature or a childlike animal in the undeniable world of the human mind."

14. See Edwin Fussell, *Frontier: American Literature and the American West* (Princeton: Princeton University Press, 1965), p. 238: [in *Typee*] "Melville established the central line he would follow in book after book, a line falling between European civilization, as played at by the Americans, and reversion to barbarism, another New World pastime. Like all the major writers in the tradition of Cooper, he had somehow to discover a neutral ground including the best of each and transcending both."

15. See A. Carl Bredahl, Jr., *Melville's Angles of Vision* (Gainesville: University of Florida Press, 1972) for a general discussion of perspectivism in *Typee*.

16. See Richard H. Brodhead, *Hawthorne, Melville, and the Novel* (Chicago: University of Chicago Press, 1976), p. 4: "Both men [Hawthorne and Melville] possess imaginations which are in a fundamental way hostile to the kind of formal procedure that the novel's organization requires. As a result . . . all of their work is characterized by a powerful tension between their visions and the nature of the genre they chose to work in."

17. Throughout Melville's early writings the sea carries a value of "possibility" and land that of "actuality." All Melville's protagonists, from Tommo through Taji, Redburn, White-Jacket, and Ishmael, are satisfied neither at sea nor on land.

18. Probably the best interpretive discussion of *Omoo* to date is Edwin M. Eigner's "The Romantic Unity of Melville's *Omoo*," *Philological Quarterly* 46 (January 1967):95–108. Eigner posits a diphasic structure in *Omoo* whereby the despair of the Tahitians finds an analogue in the despair of the *Julia*'s crew. Although the mutiny aboard the *Julia* does signify real despair, Tommo's disengagement from the *Julia* and the crew signifies his reassertive attempt to overcome despair and reintegrate his world.

19. Herman Melville, *Omoo*, ed. Harrison Hayford, Hershel Parker, and G. Thomas Tanselle (Evanston and Chicago: Northwestern University Press and the Newberry Library, 1968). Future references citing chapter and page numbers will be included in my text, with *Omoo* abbreviated as *O*.

20. See T. Walter Herbert Jr., *Marquesan Encounters: Melville and the Meaning of Civilization* (Cambridge: Harvard University Press, 1980), passim, for a summary view of the motivations, behavior, and results of the Christian mission in Polynesia.

21. Granted, the Tamai passage was a transplant from the original *Typee* material, and consequently might well appear disjunctive in a different narrative; however, Melville did insert the episode where it stands, and he did relate its intrinsic value to the rest of the narrative movement.

22. See Leon Howard, *Herman Melville: A Biography* (Berkeley: University of California Press, 1958), p. 68: "Not until he visited Honolulu, he wrote later, did he become aware of the fact that the natives 'had been civilized into draft horses, and evangelized into beasts of burden.' The impressions he had begun to form in the Marquesas and Tahiti were crystallized in the Hawaiian Islands."

CHAPTER TWO

1. Herman Melville, *Mardi*, ed. Harrison Hayford, Hershel Parker, and G. Thomas Tanselle (Chicago and Evanston: Northwestern University Press and the Newberry Library, 1970). Future references citing chapter and page numbers will be included in my text, with *Mardi* abbreviated as *M*.

2. Milton R. Stern, *The Fine Hammered Steel of Herman Melville* (Urbana: University of Illinois Press, 1957), pp. 70–71, and Edgar A. Dryden, *Melville's Thematics of Form: The Great Art of Telling the Truth* (Baltimore: Johns Hopkins University Press, 1968), p. 47, are two critics who see a unity amid the seeming fragmentation of *Mardi*.

3. See Edwin M. Eigner, *The Metaphysical Novel in England and America: Dickens, Bulwer, Melville, and Hawthorne* (Berkeley: University of California Press, 1978), p. 77: "Those critics who contend that *Mardi* begins like *Typee* and *Omoo*, as a realistic narrative of facts, ought to bear at least these two differences in mind: (1) that the narrator here is not jumping ship in some interesting South Sea port, but, against all rational advice, on the high seas, some thousand miles from the nearest land; and (2) that he defects in *Mardi* not, as in the earlier works, because the ship is physically intolerable, but because it represents a vaguely spiritual deficiency." See also Dryden, *Melville's Thematics of Form*, p. 50.

4. See William B. Dillingham, *An Artist in the Rigging: The Early Works of Herman Melville* (Athens: University of Georgia Press, 1972), p. 124: "*Mardi* is Emerson's *Nature* turned inside out. Emerson's favorite idea of a man-centered universe and his repeated insistence upon the unity that underlies diversity led him to an unqualified optimism. If Melville seems to be making the same points, his conclusion is diametrically opposite."

5. See John D. Seelye, *Melville: The Ironic Diagram* (Evanston: Northwestern

University Press), p. 35: "Traveling the complete circuit of the archipelago in search of Yillah, the unattainable ideal which the Faustian man is committed to pursue, Taji is predictably unsuccessful." I do take issue with Seelye's sense of "predictability," which seems to me to be predicated upon a modern assumption of the futility of all quests. What is predictable for us was a hard-won, unwanted discovery for Melville.

6. See Stern, *The Fine Hammered Steel*, p. 124: "Ideal must be actualized, humanized.... The ideal needs humanity and experience in which to exist at all, but once it touches humanity and experience, it undergoes another transformation which is the death of the pure state, the death of Yillah." See also Charles R. Feidelson, Jr., *Symbolism and American Literature* (Chicago: University of Chicago Press, 1953), p. 171: Taji "is unable to regard Yillah simply as the putative end of an infinite process. He seeks her as a finite object and is thereby thrown into a terrible dilemma.... He is doomed to apply the endless journey to a purpose for which it was never intended—that is, to attain an end."

7. Lawrance Thompson, *Melville's Quarrel with God* (Princeton: Princeton University Press, 1952), p. 67: "For Melville, perhaps the major value of his having employed the allegorical device of representing Taji's disillusionment . . . as a form of psychological fragmentation . . . was that he could project his own conflicting hopes and doubts by letting these three characters explore the meaning of the word 'Truth.'" See also Eigner, *The Metaphysical Novel in England and America*, p. 80.

8. Merrell R. Davis, *Melville's "Mardi": A Chartless Voyage* (New Haven: Yale University Press, 1952) identifies this epistemological quest with Babbalanja (p. 182) and distinguishes between Babbalanja's search and Taji's quest for Yillah; however, Babbalanja's questions—"How much can man know?" and "What is certain knowledge?" (Davis, p. 182)—are inextricably linked to the search for Yillah.

9. See Leon Howard, *Herman Melville: A Biography* (Berkeley: University of California Press, 1958), p. 119: "Through his characters, he [Melville] had gone even further than he had dared to go in his own proper person by allowing his philosopher to disavow Christianity . . . and by attributing to his poet the disillusioning discovery that the highest religious authority dwelt in an almost complete symbolic darkness."

10. See T. Walter Herbert Jr., *Moby-Dick and Calvinism: A World Dismantled* (New Brunswick, N. J.: Rutgers University Press, 1971), pp. 78–79, on the conclusion of Mardi and Melville's ongoing struggle with theodicy: "the liberal optimism of Serenia might be said to rest upon a bomb, whose hidden fuse could be ignited by a fearless inquiry into the mad meanings of radical evil." For a positive reading of the values of Serenia, see Willard Thorp, *Herman Melville: Representative Selections* (New York: American Book Company, 1938), "Introduction," p. civ.

11. On the ambiguity of Hautia and her relationship to Taji and Yillah, see Martin Leonard Pops, *The Melville Archetype* (Cleveland: Kent State University Press, 1970), p. 42.

12. See Robert D. Richardson, *Myth and Literature in the American Renaissance* (Bloomington: Indiana University Press, 1978), p. 210, for a view of *Mardi* as tragic unresolved myth: "The reason the narrative of *Mardi* returns to the mythic level at the end is to drive home the point that the book *Mardi* is itself a myth. . . . Far from being a story of the triumph of Psyche or the Soul, the Yillah story in *Mardi* is a tragic story of the death of the myth of the soul."

CHAPTER THREE

1. Herman Melville, *Redburn, His First Voyage*, ed. Harrison Hayford, Hershel Parker, and G. Thomas Tanselle (Evanston and Chicago: Northwestern University Press and the Newberry Library, 1969). Future references citing chapter and page numbers will be included in my text, with *Redburn* abbreviated as *R*.

2. In "Melville's *Redburn*: Initiation and Authority," *New England Quarterly* 46 (December 1973): 558–72, Michael Davitt Bell stresses that *Redburn* cannot be viewed as a typical novel of initiation, for Redburn does not come to a proper understanding of his culture. See, also, William B. Dillingham, *An Artist in the Rigging: The Early Works of Herman Melville* (Athens: University of Georgia Press, 1972), pp. 48–49, 54; Edwin Haviland Miller, *Melville* (New York: George Braziller, 1975), p. 161; and Edward S. Grejda, *The Common Continent of Men: Racial Equality in the Writings of Herman Melville* (Port Washington, N. Y.: Kennikat Press, 1974), p. 57.

3. A. R. Humphreys, in *Herman Melville* (New York: Grove Press, 1962), p. 29, is one of a handful of readers genuinely and unqualifiedly enthusiastic about Melville's artistry in both *Redburn* and *White-Jacket*: "Both works are in fact strikingly good. By drastic revulsion, however unwilling, from the manner of *Mardi*, the writing becomes direct, sensitive, and intense. . . ."

4. One of surprisingly few discussions of the fort scene in *Redburn* is to be found in Charles Haberstroh's "*Redburn*: The Psychological Pattern," *Studies in American Fiction* 2 (Autumn 1974):133–44. For Haberstroh, "The image of the fort—with its serenity and safety—embodies Redburn's sense of his own boyhood. He would, obviously, give anything to return to it. It is understandable that his mind, in musing about England, fixes itself primarily on images of quiet pastoralism, images that reflect his experience of the fort and his hope that England may somehow be like that June day on the Narrows" (p. 138). John D. Seelye, in *Melville: The Ironic Diagram* (Evanston: Northwestern University Press, 1970), pp. 49–52, comments on the antithesis [ironic diagram] between the garden within the fort and the garden of the gambling house in London.

5. See Harold T. McCarthy, "Melville's *Redburn* and the City," *Midwest Quarterly* 12 (July 1971):395–410. Throughout his essay McCarthy comments on Redburn's association and identification of Liverpool with New York—as together they present a telling image of the "secular city."

6. See and compare John 20:13–14.

7. See McCarthy, "Melville's *Redburn*," p. 402: "Melville's technique of ironic association, which links the figure of dying Nelson and his slave-like captives with the figures of the dying mother and children and the bodies gathered for public inspection in the Death-House suggests the entire city is a house of the dead."

8. *Redburn* contains numerous references to death; as Edwin Miller puts it so trenchantly, "references to death are rarely absent" (*Melville*, p. 154). Nevertheless, there has been little close analysis of the death scenes as a structural element in the novel.

9. Herman Melville, *White-Jacket; or, The World in a Man-of-War*, ed. Harrison Hayford, Hershel Parker, and G. Thomas Tanselle (Evanston and Chicago: Northwestern University Press and the Newberry Library, 1970). Future references citing chapter and page numbers will be included in my text, with *White-Jacket* abbreviated as *W-J*.

10. One of the earliest and best discussions of the infamous Cadwallader Cuticle is to be found in Chapter 11 of Howard P. Vincent's *The Tailoring of "White-Jacket"* (Evanston: Northwestern University Press, 1970). In that chapter Vincent explores the literary sources for Cuticle and also illuminates Melville's probable researches into medical practices and theory in the 1840s.

11. In Chapter 12 of *The Tailoring of "White-Jacket,"* Vincent explores Melville's source for this scene in John Sherburne Sleeper's *Tales of the Ocean*, in which the murder-suicide that White-Jacket contemplates is actually carried out by an impressed American sailor aboard an English ship.

12. According to Vincent, White-Jacket's survival shows us that "Melville, far beyond Ames, jubilantly affirms the sheer goodness of being alive, coiled monsters though there be nearby" (*The Tailoring of "White-Jacket,"* p. 216); for Robert C. Albrecht, in "White Jacket's [*sic*] Intentional Fall," *Studies in the Novel* 4 (1972):23–24, "White Jacket's [*sic*] recognition of the impulse to life signifies the emergence of his true self, his movement towards the 'courage to be' in Tillich's words." Larry J. Reynolds, whose overall argument is quite persuasive, undercuts his own argument with an inexplicable reading of the novel's ending: "The loss of the jacket ... results not from White-Jacket's acquiring a new vision of and attitude toward his fellows—a development for which there is no motivation or evidence in the work—but rather from the arrival of the *Neversink* in port and the termination of White-Jacket's naval experience" ("Antidemocratic Emphasis in *White-Jacket,*" *American Literature* 48 [March 1976]:26). The novel ends, of course, with the *Neversink* still at sea—merely homeward *bound*.

13. See Richard Boyd Hauck's argument in *A Cheerful Nihilism: Confidence and the Absurd in American Humorous Fiction* (Bloomington: Indiana University Press, 1971), p. 90: "His [White-Jacket's] reasoning, of course, is entirely circular. He says in one breath that God will intercede, and in another he demonstrates that He cannot or will not intercede." Unlike Hauck, I don't see White-Jacket's self-negating reasoning as "a function of White-Jacket's sense of humor," and I therefore fail to see its "power to enable White-Jacket to live with ambivalence."

CHAPTER FOUR

1. David Hume, *A Treatise of Human Nature: Being an Attempt to introduce the experimental method of Reasoning into Moral Subjects*, 2 vols. (London, 1739), pp. 457–58.

2. Herman Melville, *Moby-Dick*, ed. Harrison Hayford and Hershel Parker

(New York: W. W. Norton, 1967). Future references citing chapter and page numbers will be included in my text, with *Moby-Dick* being abbreviated as *M-D*.

3. On Ishmael's role and identity at the beginning of the novel, see Harrison Hayford's fine article "Loomings," in *Artful Thunder: Versions of the Romantic Tradition in American Literature in Honor of Howard P. Vincent*, ed. Robert J. DeMott and Sanford E. Marovitz (Cleveland: Kent State University Press, 1975), pp. 119–37.

4. See Michael Davitt Bell, *The Development of American Romance* (Chicago: University of Chicago Press, 1980), p. 217: "Like Taji, he takes to the sea as a substitute for acting out suicidal compulsions. Not even, perhaps, as a substitute; for the attraction he feels for the 'nameless perils of the whale' and the somber testimony of the memorial tablets in the Whaleman's Chapel hint that he may embrace whaling as *a form of* suicide."

5. The most perceptive discussion of the Mapple chapters to date is to be found in Bainard Cowan's *Exiled Waters: "Moby-Dick" and the Crisis of Allegory* (Baton Rouge: Louisiana State University Press, 1982), pp. 77–86. Cowan takes issue with the prevailing view that Father Mapple's sermon represents "an eloquent expression of Christian faith" and argues that the "Chapel," "Pulpit," and "Sermon" chapters "reveal the dead end of Christianity in American Calvinism" (p. 81). In the course of his discussion, Cowan presents a persuasive interpretation of the cenotaph-tablets in the chapel, which in his view reinforce the misdirection and doom of Mapple's sermon.

6. On the complex relationship between perception, reality, and being see Paul Brodtkorb, Jr., *Ishmael's White World: A Phenomenological Reading of "Moby-Dick"* (New Haven: Yale University Press, 1965), pp. 128–29 and passim. Also see Charles Feidelson Jr., *Symbolism and American Literature* (Chicago: University of Chicago Press, 1953), pp. 32 ff. and passim, for the relationship between perception and symbolism in the novel.

7. See the "Preface" to T. Walter Herbert Jr.'s *Moby-Dick and Calvinism: A World Dismantled* (New Brunswick: Rutgers University Press, 1977) for a lucid summation of Melville's "theological" stance in *Moby-Dick*.

Commenting on the essential difference between Melville and the "post-modernist" cult of absurdity, Henry Nash Smith astutely observes: "What lies behind the pasteboard mask of appearances in *Moby-Dick* may be the colorless all-color of atheism, but this is still only a possibility, and the ambiguity lends a dimension to Melville's fictive world that makes it, although certainly not simpler or safer, undeniably bigger and more complex than the programmatic meaninglessness of the world of the Keseys and Hellers and Pynchons" (*Democracy and the Novel: Popular Resistance to Classic American Writers* (New York: Oxford University Press, 1978), p. 55.

8. See Richard H. Brodhead, *Hawthorne, Melville and the Novel* (Chicago: University of Chicago Press, 1976), p. 158:

Time in Ishmael's narrative takes the form Frank Kermode calls *chronos*: instead of seeming to possess a larger order it unfolds as "one damn thing after another." We move through the perpetual present of Ishmael's perception and inventively responsive imagination. But in the narrative associated with Ahab time takes the form Kermode calls *kairos*: its moments are felt as "significant seasons," as "charged with a meaning derived from its relation to the end." We see a cunning meaning in its incidents because they lead us forward to contemplate Ahab's final encounter with Moby Dick.

9. On Ishmael's "colorless, all-color" voice in "The Whiteness of the Whale," see James Guetti, *The Limits of Metaphor: A Study of Melville, Conrad, and Faulkner* (Ithaca: Cornell University Press, 1967), pp. 26–27.

10. See A. Robert Lee, "*Moby-Dick*: The Tale and the Telling" in *New Perspectives on Melville*, ed. Faith Pullin (Edinburgh: Edinburgh University Press, 1978), p. 108: "Even allowing that Melville got some of the originals wrong by error (the Hebrew is slightly askew, as are the Greek and the Anglo-Saxon), the point of the list ['Extracts' and 'Etymology'] is to mock our expectations of ever assigning exact, or correct, etymologies and words to the whale." For a similar view, see also Cowan, *Exiled Waters*, p. 63.

11. W. H. Auden, *The Enchafèd Flood: or, The Romantic Iconography of the Sea* (New York: Random House, 1950), pp. 134–36, sees Ahab and Pip bound together, but as antitypes of strength and humility.

12. See Cowan, *Exiled Waters*, p. 60: "It is of the very character of *Moby-Dick* as allegory that it begin retrospectively, long after the disastrous whale hunt is past, when the sole survivor of the *Pequod* has had sufficient time to meditate on and interpret his mysterious and overwhelming experience."

More specifically to the point of my argument, see William B. Dillingham, "The Narrator of *Moby-Dick*," in *English Studies* 49 (No. 1, 1968): 20–29. Dillingham makes a number of explicit identifications of Ishmael with Coleridge's Ancient Mariner and concludes summarily, "the ordeal of the Ancient Mariner, his facing of almost unendurable loneliness, is basically the ordeal of Ishmael" (p. 28). I find the whole of Dillingham's argument, particularly with regard to Ishmael's accidental survival (pp. 25–26), quite congenial to my own views of Melville's conception of Ishmael's role in the novel. Perhaps the most helpful overall reading of the "Epilogue" and the light it casts on Ishmael's survival is found in Ted N. Weissbuch and Bruce Stillians, "Ishmael the Ironist: The Anti-Salvation Theme in *Moby-Dick*," *English Society Quarterly* 31 (2d Quarter, 1963):71–75. For Weissbuch and Stillians, Ishmael "retains a detached awareness rather than a thorough understanding of his experience aboard the *Pequod*" (p. 72). See also Michael J. Hoffman, *The Subversive Vision: American Romanticism in Literature* (Port Washington, N. Y.: Kennikat Press, 1972), p. 97.

13. See Martin Leonard Pops, *The Melville Archetype* (Cleveland: Kent State University Press, 1970), p. 71: "Nothing is more indicative of the Ahabian aspect of Ishmael's personality than the fact that even after the cataclysmic disaster of the *Pequod* and his survival on the open sea, he sails again (and presumably again and again) on a whaler."

CHAPTER FIVE

1. Herman Melville, *Pierre; or, The Ambiguities*, ed. Harrison Hayford, Hershel Parker, and G. Thomas Tanselle (Evanston and Chicago: Northwestern University Press and the Newberry Library, 1971). Future references citing book, chapter, and page numbers will be included in my text, with *Pierre* abbreviated as *P*.

2. See Brian Higgins and Hershel Parker, "The Flawed Grandeur of Melville's *Pierre*" in *New Perspectives on Melville*, ed. Faith Pullin (Edinburgh: Edinburgh University Press, 1973), p. 162, who comment on the relationship between and the shift in perspectives from *Moby-Dick* to *Pierre*:

> Melville in *Moby-Dick* had attempted to convert the whaling narrative, a flourishing division of nautical literature, into a vehicle for the philosophical and psychological speculations a pondering man like him was compelled toward. *Pierre* is his comparable attempt to convert the gothic romance (in one of its late permutations as sensational fiction primarily for female readers) into a vehicle for his psychological and philosophical speculations (now in this order of importance).

3. On Melville's use of the third-person narrator in *Pierre* and the later fiction see John. D. Seelye, *Melville: The Ironic Diagram* (Evanston: Northwestern University Press, 1970): "As he entered that phase of his career which ends with *The Confidence-Man*, the gap of empathy between narrator and quester continued to widen, each change in attitude moving Melville farther from subjective participation toward disinterested observation" (p. 76). See also Karl F. Knight, "The Implied Author in Melville's *Pierre*," in *Studies in American Fiction* 7 (Autumn 1979): 163–74: "the baffling complex manner in which the narrator [in *Pierre*] is used suggests that he is a created figure distinct from Herman Melville and, further, that he is used precisely for the purpose of compounding the ambiguities of the book . . ." (p. 164).

4. On Pierre's essentially Ishmaelian character, see Nathalia Wright, *Melville's Use of the Bible* (Durham: Duke University Press, 1949), p. 52: "The angel who gave Hagar the name for Ishmael before his birth also prophesied his nature: 'And he will be a wild man; his hand will be against every man, and every man's hand against him; and he shall dwell in the presence of all his brethren.' To a greater degree than any other hero of Melville's, Pierre is such a wild man, or wild ass of a man, as a literal translation has it."

5. E. H. Eby, "[A Literary Experiment and the Destruction of Certainties]" in *Critical Essays on Herman Melville's "Pierre; or, The Ambiguities,"* ed. Brian Higgins and Hershel Parker (Boston: G. K. Hall, 1983), p. 187, sees both *Moby-Dick* and *Pierre* as Melville's critiques on Emersonian optimism. In other contexts, Michael J. Hoffman, in *The Subversive Vision: American Romanticism in Literature* (Port Washington, N. Y.: Kennikat Press, 1972), p. 87, sees Ahab as Melville's "parody of the Transcendentalist 'great man,'" whereas Stephen E. Whicher, in *Freedom and Fate: An Inner Life of Ralph Waldo Emerson* (Philadelphia: University of Pennsylvania Press, 1953), p. 25, calls Ahab the "archetype of . . . radical self-reliance."

6. See Robert Milder, "Melville's 'Intentions' in *Pierre*," *Studies in the Novel* 6 (Summer 1974): 190: "*Pierre* was written and conceived as what might be termed a 'negative *bildungsroman*,' a deliberate reductio ad absurdum of all metaphysics, all ethics, and all psychology, founded on the proposition that nothing can be known, least of all the knower himself."

7. Again see Milder, "Melville's 'Intentions' in *Pierre*," p. 196: "He [Melville] had come to doubt the most fundamental premises of moral and religious belief,

not least of them the integrity of the individual soul. . . . His will to believe—in God and Truth, if it were possible; in himself, if it were not—balked at this revelation of nothingness. . . ."

On the extremity of Pierre's (and Melville's) position in *Pierre*, see one of the fine early interpretations of the novel, S. Foster Damon's "Pierre the Ambiguous" in *The Hound and Horn* 2 (January–March 1929): 118: "There are two schemes of salvation: the Pagan and the Christian. The first is summarized by the famous inscription over the gateway to the temple at Delos: 'Know Thyself'; the Golden Rule summarizes the other. Whether knowingly or not, Melville so contrived his book [*Pierre*] that it might prove both of them impossible."

8. Milder argues (in "Melville's 'Intentions' in *Pierre*") that the novel as it was published reveals a unified conception and that whatever changes in direction occurred in the last half of the novel were essentially integrated into Melville's overriding purpose. Pierre's rebellious nature as a writer is consistent with his social and moral rebellion in the first half of the novel, and his literary rebellion only makes sense as an outgrowth of his earlier rebellion and the response to it by family, friends, and society in general.

9. In spite of the great deal of attention devoted to Plinlimmon and his pamphlet, no one to my knowledge has emphasized the striking analogue and possible source to be found in John Calvin and his *Institutes*. For example, in the *Institutes*, 4, xx, 1, Calvin states that "whoever knows how to distinguish between body and soul, between this present fleeting life and that future eternal life, will without difficulty know that Christ's spiritual Kingdom and the civil jurisdiction are things completely distinct." Even more to the point, when Calvin discusses this "twofold government in man," the spiritual and the political, he concludes: "Now these two, as we have divided them, must always be examined separately; and while one is being considered, we must call away and turn aside the mind from thinking about the other. There are in man, so to speak, two worlds, over which different kings and different laws have authority" (*Institutes*, 3, xix, 15). See John Calvin, *Institutes of the Christian Religion*, 2 vols., ed. John T. McNeill, trans. Ford Lewis Battles (London: S. C. M. Press, 1961), passim.

10. See Warner Berthoff, *The Example of Melville* (Princeton: Princeton University Press, 1962), p. 54: "The highest flight of eloquence in *Pierre* is, prophetically, on the Carlylean theme of the necessity of Silence, and the later stages of the novel are overrun with observations on the essential 'namelessness' or 'unspeakableness' of what lies deepest in existence. It is an awkward point of arrival for a writer who had thus far been committed to completeness and explicitness of statement as the true earnest of literary virtue."

11. See Milton R. Stern, *The Fine Hammered Steel of Herman Melville* (Urbana: University of Illinois Press, 1957), p. 192: "The non-being of Plinlimmon's repose and the selfishly anti-idealistic orientation of whatever ideas the Apostles has written into 'IF' indicate that Plinlimmon had had his insight into the true nature of God as zero." Lawrance Thompson, in *Melville's Quarrel with God* (Princeton: Princeton University Press, 1952), devotes several pages (pp. 272–79) to the intricate values of Plinlimmon and his pamphlet within the overall context of *Pierre*. Thompson sees Plinlimmon's pamphlet as "the high-water

mark of Melville's own private myth as to the deceptiveness with which God Himself hoaxes and gulls human beings into believing a great deal of falsehood about Himself" (p. 276).

12. See Richard H. Brodhead, *Hawthorne, Melville, and the Novel* (Chicago: University of Chicago Press, 1976), p. 188: "'Ye know him not!' The last line of *Pierre* leads us back to the ending of *Moby-Dick*; it reminds us that finally we know no more about who Pierre is or what his life has meant than we do about the white whale that surfaces, destroys, vanishes.... As it does in *Moby-Dick*, ... our adventure in knowledge culminates in a discovery of the permanence of our ignorance."

CHAPTER SIX

1. Herman Melville, "The Encantadas" in *The Complete Stories of Herman Melville*, ed. Jay Leyda (New York: Random House, 1949), p. 50. All future citations of Melville's short stories will refer to the Leyda edition and will be included in my text. For economy of reference I will employ the following abbreviations for the short stories: "The Encantadas": "En"; "The Piazza": "Piazza"; "Benito Cereno": "BC"; "Bartleby": "B"; "The Lightning-Rod Man": "L-R M"; and "The Bell-Tower": "B-T."

2. See John D. Seelye, *Melville: The Ironic Diagram* (Evanston: Northwestern University Press, 1970), p. 91: "Unlike Taji and Ahab, who hurl themselves across a cosmos, or even Pierre, who has a metropolis to baffle him, the questers of Melville's short stories have literally no place to go. Their quests, correspondingly, are not plunges into mystery, but mere wavering, often bewildered, advances and retreats, attempts to come to terms with a situation beyond their limited understanding."

Kingsley Widmer, of all Melville's critics, sees the late fiction in the most absolute terms. In "The Perplexity of Melville: *Benito Cereno*," in *Studies in Short Fiction* 5 (Spring 1968):225, he asserts that "the analogous material of the three major novellas—*Benito Cereno, Bartleby, Billy Budd*—provides ground for meditating on the unanswerable." And in *The Ways of Nihilism: A Study of Herman Melville's Short Novels* (California State Colleges, 1970), pp. 135–36, he puts his case in the most summary terms: "the nihilistic implications of Melville's fables, as I have interpreted them, deny ameliorist possibilities.... These stories rightly terrify because of what we would have to choose to go beyond such nihilism." Although Widmer has a keen sense of the bleak tonality of Melville's late fiction, this bleakness does not derive from a doctrinal, dogmatic nihilism operating in Melville (Widmer's view). Rather, Melville's conception and depiction of negation arise directly from his nineteenth-century concepts of affirmation and completion and, hence, negation in Melville's art has the force of vacated presence rather than of the void that we associate with twentieth-century comedy of the absurd and Kafka (See Widmer, "The Negative Affirmation: Melville's 'Bartleby,'" *Modern Fiction Studies* 8 [Autumn 1962]:276). See also Scott Donaldson, "The Dark Truth of *The Piazza Tales*," *PMLA* 85 (October 1970):1082–86.

3. See Helmbrecht Breinig, "The Destruction of Fairyland," *ELH* 35 (June 1968):254–83. Since Breinig's excellent article on "The Piazza," more and more critics have begun to see the centrality of the tale to Melville's purposes in the rest of the collection. See, for example, Marvin Fisher, *Going Under: Melville's Short Fiction and the American 1850's* (Baton Rouge: Louisiana University Press, 1977), pp. 15–16: speaking of the centrality of "perspectives" in the tale, Fisher concludes that "these subtleties determine the significance and position of 'The Piazza' as well as define the problem and inform the meaning of such stories as 'Bartleby,' 'Benito Cereno,' 'The Two Temples,' or 'Jimmy Rose.'" See also Richard S. Moore, *That Cunning Alphabet: Melville's Aesthetics of Nature* (Amsterdam: Rodopi Editions, 1982), p. 1: "Simple in plot but allegorical and turgidly allusive in manner, 'The Piazza' is a landscape sketch that establishes with great subtlety the frame of reference for the stories that follow it."

4. See Breinig, "The Destruction of Fairyland," p. 269: "The world of fairies is evoked over and over again, the Piazza is placed in a 'charmed ring' and the mountain-hut in 'fairyland,' but both realms prove to be illusions and have no healing power, neither for the inhabitants nor for the visiting pilgrims." William B. Dillingham, in *Melville's Short Fiction, 1853–1856* (Athens: University of Georgia Press, 1977), defines "Fairyland" within the story as "that unknown region of the inner self" (p. 327) and concludes: "In search of peace and joy the narrator sets out into the inner sea of the half-known life to find a Tahiti that as Ishmael warns, is forever lost. The narrator's quest is therefore doomed to failure from the start, and he voyages among the 'horrors' of the hidden self at his own risk."

5. Seelye, *The Ironic Diagram*, pp. 24–25, is almost alone in seeing the narrator as not being disillusioned by his experience. The more prevailing view is that the story "deals with a sensitive thinker who seeks enlightening truth but encounters despair" (Dillingham, *Melville's Short Fiction*, p. 320), and that the narrator's experience "exposes the deceptiveness of sensation as well as an impassable gulf between the actual and the ideal" (Moore, *That Cunning Alphabet*, p. 42).

6. Both Fisher and Dillingham emphasize this particular scene. For Dillingham, "the narrator thus is cursed because he is incapable of sustaining any optimism, pleasure, or tranquility" (*Melville's Short Fiction*, p. 84). For Fisher, somewhat more dramatically, "the penitential tortoises emblematically extend their Tartarean existence from the fallen world of the Encantadas into the somewhat less anguished world of mid-nineteenth-century America, a promised land that Melville was not alone in apprehending in penitential terms of quiet desperation" (*Going Under*, p. 37).

7. Robert C. Albrecht, "The Thematic Unity of Melville's 'The Encantadas,'" *Texas Studies in Literature and Language* 14 (Autumn 1972): 463–77, cites Dante's *Inferno* as a major source for the sketches and sees Melville, whom he identifies with the narrator, as "our Virgil," (pp. 463–64).

8. Warwick Wadlington, in *The Confidence Game in American Literature* (Princeton: Princeton University Press, 1975), p. 125, astutely observes that "the

storytelling in 'Benito Cereno' is remarkable for maintaining a pace that tests the bounds of delayed narrative closure." But he is less astute when he continues, "the narrative patience of 'Benito Cereno' is a schooling in patience for the reader whereby he is instructed to see, in the appearance of things, warped, one-sided versions of whole potentials that with thoughtfully sympathetic application can be intuited in their fullness." It is precisely "fullness" of perception and intuition and understanding that "Benito Cereno" denies.

9. See Ruth B. Mandel, "The Two Mystery Stories in Benito Cereno," *Texas Studies in Literature and Language* 14 (Winter 1973):640–41: "In *Benito Cereno* Melville is true to the sense of the novel expressed in *Pierre*, attacking books which present vast mysteries only to unravel them at the end. At first *Benito Cereno* seems to do just that, but its surface clarity is misleading, and its art ultimately upholds a vision of mystery." Dillingham also points to the tale's insoluble mystery when he points out that "despite the insistence of numerous critics that 'Benito Cereno' *contrasts* appearance with reality, the underlying conclusion reached in the story is that both appearance and what passes for reality are false and thus in a sense not opposites but similitudes. Whenever one layer of false perception has been cut away in order for bare reality to be seen below, that reality proves to be only another layer of appearance" (*Melville's Short Fiction*, pp. 229–30).

10. Although for the sake of emphasis I wish to comment on the "knot scene," it is difficult not to agree with Eric J. Sundquist that "the conversation about the knot is a tableau whose figurative message so closely approaches the literal that its unfolding takes the form of tautology" ("Suspense and Tautology in *Benito Cereno*," *Glyph* 8 [1981]:117).

11. Again Dillingham is illuminating when he points out that "Delano's vision is wilfully myopic. He must see things close up where all the details stand out but where similitudes are obscured" (*Melville's Short Fiction*, p. 249).

12. A most thoughtful essay on the belabored subject of slavery in "Benito Cereno" is Kermit Vanderbilt's "'Benito Cereno': Melville's Fable of Black Complicity," *Southern Review* 12 (April 1976):311–22. Viewing slavery as Melville's metaphor for man's fate, Vanderbilt contends that the story takes on "a spiraling design of intolerance and oppression that will continue throughout human history; and slavery becomes a metaphor of the black complicity of mankind" (p. 313). See also Bernard Rosenthal, "Melville's Island" *Studies in Short Fiction* 11 (Winter 1974): 1–9, who argues that "the story is more about metaphysics than politics" (p. 2) and sees the religious and political symbols of the story converging upon "a moment of moral and spiritual failure in a universe presided over by nothing" (p. 8).

13. See Sundquist, "Suspense and Tautology in *Benito Cereno*," p. 106: "If the deposition limits and contains the violence, and ultimately the moral significance, of the events barely held in check in the first part of Melville's story, it does so incompletely; for the final scenes of the executed Babo and the ruined Benito Cereno emerge as a shadow which the language of the court and the coldblooded documents of history cannot fully *contain*."

14. Virtually everyone reading the story comments upon Delano's blindness, sunny self-righteousness, and insensibility. However, Delano's inability to see his world clearly, and his unwillingness to face the unpleasant truths that the world thrusts upon him, mark him more as a norm than an oddity in the context of Melville's fiction in the 1850s, the final irony being that he survives his own ignorance unscathed.

15. Milton R. Stern, "Towards 'Bartleby the Scrivener' " in *The Stoic Strain in American Literature: Essays in Honour of Marston La France* (Toronto: University of Toronto Press, 1979), pp. 19–41, provides a judicious and equitable summary analysis of the many well-known "approaches" to "Bartleby." I will cite only those critics whose views are and have been most helpful in clarifying my own thinking.

16. See A. N. Kaul, *The American Vision: Actual and Ideal Society in Nineteenth-Century Fiction* (New Haven: Yale University Press, 1963), pp. 275–76, who sees "The Encantadas" as "the opposite of the social hopefulness that Melville had celebrated earlier" and sees Bartleby as representing "the flotsam and jetsam that has irrevocably broken down as a society." In spite of the plethora of articles written on "Bartleby," again it is the case that relatively few critics have looked at the story in the larger context of Melville's total career; R. Bruce Bickley, Jr. *(The Method of Melville's Short Fiction* [Durham, N. C.: Duke University Press, 1975]) and William B. Dillingham *(Melville's Short Fiction*) are notable exceptions.

17. See Mordecai Marcus, "Melville's Bartleby as a Psychological Double" in *Bartleby the Inscrutable: A Collection of Commentary on Herman Melville's Tale "Bartleby the Scrivener,"* ed. M. Thomas Inge (Hamden, Conn.: Anchor, 1979), pp. 107–8. Although I don't agree with Marcus's extreme view that Bartleby is to be viewed as a psychological projection of "the lawyer's mind," I do agree that "Bartleby appears to the lawyer chiefly to remind him of the inadequacies, the sterile routine, of his world."

18. On Bartleby's negative preference and its implications, see Bickley, *The Method of Melville's Short Fiction*, p. 42.

19. See Walter R. Patrick, "Melville's 'Bartleby' and the Doctrine of Necessity," in *Bartleby the Inscrutable*, ed. Inge, pp. 143–58 (a revised version of his essay that first appeared in *American Literature* 41 [March 1969]:39–54). Commenting on this particular scene, Patrick rightly concludes that "from this scene forward, . . . the attorney's sense of identification with Bartleby, together with his awareness of the common bond of humanity, grows stronger and stronger" (pp. 153–54). For an opposing view of the lawyer's sensibilities, see Allan Moore Emery, "The Alternatives of Melville's 'Bartleby,' " *Nineteenth-Century Fiction* 31 (September 1976): 170–87. Emery sees the lawyer as smug, self-satisfied, and oblivious to the causes of Bartleby's plight.

20. Again Patrick, in *Bartleby the Inscrutable*, ed. Inge, p. 155, is correct I think in seeing the lawyer's "offer to take Bartleby into his own dwelling" as the "high point in the attorney's growth in sympathy."

21. Surprisingly few critics even mention this electric touch, which is so cru-

cial to understanding the lawyer's response to Bartleby. Stern, however, in "To-wards 'Bartleby the Scrivener,' " p. 26, comments upon this scene as revealing the change that takes place in the narrator in the course of the story and observes that "nowhere in the first half [of the story] is there a physico-psychic jolt of current running between the narrator and Bartleby as there is in the death scene in the Tombs." See also Stanley Brodwin, "To the Frontiers of Eternity" in *Bartleby the Inscrutable*, ed. Inge (first publication), p.xx: "his 'shiver' told him [the lawyer] more than the fact of Bartleby's death; it told him that his vaunted safety was, in the end, the most destructive and vulnerable illusion of all. And not unlike Ishmael or the messenger in Job, he has escaped to tell us."

22. Hershel Parker, "The Sequel in 'Bartleby,' " in *Bartleby the Inscrutable*, ed. Inge (first publication), p. 162, clearly defines the terms of reference in the sequel: "The report of the 'one little item of rumor' about Bartleby's past employment rests upon no known basis and possesses no demonstrable truth. What is important about the rumor is not what it tells about Bartleby, since it may be false, but what it tells about the narrator, who has found it to be not without 'a certain strange suggestive interest,' however sad, and who assumes that 'it may prove the same with some others.' " I do not agree, however, with Parker's conclusion that "in his self-conscious eloquent sequel, after all, the lawyer has merely made his last cheap purchase of a 'delicious self-approval' " (p. 164).

23. See Stern, "Towards 'Bartleby the Scrivener,' " p. 35: "the uncertain rumour about the Dead Letter Office at once universalizes Bartleby and keeps the focus exactly where Melville wants it—on the effect of Bartleby's condition, not on the cause of it."

24. Dillingham, *Melville's Short Fiction*, pp. 172–82, is one of the few critics to note the inherent ambiguity of both salesman and narrator, concluding that "Melville's purpose is not to present one character as good and the other as evil but to show through the ironic use of a Christian frame of reference how each views the other" (pp. 181–82).

25. On the "structure and narrative method" of the diptychs, see Bickley, *The Method of Melville's Short Fiction*, pp. 76–77.

26. See Alan Lebowitz, *Progress into Silence: A Study of Melville's Heroes* (Bloomington: Indiana University Press, 1970), p. 182: "for Israel there is never a rebirth, only a series of repeated opportunities, all of which prove futile and renew for yet another term his captive, deathlike life." See also Charles Feidelson, Jr., *Symbolism and American Literature* (Chicago: University of Chicago Press), pp. 182–83, on Israel's passive hopelessness.

27. Herman Melville, *Israel Potter, His Fifty Years of Exile*, ed. Harrison Hayford, Hershel Parker, and G. Thomas Tanselle (Evanston and Chicago: Northwestern University Press and The Newberry Library, 1982). Future references citing chapter and page numbers will be to this edition and will be included in my text, with *Israel Potter* abbreviated as *IP*.

28. Although countless critics of the novel have seen and responded to the book's blackness and bleakness of vision, most shy away from following the Cosmopolitan into the darkness that ends the book. Thus, for example, Elizabeth Foster in her introduction to the Hendricks House edition (New York, 1954)

backs off from the implications of her own argument when she concludes that "however disillusioned, Melville stops short of Timonism. One cannot trust God; one cannot trust nature; but one must cling to some faith in man, for the alternative is too frightful" (p. lxxxix). Too frightful for Foster perhaps, but not I think for Melville. Similarly, Richard Boyd Hauck, one of the best recent readers of the novel, can argue on the one hand that "the humor of the Confidence-Man and *The Confidence-Man* teaches us ... that understanding reveals the absolute ambiguity underlying all phenomena, including understanding itself" and nevertheless conclude that "the moral of both the masquerade and the book is that charity cannot arise from experience and must therefore be continually invented in an act of confidence, in spite of the horrendous risk of being defrauded or being thought a fraud" ("Nine Good Jokes: *The Redemptive Humor of the Confidence-Man* and The Confidence-Man," in *Ruined Eden of the Present: Hawthorne, Melville and Poe; Critical Essays in Honor of Darrel Abel* [West Lafayette, Ind.: Purdue University Press, 1981], pp. 280–81).

29. Herman Melville, *The Confidence-Man, His Masquerade*, ed. Harrison Hayford, Hershel Parker, and G. Thomas Tanselle (Evanston and Chicago: Northwestern University Press and the Newberry Library, 1984). Future references citing chapter and page numbers will be to this edition and will be included in my text, with *The Confidence-Man* abbreviated as *C-M*.

30. Hauck, "Nine Good Jokes," pp. 257–58, is surely right in arguing that "the opening scene of the book displays the pattern of unresolved dialectic which governs the whole": "these two signs [the deaf-mute's and the barber's] and the aphorisms on the slate represent the terms of the book's unresolved dialectic, and the crowd is caught between them."

31. See John G. Cawelti, "Some Notes on the Structure of *The Confidence-Man*," *American Literature* 29 (November 1957):278–88. Cawelti's definition of what he calls the "incomplete reversals" that permeate the book on every level is very helpful here: "something is presented, a character, an incident, an idea, anything which might give the reader some clue to the interpretation of the represented reality; then a counter incident or idea appears, powerful enough to destroy the usefulness of the first clue, but insufficient to provide a foundation for a new interpretation of what has been presented. We are left in the air with no way of resolving two mutually exclusive possibilities" (pp. 282–83). See also D. E. S. Maxwell, *American Fiction: The Intellectual Background* (New York: Columbia University Press, 1963), pp. 167–73, on the instabilities of the "counterpointing of ideas" and the dissimulations in the novel.

32. See Philip Drew, "Appearance and Reality in Melville's *The Confidence-Man*," *ELH* 31 (December 1964):418–42. Drew clearly defines the book's ambiguous definition of confidence when he observes "that there are two possible responses to a man appealing for your confidence. You can mistrust him, even if this shows your lack of heart, or you can have faith in him, even if this shows your lack of sense. These responses are incompatible, and each may be wrong in certain circumstances" (p. 437). I would merely add that in the book no one can determine whether trust or skepticism is misplaced until after the choice has been made.

33. See James Duban, *Melville's Major Fiction: Politics, Theology, and Imagination* (DeKalb: Northern Illinois University Press, 1983). Duban emphasizes "the impact of *The Confidence-Man's* skeptical epistemology," asking us to "recall how liberal Christian claims to regeneracy presuppose the mind's ability to distinguish truth. 'To reject human nature and declare it unworthy of confidence,' claimed Orestes A. Brownson, 'is—whether we know it or not—to reject all ground of certainty, and to declare that we have no means for distinguishing truth from falsehood.' "

34. Any discussion of *The Confidence-Man* should take into account Cecilia Tichi's brilliant essay, "Melville's Craft and Theme of Language Debased in *The Confidence-Man*," *ELH* 39 (December 1972):639–58. Her essay focusses upon the endless linguistic difficulties Melville places in the path of his readers and concludes that for Melville "language has become the meanest stuff of swindle because it was severed from its ethical and communicative functions" (p. 640). In these terms the book's irresolute ending is to be seen not as an anomaly but as a necessity, for in effect there is no legitimate way to conclude a non-statement. See also Edgar A. Dryden, *Melville's Thematics of Form* (Baltimore: Johns Hopkins University Press, 1968), p. 191, who sees the final chapter as "an epitome of the entire novel" in which the Christian cosmos is destroyed and replaced by the "Drummond Light" of the Cosmopolitan/Confidence-Man.

35. Commenting on the last line of the novel, Leon F. Seltzer concludes that "we are eventually forced to accept the novel's radically limited narrative perspective as symbolizing our own limited capacity to 'see' what goes on around us" (*The Vision of Melville and Conrad: A Comparative Study* [Athens: Ohio University Press, 1970], p. 52).

CHAPTER SEVEN

1. Herman Melville, *Clarel: A Poem and Pilgrimage in the Holy Land* , ed. with Introduction by Walter Bezanson (New York: Hendricks House, 1960), IV, xv:11. 48–62. Future references to *Clarel*, citing part, canto, and line numbers, will be included in my text.

2. Herman Melville, *Poems: Containing Battle Pieces, John Marr and Other Sailors, Timoleon, and Miscellaneous Poems* (New York: Russell and Russell, 1963), p. 3.

3. It is commonplace to link *Clarel* and *Billy Budd* (see Vincent Kenny, *Herman Melville's "Clarel": A Spiritual Autobiography* [Hamden, Conn.: Archon Books, 1973], Chapter 4, "A Century of Readers," for a summary overview), but the lack of consensus about both works makes those links anything but uniform or stable.

4. See Bernard Rosenthal, "Herman Melville's Wandering Jews" in *Puritan Influences in American Literature*, ed. Emory Elliott (Urbana: University of Illinois Press, 1979), pp. 167–89. Rosenthal sees Melville in *Clarel* as "probing the possibility of nothingness" (p. 168) and argues that Melville "began explicitly with the premise that the Christian era was closing" (p. 169). I would merely put "closed" for "closing."

5. Kenny, *Herman Melville's "Clarel*," pp. 225–26.

6. "Introduction" to Herman Melville, *Billy Budd, Sailor (An Inside Narrative)*, ed. Harrison Hayford and Merton M. Sealts, Jr. (Chicago: The University of Chicago Press, 1962), p. 135. See also Loren Baritz, *City on a Hill: A History of Ideas and Myths in America* (New York: John Wiley and Sons, 1964), p. 329: "The tale [*Billy Budd*] is an integral part of Melville's total work, it but continues the great themes that had occupied him from the first."

7. See Morse Peckham, "Hawthorne and Melville as European Authors" in *Hawthorne and Melville in the Berkshires*, ed. Howard P. Vincent (Cleveland: Kent State University Press, 1968), p. 62: "The story is an exemplum of the discursive *Clarel*; it shows how, in a critical situation, in which everything should come clear and be focussed, nothing is clear. It is a story deliberately constructed to defy interpretation."

8. See Milton R. Stern's "Introduction" to his edition of the novel (Indianapolis: Bobbs Merrill, 1975), particularly his argument regarding the political dimensions of the tale and its critics. Stern argues that "critics unconsciously will be directed temperamentally toward certain works and writers to find importance and values according to the internal hive of ideologies, allegiances, and associations that impel them toward the particular works in the first place" (p. xlii), and in the case of *Billy Budd* it is clear that critics have frequently made it a battleground for ideologies as much political as literary, the result being that arguments frequently tell us more about the reader of the novel than about the novel itself.

9. Herman Melville, *Billy Budd, Sailor (An Inside Narrative)*, ed. Harrison Hayford and Merton M. Sealts, Jr. (Chicago: The University of Chicago Press, 1962), 3:54. Further references, citing chapter and page numbers, will be included in my text, with *Billy Budd* abbreviated as *BB*.

10. Remarkably little criticism has been directed to the function and importance of the narrator in *Billy Budd*. Paul Brodtkorb, Jr. ("The Definitive *Billy Budd*: 'But Aren't It All Sham?,'" *PMLA* 82 [December 1967]:602–12) proclaims the centrality of the narrative voice in the novel, but after a few paragraphs shifts references from the "narrator" to "Melville" and proceeds to argue *Melville's* purposes regarding Vere or Billy. For a view of the narrator as Melville, see Edward H. Rosenberry, "The Problem of *Billy Budd*," *PMLA* 80 (December 1965):491: "*Billy Budd* is narrated by an unmediated author who, unlike Chaucer, gives no hint that his 'wit is short' or his artistic distance great." Even C. N. Manlove, whose essay, "An Organic Hesitancy: Theme and Style in *Billy Budd*," in *New Perspectives on Melville*, ed. Faith Pullin (Edinburgh: Edinburgh University Press, 1978), is one of the most revealing we have on the narrative voice in the novel, errs essentially in considering the narrator as omniscient (see p. 298).

11. See Brodtkorb, "The Definitive *Billy Budd*," p. 604: "the narrator is engaged throughout in trying to understand his characters; in trying, that is, to get at the always problematic nature of the other," and again: "he [the narrator] is a man trying with all the resources at his command to give an account of what really happened, an 'inside narrative' " (p. 603).

12. For a persuasive analysis of the narrator's style and its relationship to the overall purposes of *Billy Budd*, see Manlove, "An Organic Hesitancy." Comment-

ing on the precision to be found in certain narrative-descriptive passages, Manlove concludes that "the lack of it in other passages could be deliberate" (p. 291).
In a more general but still helpful way, Robert T. Eberwein comments on the
"various barriers" confronting the narrator as he tries to tell his story: "He must
rely on references to biblical material probably ignored by most of his audience,
depend on his readers to accept his veracity and his manner of narration, and,
finally, resort to conjecture and speculation on the vitally important issues of
Claggart's nature, Vere's madness, and the final interview between Billy and the
Captain" ("The Impure Fiction of *Billy Budd*," *Studies in the Novel* 6 [Fall
1974]:323).

13. Comments on Billy's speech defect are commonplace, but in the context
of the confrontation between Billy and Claggart, Manlove's observation is suc-
cinct and relevant: "Billy's very defect is one whereby nature makes him more
surely her own. Speech is the fabric of civilization, and of this when deeply stirred
Billy becomes incapable. His stutter thus precisely delineates his remoteness
from civilized man" ("An Organic Hesitancy," p. 282).

14. See Milton R. Stern, "Introduction" to *Billy Budd*, p. xxxix: "Once more I
insist that *Billy Budd* is a politically conservative tale made complex by all the
bitterness Melville feels about fallen man, the doom of prelapsarian Billy, and
historical necessity." Stern goes on to argue that the "creation of measured forms
became for Melville the highest expression of the human spirit in its struggle
with the overwhelming, dark forces of an incomprehensible universe both inside
and outside man—the unconquerable, double vastness he indicated in *Moby-
Dick* and *Pierre*" (p. xiv). See also Bernard Rosenthal, "Elegy for Jack Chase,"
Studies in Romanticism 10 (Summer 1971):213–29. Rosenthal argues that
Vere, Billy, and Claggart are all victims of their common, fatally flawed, humanity
and concludes, darkly but accurately I think, that "any promise of redemption,
any hope of escape from the sentence that all mankind must have executed upon
it is fraudulent" (p. 229).

15. Mary Everett Burton Fussell, "*Billy Budd*: Melville's Happy Ending," *Studies in Romanticism* 15 (Winter 1976):55–56, stresses the incompleteness of the
Billy Budd manuscript and cites this scene in particular as a "most glaring deficiency." Yet a few sentences later in her argument she moves toward the position
I am arguing when she conjectures that the ellipsis in this scene "is perhaps not
so much a cover-up for a missing section as a grandly modest statement of the
structure of the whole book" (p. 56).

Index

Acushnet, the, 8

Ahab: definition, 106–7; relationship to Ishmael, 104–6; relationship to Pip, 115–17; tragedy, 117

Albrecht, Robert C., 90(n12), 155(n7)

Aleema (in *Mardi*), 32–33

America: in "Benito Cereno," 150; in *Israel Potter,* 178–79; in *Mardi* (satirized), 49–50; in *Pierre* (young America in literature satirized), 137–39; in *Redburn,* 66–67, 71; in *White-Jacket* (ideals and the U.S. Constitution), 80–81

Alter-egos: in "Bartleby" (Bartleby and the narrator-lawyer), 172–73; in *Mardi,* 29, 39–40, 52; in *Moby-Dick* (Ahab and Ishmael), 110–11; in *Redburn,* 62, 72–73; in *White-Jacket,* 81–86

Anderson, Charles R., 8(n8)

Arnold, Matthew, ("Stanzas from the Grande Chartreuse"), 12

Auden, W. H., 116(n11)

Baritz, Loren, 8(n8)

"Bartleby" [165–76]: alter-egos (Bartleby and the lawyer), 172–73; and "Benito Cereno," 175; a closed world, 166–69; Dead Letter Office, 175–76; death, 175–76; death of the quest, 166–69; the negated self, 171–72; physical setting, 167–68; social disintegration, 168; time, 169

"Battle Pieces," [190–91]

Bayle, Pierre, (radical skepticism), 165

Bell, Michael Davitt, 58(n2), 95(n4)

"The Bell-Tower" [176–77]: as allegory, 177; and Hawthorne's "The Birthmark," 177

"Benito Cereno" [158–65]: American ideals (in Delano), 159; and "Bartleby," 175; emblematic devices, 160; law and society (the tribunal), 163–65; narrative voice, 158; as problem narrative, 159–60; sentimentalism and rationalism (in Delano), 159; as suspense narrative, 158; the worst of all possible worlds, 158

Benton, Thomas Hart, 50

Berthoff, Warner, 141(n10)

Bezanson, Walter, 190(n1)

Bickley, R. Bruce, 166(n16), 171(n18), 177(n25)

Bildad and Peleg (in *Moby-Dick*), 100–101

Billy Budd [192–211]: the *Bellipotent* as microcosm 196, Claggart (compared to Billy), 197–98, (as Milton's Satan), 197; critical difficulties, 193–94, echoes of earlier works, 193, 203, as "inside narrative," 194, law 194 (the trial), 205–7; narrative voice, 194–95, (and Claggart), 199–200, and Captain Vere, 200–201; Captain Vere (and Claggart), 201–2, (and Nelson), 200, and Plinlimmon's